SERVANT OF GOD

# JOSEPH DUTTON

### HIS LIFE * HIS SERVICE * HIS LEGACY

April 27/1923.
80 Years,

Joyfully Yours,
Joseph Dutton
Kalawao, Molokii
Hawaii.

SERVANT OF GOD
# JOSEPH DUTTON
HIS LIFE * HIS SERVICE * HIS LEGACY

*The view from 2023*

*With tribute to ALL who braved risk of leprosy*
*to serve the least of God's people*

December 22, 2023

Dear Brothers and Sisters,

Peace be with you!

St. Damien DeVeuster is known throughout the world for his heroic and saintly work among the patients with leprosy who were forcibly exiled to the tiny Kalaupapa Peninsula on the Island of Molokai. Also well-known now is St. Marianne Cope, a Franciscan Sister who generously responded to the call to serve those same exiled and suffering people. This book is intended to introduce many to yet another person of heroic virtue who dedicated forty-four years of his life to serving those stricken by leprosy (now called Hansen's disease): Servant of God Joseph Dutton, Layman.

This book brings Joseph Dutton to life through his own words. Dutton experienced the horrors of death as a young Civil War soldier, assigned to recover the bodies of over 6,000 fallen soldiers who were hastily buried on the battlefields and transfer them to a more respectable resting place. He found post-war adjustments difficult, likely suffering what we now refer to as post-traumatic stress disorder (PTSD). This led him to a failed marriage and to a problem with heavy drinking and all the dark behaviors that came with it. But he emerged from this darkness to find a compassionate God, and he dedicated himself to serve the most desolate outcasts by volunteering – for forty-four years! – to care for the patients with leprosy in Kalaupapa, Molokai. His story of conversion to the Lord from his sinfulness, and to humble service and dedication, is inspiring for all.

The Kalaupapa Peninsula began as a settlement for people with leprosy in 1866 when the first twelve patients were exiled there, taken away from their families and the livelihoods. It continues as such to this day, though the patients are no longer contagious and are free to come and go as they choose. The stories of the approximately 8,000 patients who lived there during this time are worth remembering forever, and the current patients greatly desire that the story of light and love in the midst of darkness will carry their legacy to generations to come. Joseph Dutton is one, who through his heroic life of dedication to them, can be their storyteller to many future generations. If it is God's will that he formally declared a saint, the story will have an even wider audience for all generations.

May this book about Servant of God Joseph Dutton, Layman inspire many to be servants of God in whatever way they can, bringing the light of faith in the darkness; hope into situations that could easily lead to despair, and love even in the most challenging and difficult circumstances.

Sincerely yours in Christ,

+ Larry Silva

Most Reverend Larry Silva
Bishop of Honolulu

**Office of the Bishop** • Diocesan Chancery • 1184 Bishop Street, Honolulu, HI 96813-2859
Phone: 808.585.3356 • Fax: 808.585.3384 • Email: bishop@rcchawaii.org • www.catholichawaii.org

5

# Table of Contents

*Only in finding our Molokai
can we find true joy that can never be taken away.*

*For those of us who have heard the story of Joseph Dutton,
who find it to be inspiring,
who want to know more about him and to become his friend,
finding our Molokai is not an option.*

*Finding our Molokai, today, is what we are called to do.*

~Father John Paul Kimes
de Nicola Center for Ethics and Culture
University of Notre Dame
November 9, 2022

# *Preface*

This book will give readers insight into the personality, faith and courage of Servant of God Joseph Dutton. Read his own words in his autobiography, *Joseph Dutton – His Memoirs*, edited by Howard Case, 1931, fully included in this book.

*Joseph Dutton – His Life * His Service * His Legacy* is a project of the Joseph Dutton Guild. The purpose is to bring the Molokai story up to date and provide additional stories and materials so the reader can better appreciate the sacrifice that Joseph Dutton made when he landed on Molokai in 1886.

So much has happened since he died in 1931:

- The cause of Leprosy was discovered by Dr. Hansen and the disease, formerly Leprosy, is now readily cured.
- Father Damien was canonized in 2009 and is now St. Damien.
- Mother Marianne Cope was canonized in 2012 and is now St. Marianne.
- The settlement at Kalaupapa, with five patients remaining as of December 2023, is now a US National Park "co-administrated" by the State of Hawaii Department of Health.
- In 2016, the Damien-Marianne Catholic Conference (DMCC) was started in Honolulu, focused on evangelization in Hawaii and beyond.
- In 2021, Bishop Larry Silva opened the "cause" for Joseph Dutton's canonization with the Joseph Dutton Guild having been formed several years earlier in Honolulu.

- Two Catholic Churches have honored Joseph Dutton – In 1927 Beloit, WI with the Brother Dutton Elementary School at St. Jude Parish; and in 1948 in Stowe, VT, his birthplace, with Blessed Sacrament Church dedicated to him with unique art.
- Servant of God Joseph Dutton has long enjoyed an authentic reputation of holiness amnong the family in Hawaii, Wisconsin, and Vermont.
- January 21, 2024, Bishop Larry Silva issued an edict, declaring the evidence gathered (2000 pages worth!) completes the diocean phase of the cause. The evidence will be sent to the Dicastery for the Causes of the Saints in Rome.
- Kalawao is pronounced Kaa • La • Wow
- Kalaupapa is pronounced Kaa • Lau • Paa • Puh

~ Lynn P. Altadonna
Stowe, Vermont
December 2023

## With Respect for All
## Who Experienced Life on Kalaupapa

This book is inspired by Servant of God Joseph Dutton, Layman. In so honoring him, we honor St. Damien, St. Marianne and all those who were patients or who cared for the patients on the Kalaupapa Peninsula on Molokai. The Sisters of St. Francis continue to serve the souls, bodies and memories of the Hawaiian people who were affected by Hansen's disease.

Worldwide, the disease is usually referred to as leprosy, but the word "leper" to describe a person is very derogatory and hurtful to people and families who experienced the disease, with all its overtones of "unclean;" and somebody to be shunned or banished. Accordingly, the word is avoided and in Hawaii we use "Hansen's" to describe the disease, and "patient" or "resident" when referring to someone with Hansen's disease who lived on the Kalaupapa Peninsula.

In this book, the word was commonly used in the old documents, and, if that is the word in a quoted document, it is left as is to preserve the integrity of the document. However, the reader is encouraged not to use the former word when speaking or writing. In this book, the Guild has respectfully used the preferred words in newly written material in place of the old words to ease the personal stigma Hawaiians attach to those words.

Jesus taught that when we "serve the least of my people, you serve me". It is a privilege to be called to serve others as Jesus teaches us.

Respectfully,
~ Editors for Joseph Dutton Guild
Honolulu, Hawaii
December 2023

ROMAN CATHOLIC CHURCH IN THE STATE OF HAWAII

# DIOCESE OF HONOLULU
WITNESS TO JESUS

## HONOLULU
## BEATIFICATION AND CANONIZATION
## OF THE SERVANT OF GOD JOSEPH DUTTON, LAYMAN

### EDICT
### TO THE FAITHFUL OF THE DIOCESE OF HONOLULU

At the request of the "Joseph Dutton Guild", Dr. Waldery Hilgeman, Diocesan Postulator, has presented me with the Written Request, required by Canon Law, to initiate the Cause for the Beatification and Canonization of the Servant of God Joseph Dutton.

The Servant of God Joseph Dutton was born in Stowe, Vermont on April 27, 1843, and was raised in Wisconsin. He was a soldier in the United States Civil War, serving in the Union Army. After the War, he entered a difficult marriage, which lasted only about a year, and he took to drinking heavily. At the age of 40, he had a conversion experience and became a Catholic. He wanted to do penance for what he considered a wayward life, so he entered a monastery, only to discern that this was not his vocation. He heard about Father Damien De Veuster and Sister Marianne Cope and their heroic work with the patients with leprosy in Molokai. He volunteered to go there to help them, arriving on July 29, 1886. He humbly and faithfully served the patients of the settlement for 44 years, primarily caring for the young boys who lived at the Baldwin Home. He became ill and was transferred to St. Francis Hospital in Honolulu, where he died on March 26, 1931. [For more biographical information go to https://josephdutton.org.]

I hereby request that you present to this Diocese of Honolulu any pertinent information that you might have for or against the eventual Beatification and Canonization of the Servant of God.

Any and all information, which will remain secret, may be sent by email to Father Siegfred Dosdos, Vice-Postulator of the Cause, at sainthoodfordutton@rcchawaii.org or by regular mail at 84-5140 Painted Church Road, Captain Cook, HI 96704-8409.

All information must be received no later than June 30, 2021.

Finally, we ask for your prayers that the Holy Spirit may guide this Cause according to the will of God.

Given at the Chancery of the Diocese of Honolulu on the 29th day of May A.D. 2021.

+ Clarence Silva          Dcn. Keith Cabiles

Most Reverend Clarence (Larry) Silva          Deacon Keith Cabiles
Bishop of Honolulu          Chancellor of the Diocese

NOTE: This EDICT is to be posted through June 30, 2021 on the doors of the Cathedral Basilica of Our Lady of Peace, Honolulu, of St. Francis Church, Kalaupapa and of St. Damien of Molokai Church, Kaunakakai; as well as in the Diocesan Newspaper, *Hawaii Catholic Herald*; on the diocesan website www.catholichawaii.org; and in the diocesan eNews.

# The Joseph Dutton Guild
## His Cause for Canonization

## Our Vision

We, the members of the "Joseph Dutton Guild", are a group of Catholic men and women of Hawaii who have petitioned Bishop Larry Silva, Bishop of Honolulu, to initiate the Cause of Canonization of the Servant of God Joseph Dutton, the layman who worked for many years on the Island of Molokai together with Saint Damien De Veuster and Saint Marianne Cope. The Guild was created also to support and promote God's plan of love and service to the poor and abandoned, and to put that love into action here in Hawaii and around the world.

## Mission

With the grace of God and through our awareness, devotion, and support, our mission is to promote the Cause of Canonization of the Servant of God Joseph Dutton that will lead, if it be God's will, to the beatification and canonization of the Servant of God. We are also seeking to make people more aware of the dedication and service of the Servant of God Joseph Dutton to the poor and abandoned, thus encouraging them to imitate his lively faith and active charity.

## Objectives

The Joseph Dutton Guild strives to be of service and assistance in all those things of the process that may lead to the eventual canonization of the Servant of God Joseph Dutton, Layman of Molokai. Moreover, we seek to connect people by bringing to them an awareness of their particular Christian vocation, and so thus to enable them to share in the common vision of the Saints for continued growth in their relationship to Jesus Christ as they serve others.

## *World Wide Devotion*

The decision to proceed to the canonization of an individual requires the definitive approval of the Holy Father. Canonization requires a demonstration that the popular devotion to the candidate (called a reputation of holiness) has extended and grown in the Church over a period of time. Graces, favors and miracles, granted by God through the intercession of the candidate for canonization (called a reputation of intercessory power), are considered as divine proof that this popular devotion is the fruit of the work of the Holy Spirit in the hearts and minds of the faithful.

In 2022, the Catholic Church announced the "cause" for Joseph Dutton's canonization.

(from the Hawaii Catholic Herald,
Patrick Downes)

## *Officials in place, the inquiry into Dutton's cause begins*
05/25/2022

Bishop Larry Silva presided May 10 over the historic opening session of the diocesan inquiry for the cause of the beatification and canonization of Joseph Dutton, the Civil War veteran who spent the final 44 years of his life caring for the patients of Kalaupapa, Molokai. At the end of an evening Mass in the Cathedral Basilica of Our Lady of Peace, nine officials for the cause read and signed their oaths of office, opening the inquiry.

The main celebrant was Archbishop Christophe Pierre, Apostolic Nuncio of the United States since 2016, who was visiting the Diocese of Honolulu for the first time. The liturgy was for the memorial of St. Damien de Veuster, May 10. A walnut-sized bone relic of the saint was on display for veneration in a polished wood box in front of the altar.

The procedures officially launched the diocesan inquiry "into the life, the virtues, and reputation of holiness and intercessory power of the servant of God Joseph Dutton, layman."

"Servant of God" is the initial title given any candidate for sainthood.

Msgr. Robert Sarno, retired official of the Vatican Congregation for the Causes of Saints who assisted in the canonizations of Father Damien and Mother Marianne, and who now serves as the Episcopal Delegate for Dutton's cause, led the formal proceedings.

**Patrick Boland**
Historical Commission

**Father Siegfried Dosdos**
Diocesan Postulator

**Roxanne Torres**
Notary

**Father Mark Gantley**
Promoter of Justice

**Msgr. Robert Sarno**
Episcopal Delegate

**Bishop Larry Silva**
Diocesan Bishop

*Officials in place, the inquiry into Dutton's cause begins*

*Archbishop Christophe Pierre, Apostolic Nuncio to the United States,*
*preaches May 10 in Honolulu's cathedral basilica.*
*(All photos courtesy of Dann Ebina )*

The participants in the cause read and signed their oaths of office at a lectern in the church sanctuary. They included diocesan judicial vicar Father Mark Gantley as Promoter of Justice, Father Siegfried Dosdos as the Diocesan Postulator, the primary advocate of the cause, and members of the Historical Commission Father John Paul Kimes and Patrick Boland. Not present was commission member Father Joseph Badding who had been sworn in earlier, and Joan Lewis of Rome who was added to the commission later.

The diocese's Moderator of the Tribunal Roxanne Torres signed in as notary and Deacon Keith Cabiles as chancellor.

All, including Bishop Silva, "solemnly" swore to "faithfully and carefully execute the duty" committed to them, and to "keep secret" all that they may learn in the inquiry.

"In fulfilling my duty, I will keep my eyes only on God and the good of the church, so help me God," they each said.

According to the Mass's order of worship, the pen used to sign the documents was made of wood from a tree growing on the property of St. Anthony Church in Wailuku, Maui, when and where Father Damien made his auspicious choice to volunteer for Molokai.

Also introduced were members of the Joseph Dutton Guild who, for about a decade, have been laying the groundwork that led to the initiation of the cause.

The final reading acknowledged 13 actions leading up to the opening inquiry, including the creation of the guild, consultations with the faithful, the U.S. Conference of Catholic Bishops and the bishops of the metropolitan province of San Francisco, and approval by the Vatican.

After enduring more than 30 minutes of repetitious legal language in the reading and signing of the oaths of office, Bishop Silva delivered the punch line:

"Obviously, it takes a lot of people to make a saint."

That drew laughs, but also introduced a broader truth. "That it is not just the people working on the causes, but it does take a lot of people to make a saint. Joseph Dutton would not even be proposed as a candidate for sainthood had it not been for many people who were saints to him, who were inspirations to him, such as Father Damien and Mother Marianne."

"And he would not have been a candidate for sainthood had it not been for the many people that he served and who inspired him along the way. And so we thank God for all of them," he said.

"Of course we remember that the reason we have the process of the canonization of saints is so we can become saints ourselves, so that we can imitate those who have gone before us in their fidelity to Jesus. And so we thank God for this day."

## *Several tumultuous years*

Ira Dutton was born to Protestant parents in Stowe, Vermont, on April 27, 1843, and raised in Wisconsin.

He fought in the U.S. Civil War, rising to the rank of captain with the 13th Wisconsin Volunteers. Discharged from the Army in 1866, Dutton endured several tumultuous years with a failed marriage and alcohol abuse.

He worked difficult jobs to support himself, including bringing the remains of soldiers back from Civil War battlefields to the common burial ground that is now The Great Cemetery at Corinth, MS.

Dutton found solace in Catholicism and was baptized on his 40th birthday, April 27, 1883. He took "Joseph" as his baptismal name.

As an act of atonement for his turbulent post-war years, he traveled to Molokai in 1886 to join St. Damien in his work with leprosy patients. St. Damien affectionately called his American assistant "Brother."

Dutton helped St. Damien until the priest's death three years later in 1889, and remained in Kalaupapa for an additional 42 years, administering the Baldwin Home for boys and men. St. Marianne during that time cared for girls and women at Bishop Home.

Dutton died in 1931. His grave lies next to that of St. Damien on the grounds of St. Philomena Church in Kalawao.

## *The Damien and Marianne*
## *Catholic Conference (DMCC)*

In 2016, the Damien and Marianne Catholic Conference was created in Hawaii. The vision is "To be a vital platform of evangelization for the growth of the Catholic Faith in Hawaii and beyond, imitating the charism of our Hawaiian saints. The mission is to "educate, inspire and empower the DMCC Ohana. Our focus will be on the respect of human life and dignity, marriage, youth and family life, education, social justice, and evangelism.

*Bishop Larry Silva at an International Mass Damien Marianne Catholic Conference 2018*

At the outset, the purpose of the annual conferences was to bring Christ's message to the people of Hawaii and beyond and to promote an understanding of the dignity and reverence for all life.

The DMCC held their first conference in 2017 in Honolulu. The success was followed in 2018 by the second conference. The outreach from Hawaii extended west to include people across the Pacific Rim and east to include keynote speakers from Vermont and Louisiana.

The 2018 conference drew five people from Vermont — Monsignor Routhier, Mindy Parisi, Denise Cope Parry (a great-niece to St. Marianne Cope), Lynn Altadonna and Mary Skelton. The experience highlighted the role that Blessed Sacrament Church has in celebrating the life of Joseph Dutton.

In addition, the conference elevated the awareness that exists among Catholics across the world. One Mass in the Hawaii Convention Center included people from seven countries including the Philippines, Japan, Viet Nam, and the US. The Mass music was an explosion of joy that the Vermonters had never heard before.

# The Making of a Saint

*Compiled by Msgr. Robert J. Sarno, Episcopal Delegate for the Cause of Canonization of the Servant of God Joseph Dutton, Layman and Former Official of the Congregation, now called Dicastery, for the Causes of the Saints, Rome.*

All souls who are in heaven and enjoy the vision of God face to face are Saints. In the process of canonization, the Catholic Church declares as "Saints" those faithful Catholics who gave outstanding testimony of holiness lived out in one of three essential ways: (1) they accepted or tolerated a violent death that was inflicted "in hatred of the Faith" (Martyrs); (2) they offered their lives as an expression of love, and died a rather quick and unexpected death (Confessors): (3) they gave heroic example of living all the Christian virtues (Confessors); For the first 1200 years of the history of the Catholic Church, Saints were canonized in various ways. Today, the process of canonization is very complex and thorough, and governed by a strict canonical or juridical procedure established by St. Paul II in 1983. There are four phases:

- Servant of God
- Venerable Servant of God
- Blessed
- Saint

## Servant of God

A cause of canonization cannot begin until five years after the death of the eventual candidate for canonization. This period of time permits the Church, through the local bishop or eparch, to verify whether the candidate enjoys an authentic and widespread reputation of holiness and of intercessory prayer among a significant portion of the people of God. When the local bishop officially begins the cause, the candidate is given the title of "Servant of God".

The first or local phase of the process begins with the official opening of the Cause by the bishop of the diocese or eparchy where the Servant of God died, and the appointment of a Postulator, to assist in its promotion. The bishop then nominates those Officials charged with gathering all the documentary and eyewitness evidence for and against the Canonization of the Servant of God. Two theologians examine the published writings of the Servant of God to ascertain whether there is anything in them contrary to the Faith and the moral teaching of the Church, and an Historical Commission is appointed to collect all the documentary evidence in the Cause.

Finally, the testimony of eyewitnesses is taken.

## Venerable Servant of God

The second or Roman phase of the cause of canonization starts when all the evidence gathered in the first phase is studied by the Dicastery for the Causes of the Saints in Rome. If the evidence reveals authentic and exemplary holiness of the Servant of God in one of the three ways mentioned above, the Prefect of the Dicastery informs the Holy Father that the Servant of God was, indeed, either a true martyr, or offered his/her life or has lived an heroically virtuous life.

The Holy Father then orders the Dicastery to issue the "Decree" either of martyrdom, of the offering of life or of heroic virtue. The Servant of God is given the title of "Venerable Servant of God". However, no form of public, liturgical honor may be given to the Venerable Servant of God.

## *Blessed*

The Venerable Servant of God, who has been declared to be a true "martyr" by the Holy Father, may be immediately beatified, that is, declared "Blessed". If, on the other hand, the Servant of God has been declared to have offered his/her life or to have lived a life of heroic virtue, it must be proven that one miracle has been granted by God through his or her intercession. The miracle, required for beatification in these cases, must have taken place on or after the date of death of the candidate for canonization. The overwhelming majority of cases of miraculous events are cures from diseases. For a cure to be considered a true miracle, an ecclesiastical tribunal to gather all the evidence is established by the bishop of the diocese or eparchy where the event took place. It must be determined that there is no scientific explanation for the extraordinary event and that the intercession of the candidate for canonization has been proven. The Dicastery for the Causes of the Saints conducts its study and judgment of the evidence, collected by the local Church, to verify that there is no scientific explanation for the cure and that the intercession of the candidate for canonization was requested. Once again, the conclusions are presented to the Holy Father who alone can declare that the event is a true miracle. Then the Venerable Servant of God may be beatified or declared "Blessed".

When someone is declared "Blessed", public ecclesiastical veneration (liturgical cult) is permitted by the Holy Father but only in the diocese that introduced the cause of canonization and, if it be the case, in the houses of the religious community of which the Blessed may have been a member.

## *Saint*

For the canonization of all those who are already beatified, both martyrs and confessors, one miracle is required. It must be proven that this event took place through the intercession of the Blessed and after the date of his or her beatification.

When this has been proven, the Holy Father then proceeds to the solemn ceremony of canonization, which is an infallible act of the teaching authority of the Supreme Pontiff. By this act, the Church declares that a member of the Catholic faithful is a Saint in heaven with God. The canonized Saint is then granted public veneration or liturgical honor throughout the universal Church, and held up as a model for imitation and as an intercessor for all the faithful.

It should be made very clear that the Catholic Church does not "worship" the Blessed Virgin Mary and the Saints, but rather venerates them. United in the "Communion of Saints", a tenet of the Faith declared in the Creed during solemn celebrations of the Liturgy, the faithful on earth ask the faithful in heaven, who are their brothers and sisters in Christ, to join them in presenting their needs humbly and prayerfully to God.

January 21, 2024, Bishop Larry Silva signed the edict that closed the diocean phase and sent to findings to Rome, starting the Roman Phase. If the Dicastery for the Causes of the Saints agrees, Brother Dutton will be declared "Venerable Servant of God."

# The Saints of Molokai

The Diocese of Honolulu leaders have promoted the recognition of those who served the leper colony at Molokai. First the Belgian priest, Reverend Damien de Veuster is honored throughout Hawaii with statues and prayers. The story of the cause for canonization follows.

The Saint Damien story is transcribed from the pamphlet *St. Damien De Veuster, ss.cc. of Molokai*, Congregation of the Sacred Hearts of Jesus and Mary Center, Kaneohe, Hawaii. www.sscc.org.

## Saint Damien

**Joseph De Veuster** was born on January 3, 1840, in the village of Tremeloo, Belgium. He was the seventh of eight children born to Frans and Ann-Catherine De Veuster in a devout Catholic family. His father intended for him to take over the family farm someday. However, Joseph felt drawn to the religious life like two of his sisters and a brother before him. At age 19, he entered the Congregation of the Sacred Hearts of Jesus and Mary at Louvain. For his religious name, he chose Damien after a third-century physician-saint and early Christian martyr.

In 1863, Damien's older brother, Father Pamphile, was headed for the Sacred Hearts mission in the Hawaiian Islands. A case of typhus prevented him from going. Damien, with missionary zeal and unbridled enthusiasm, asked and received permission to take his brother's place. After a sea voyage of nearly five months, Damien arrived in Honolulu on March 19, the Feast of St. Joseph, in 1864. For the next two months he studied the Hawaiian language and prepared for ordination to the priesthood.

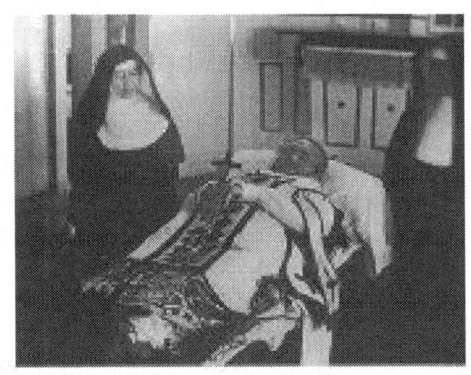

A. Damien at twenty-three just before he left Europe

B. Damien with boys of the settlement, 1889

C. Damien with some children of the settlement, probably members of the choir

D. Damien two months before his death in 1889. The lowered sling supporting his arm was given to him by Mother Marianne Cope, OSF

E. Mother Marianne Cope, OSF and Sister Leopoldina Burns, OSF prepared the funeral bed and casket of Father Damien, April 1889

The ordination of Damien and two others took place at the Cathedral of Our Lady of Peace in Honolulu on May 21, 1864. His first assignment was to the island of Hawaii. He labored there for nearly nine years - first in the Puna district, and then in an area encompassing the districts of Kohala and Hamakua. It was on Hawaii Island that Damien first witnessed leprosy patients being separated from their families and banished to the isolated peninsula of Kalaupapa on Molokai. These government-imposed measures were meant to prevent the spread of the disease, with no regard for the emotional impact this would have on those affected.

In May of 1873, Bishop Maigret blessed the first stone church of St. Anthony in Wailuku, Maui. To the assembled priests, he expressed the dire need to provide spiritual help for the people of Kalaupapa. Realizing the risks and sacrifice that this would entail, the bishop asked for volunteers on a three-month rotating basis. Damien was the first to volunteer, and accompanied the bishop to Kalaupapa. After seeing the paltry living conditions and the despair of its residents, he decided to remain there. With no house to shelter him, he slept under the canopy of a pandanus tree for several days after his arrival. The tree stood next to the small Catholic chapel erected the year before in the village of Kalawao.

Damien cared for the spiritual and physical needs of the residents of Kalaupapa. In addition to celebrating Mass and hearing their confessions, he built houses and an orphanage. He constructed churches, both in Kalaupapa and on top-side Molokai. For those who died, he made their coffins and dug their graves.

Father Damien's acts of compassion and advocacy for the patients at Kalaupapa earned him the respect and admiration of people around the world. In 1881, Princess Regent Liluokalani met Father Damien during her visit to the leprosy settlement. She later conferred upon him the decoration of the Knight Commander of the Royal Order of Kalakaua, in recognition of his dedicated service.

A medical examination in 1884 confirmed that Damien had contracted leprosy. In the face of this adversity, he stoically stated: "I have accepted this malady as my special cross." Despite his failing health, Damien continued to work up until a few days before his death on April 15, 1889. He was buried beneath the panandus tree which first sheltered him nearly 16 years earlier.

In 1936, at the request of King Leopold III, Father Damien's remains returned to his homeland. Much pomp and circumstance heralded the return of the native son of Belgium. His remains now rest in the crypt of the church where he first entered religious life.

Public acclamation of Damien's sanctity was heard even during his lifetime. But it would take 120 years after his death before he was officially recognized as a saint. Official acknowledgement began on July 9. 1977 when Pope Paul VI accorded Damien the title of Venerable. Pope John Paul II declared him Blessed on June 4, 1995. Finally, on October 11, 2009, Pope Benedict XVI proclaimed Father Damien a saint of the church. His feast day is celebrated on May 10, the first day of his arrival on the island of Molokai. A relic of Saint Damien is enshrined in the Cathedral of Our Lady of Peace, and another relic has been reinterred within his original grave site at Kalawao for veneration by the faithful.

## *Prayer to Saint Damien*

Father of Mercy, in our brother priest, Saint Damien of Molokai, ss.cc., You have given a shining witness of love for the poorest and most abandoned. Grant that, by his intercession, as faithful witness of the Heart of Your Son Jesus, we too may be servants of the most needy and rejected.

Teach us to live our lives with joy like yours, and to celebrate and contemplate the Eucharist so we might be good disciples of Jesus and Mary.

We ask this through our Lord Jesus Christ, Your Son, who lives and reigns with You and the Holy Spirit, one God, forever and ever. Amen.

## Saint Marianne Cope

The Saint Marianne Cope story is transcribed from the pamphlet – St. Marianne Cope, Beloved Mother of Outcasts, Sisters of St. Francis, Kalaupapa, HI. www.saintmariannecope.org.

Barbara Koob (now officially "Cope") was born on January 23, 1838 in Heppenheim, Germany. She was one of the 10 children born to Peter Koob, a farmer, and Barbara Witzenbacher Koob. The first year after Barbara's birth the family moved to the United States. The Koob family found a home in Utica, NY, where they became members of the St. Joseph Church and where the children attended the parish school.

Although Barbara felt called to the religious life at an early age her vocation was delayed for nine years because of family obligations. As the oldest child at home, she went to work in a factory after completing eighth grade in order to support her family when her father became ill. Finally, in the summer of 1862, at the age of 24, Barbara entered the Sisters of St. Francis in Syracuse, NY. On November 19, 1862, she received the religious habit and the name of Marianne. The following year she made her religious profession and began serving as a teacher and principal in several elementary schools in New York State. She had joined the Sisters of St. Francis with the intention of teaching, but her life soon became a series of administrative appointments. God had other plans for Sister Marianne.

As a member of the governing boards of her religious community in the 1860's, she participated in the establishment of two of the first hospitals in the central New York area. In 1870, she began a new ministry as a nurse-administrator at St. Joseph's Hospital in Syracuse, NY where she served as head administrator for six years. During this time she put her gifts of intelligence and people skills to good use as a facilitator, demonstrating the energy of a woman motivated by God alone.

Although Mother Marinane was often criticized for accepting for treatment "outcast" patients such as alcoholics, she became well known and loved in the central New York area for her kindness, wisdom, and down-to-earth practicality.

A. *Mother Marianne Cope,*OSF

B. *Sisters and patients in front of St. Elizabeth Convent, Kalaupapa*

C. *Mother Marianne Cope,*OSF *and Sister Leopoldina Burns,*OSF *prepared the funeral bed and casket of Father Damien, April 1889*

D. *Sister Concordia Eller, Sister Leopoldina Burns, Mother Marianne Cope, Sr. M. Elizabeth Gomes, Sr. M Vincentia McCormick, 1899*

E. *Mother Marianne Cope in the backyard at St. Elizabeth, November 1899*

F. *Mother Marianne on the grounds of St. Elizabeth a few days before she died on August 9th, 1918*

In June, 1883, Mother Marianne, now the provincial mother in Syracuse, received a letter from a Catholic priest assigned to the Catholic Mission in the Kingdom of Hawaii asking for help in managing hospitals and schools. The letter touched Mother Marianne's heart and she enthusiastically responded, in a letter back to Fr. Leonor on June 5, 1883: "my interest is awakened and I feel an irresistible force drawing me to follow this call..."

It wasn't until Father Leonor's visit on July 6, 1883, he told Mother Marianne the truth about the plight of Hawaii's leprosy patients. On July 12, shortly after his visit, Mother Marianne sent her answer, saying: "I am hungry for the work and I wish with all my heart to be one of those chosen ones, whose privilege it will be to sacrifice themselves for the salvation of the souls of the poor Islanders...I am not afraid of any disease; hence it would be my greatest delight even to minister to the abandoned "lepers".

Mother Marianne and six other Sisters of St. Francis arrived in Honolulu in November, 1883. With Mother Marianne as supervisor, their main task was to manage the Kakaako Branch Hospital on Oahu, which served as a receiving station for patients with leprosy (now called Hansen's disease) gathered from all over the islands. After being at the Kakaako Branch Hospital for three months, Queen Kapiolani asked Mother Marianne to open a hospital in Maui. Mother left with two other sisters for Maui. Malulani Hospital, which means "Protection of Heaven", was opened in April 1884. The hospital, now known as Maui Memorial Hospital, is still operational today. The sisters began teaching English to the Hawaiian girls and established St. Anthony's School which also still exists today.

Back at the Kakaako Branch Hospital, the sisters had quickly set to work cleaning the hospital and tending to its 200 patients. By 1885, they made major improvements to the living conditions and treatment of the patients. In November of that year, they also founded the Kapiolani Home for Girls inside the hospital compound, established to care for the healthy daughters of leprosy disease patients at Kakaako and Kalawao. The unusual decision to open a home for healthy children on the leprosy hospital premises was made because only the sisters would care for those so closely related to people with the dreaded disease.

Mother Marianne met Father Damien deVeuster, SS.CC. for the first time in January 1884 when he was in apparent poor health. Two years later, in 1886, after he had been diagnosed with Hansen's disease, Mother Marianne alone gave hospitality to the outcast priest upon hearing that his illness made him an unwelcome visitor to church and government leaders in Honolulu. In 1887, when a new government took charge of Hawaii, its officials decided to close the Oahu hospital and receiving station and to reinforce the former alienation policy. The unanswered questions were: Who will care for the sick? Who once again would be sent to a settlement for exiles on Kalaupapa peninsula on the island of Molokai? The Hawaiian government had decided to close the Kakaako Receiving Station and to send the patients directly to Kalaupapa.

In November 1888, Mother Marianne again responded to the plea for help and said: "We will cheerfully accept the work..." She arrived in Kalaupapa together with Sister Leopoldina Burns and Sister Vincentia McCormick several months before Father Damien's death and was able to console the ailing priest by assuring him that she would provide care for the patients at the Boys' Home at Kalawao that he had founded.

Together the three sisters ran the Bishop Home for 103 girls and over 100 boys. Once the new Baldwin Home, which had been established after Father Damien died was completed, Mother Marianne and the sisters returned to Bishop Home and joined the other sisters in caring for the women and girls. The workload was extreme, and the burden at times seemed overwhelming. In moments of despair, Sister Leopolidina reflected: "How long, O Lord, must I see only those who are sick and covered with leprosy?" Mother Marianne's invaluable example of never failing optimism, serenity and trust in God inspired hope in those around her and allayed the sisters' fear of contracting leprosy. She taught her sisters that their primary duty was "to make life as pleasant and comfortable as possible for those of our fellow creatures, who God has chosen to afflict with this terrible disease..."

Mother Marianne never returned to Syracuse. She died on Kalaupapa on August 9, 1918 of natural causes and was buried on the grounds of Bishop Home.

Her body was exhumed in January 2005 and returned to Syracuse, NY. A shrine in her honor was erected in the motherhouse chapel in Syracuse. She was beatified on May 14, 2005 and canonized on October 21, 2012. In July, 2014, her remains were brought back to Hawaii and are enshrined at the Cathedral Basilica of Our Lady of Peace in Honolulu.

And her legacy in Hawaii continues: The Sisters of St. Francis are still present in Kalaupapa, and they staff care centers, hospitals, nursing homes, diocesan schools, and run a flagship education center - St. Francis School in Honolulu founded in 1924; and St. Francis Healthcare System of Hawaii founded in 1927.

## *Prayer to Saint Marianne Cope*

Lord, Jesus, you who gave us your commandment of love of God and of neighbor and identified yourself in a special way with the most needy of your people, hear our prayer. Faithful to your teaching, Mother Marianne Cope loved and served her neighbor, especially the most desolate outcast. Giving herself generously and heroically for the victims of leprosy, she alleviated their physical and spiritual sufferings, thus helping them to accept their afflictions with resignation, as a pledge of God's love and their eternal happiness. Through her merits and intercession, grant us the favor which we confidently ask of you (mention request) so that the People of God, following the inspiration of her life and apostolate, may practice fraternal charity, according to your word and example. Amen. St. Marianne Cope, Pray for us.

*Joseph Dutton*
*His Memoirs*

THE STORY OF FORTY-FOUR YEARS OF SERVICE
AMONG THE LEPERS OF MOLOKAI, HAWAII

# NOTE FROM THE PUBLISHER

*Joseph Dutton : His Memoirs* is included in its entirety. We have made several changes to aid the reader in 2023:

- We have reordered several chapters to present Brother Dutton's story and writings in chronological order where logical.
- We have moved several chapters that are focused on Molokai, Kalaupapa, and Leprosy to Appendices at the end of the Memoirs section to focus the main body of the book on Brother Joseph Dutton and his story.
- We have moved several photographs to places in the text that are more appropriate and illustrative to the reader.
- We have added several new photographs and images to aid the readers understanding of the content. Some of these new images were not available in 1931 at the time of original publication. These additions are indicated with an asterisk (*) in the caption.
- We have corrected obvious typographical errors and updated spelling and grammatical constructs where appropriate if we felt they might be unclear to the reader, but we left the vast majority of the content as is to reflect the sensibilities and writing of the early 1930s.

# CHAPTER 2

# *Joseph Dutton*
# *His Memoirs*

## THE STORY OF FORTY-FOUR YEARS OF SERVICE
## AMONG THE LEPERS OF MOLOKAI, HAWAII

The latest photograph of Joseph Dutton, taken in January, 1931, at the St. Francis Hospital, Honolulu, to which he was removed for an eye operation. When he went to Honolulu he left Molokai, and his work among the lepers, for the first time in 44 years.

JOSEPH DUTTON
[HIS MEMOIRS]

The Story of Forty-four Years of Service
Among the Lepers of Molokai,
Hawaii

Edited by
HOWARD D. CASE

From the Press of
The Honolulu Star-Bulletin, Ltd.
Honolulu.
1931

# JOSEPH DUTTON

## HIS MEMOIRS

The Story of Forty-Four Years of Service
Among the Lepers of Molokai, Hawaii

Edited by
Howard D. Case

FROM THE PRESS OF
THE HONOLULU STAR-BULLETIN, LTD.
HONOLULU
1931

JOSEPH DUTTON : HIS MEMOIRS

## *Table of Contents*

*Read his story,*
*and whether you be prince or pauper,*
*it will urge you on*
*to better deeds and more faithful attention*
*to the real, first things of life.*

# *Foreword*

Lives that live forever are lives of self-sacrifice. So the deeds of Joseph Dutton will live in the minds of men and be retold for generations, while those of his day generally classed as successful will be dead, forgotten. There is a whole sermon on things worth while to be found in the good works of Joseph Dutton. And it rises above the romantic glamor of traditional imaginary horror generally associated with the pestilential isolation of leprosy. Joseph Dutton did not go to the Kalawao Settlement to gain fame or be the subject of a book. He went there to lose himself in the service of his fellow man. He loved his work. He radiated healthful good cheer in a little world that could be dreadful and drear. And as he went along the pathway of more than two score years he kept in touch with the old friends of the old days, not pleasanter days but full of pleasant memories. Romantic interest surrounds such a life. Above all it is an inspiration. No words of mine can add luster to the life and work of Joseph Dutton, but like so many others who know him, I gladly offer my tribute of respect and appreciation. Of whatsoever things are worthwhile, he garnered a great and beautiful harvest. It is especially gratifying that one of his friends has given the time and thought to make a permanent record and readable account of one who so completely gave his life for his fellows. No wonder he celebrated his eighty-seventh birthday with health and a wonderfully youthful outlook on the added years of service for which we all hope he may be spared. Read the story, and whether you be prince or pauper, it will urge you on to better deeds and more faithful attention to the real, first things of life.

WALLACE R. FARRINGTON,
PUBLISHER OF THE HONOLULU STAR-BULLETIN
FORMER GOVERNOR OF HAWAII.

*His message to the world,*
*not of words but of deeds,*
*has been one of patience,*
*of self–sacrifice,*
*of unfaltering belief in God and His teachings.*

# *Introduction*
## 1931

To me, a newspaper reporter, schooled to avoid "fine" writing, it has been an altogether pleasant and inspiring task to set down here the memoirs, the life story, of Joseph (formerly Ira) Dutton, who for the last forty-four years has performed one of the most notable humanitarian tasks in the history of America—the devotion of the best years of his life in the service of the afflicted of his fellow man, the lepers of Molokai.

These memoirs came to be written as a part of the routine of a busy newspaper office. I was assigned to go to Molokai, visit Joseph Dutton, obtain his life story and his consent to its publication by The Honolulu Star-Bulletin. I made several trips into the forbidden territory, with the assistance of Dr. Frederick E. Trotter, president of the territorial board of health, and the late John D. McVeigh, then superintendent of the leper settlement, and came away finally with my "story."

My greatest task was, I believe now, in convincing Joseph Dutton of the advisability of publishing his memoirs; of letting the whole world know through the printed word the details of his long life of service among the lepers; of baring for the first time the innermost secrets of his heart; of stating without hesitancy the primary reasons which led him to forsake the world and hide himself away upon an island which, up until only a comparatively few years ago, was a place to be shunned.

What appears in the following pages is largely in Joseph Dutton's own words, edited somewhat to conform to present-day methods of presentation of material of this sort, and supplemented here and there by letters, manuscripts and other documents. In other words, it is Joseph Dutton's own story, told to me by a man in splendid control of his every faculty despite his advanced age.

I would like to make it clear that this volume is confined to the memoirs of Joseph Dutton, and no attempt has been made to present a complete history of the leper settlement, nor of leprosy in the Hawaiian Islands. Historical matter regarding these subjects has been brought out only as it relates directly to the personal labors and sacrifices of the subject of these memoirs.

Despite the isolation of forty-four years, Joseph Dutton is known throughout the world. He has friends in every part of the globe—countless persons who have read of his work and who have become his steady correspondents. In many places in America he is honored annually—at Milton College, where he was educated; at Grand Army of the Republic posts, and elsewhere when old, old friends, the friends of his youth, gather to pay him tribute.

The great cliffs of Molokai, shoved back by Nature's hand from the rocky shores of Kalawao, shelter the tiny whitewashed frame building where of nights Joseph Dutton sat and wrote for so many years by the feeble light of a candle, keeping in touch with his friends in the great outside. His message to the world, not of words but of deeds, has been one of patience, of self-sacrifice, of unfaltering belief in God and His teachings. And his task will not end until, when God wills, the light fades forever from his bright, smiling eyes.

H. D. C.

(FROM THE HONOLULU STAR-BULLETIN, JULY 14, 1928.)

# President Coolidge Gives High Praise To Joseph Dutton, Aide Of Lepers

(ASSOCIATED PRESS BY WIRELESS)

JANESVILLE, Wis., July 14—Direct acknowledgement of the great work of Brother Joseph Dutton and his appreciation of his service to humanity in his ministrations to the leper colony on the island of Molokai, Hawaii, was made yesterday by President Calvin Coolidge.

President Coolidge yesterday personally acknowledged a gift from Brother Dutton sent to him through Stephen Bolles, editor of the Janesville Gazette. President Coolidge also announced in his letter to Bolles that he was sending a letter direct to Brother Dutton, thanking him for the gift.

Brother Dutton, 85-year-old Civil war veteran and former resident of Janesville, sent President Coolidge a picture of his birthplace at Stowe, VT. He also sent a photograph of his mother to Mrs. Coolidge.

In forwarding the mementoes, Bolles told President Coolidge of Dutton's life in Molokai, and in referring to his work, said: "Brother Dutton is standing alone in the world with this service he is rendering at Molokai."

Bolles received the following reply from President Coolidge:

"Dear Mr. Bolles: Accept my sincerest thanks for your letter of July second, and for your kindness in sending me the parcel from Brother Joseph Dutton, head of the leper colony at Molokai, Hawaiian islands.

What you tell me of Brother Dutton is most interesting. It is good of you to write me so fully about him.

I have been greatly pleased and touched by his thought of me and I am writing him a direct word of appreciation of this.

Mrs. Coolidge and I are thoroughly enjoying our visit to this state and are finding our stay at Cedar Island Lodge delightful in every way. I was very glad indeed to hear from you."

Very truly yours,
CALVIN COOLIDGE

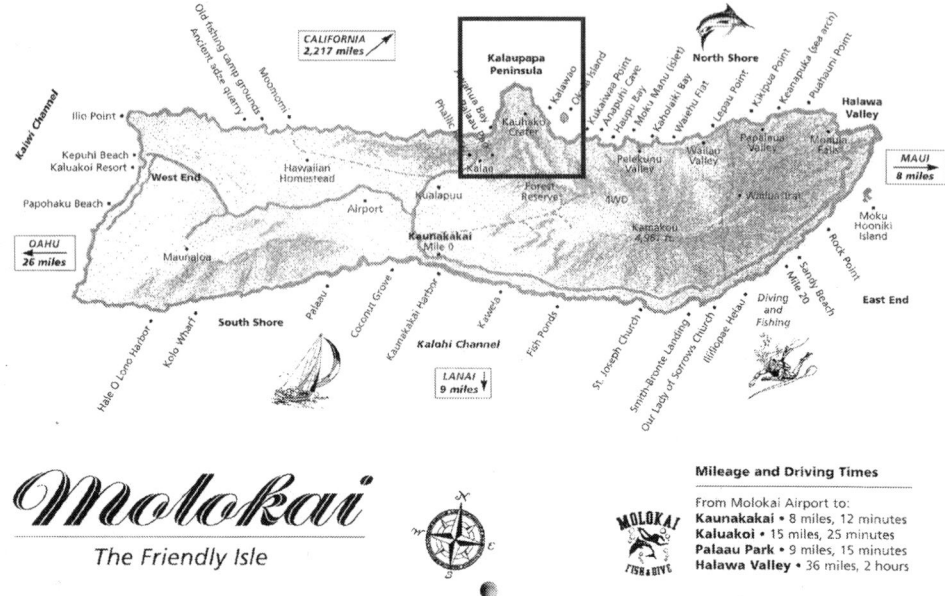

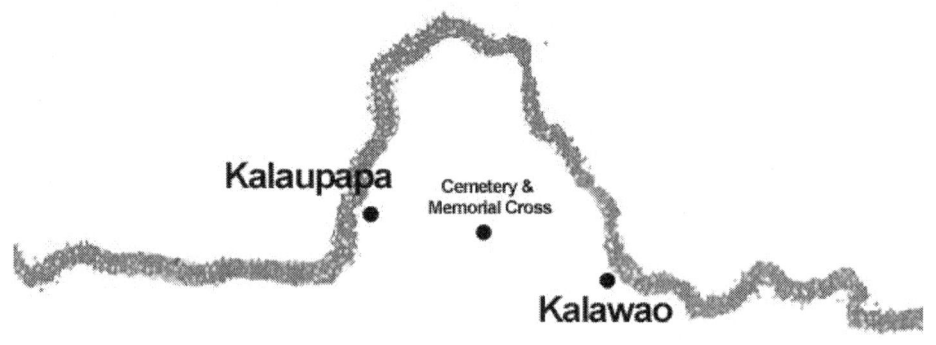

## MOLOKAI: PAST AND PRESENT
### 1931

The very mention of Molokai, fifth in size of the eight principal islands comprising the Hawaiian group, is apt to leave a bitter taste in the mouths of those unfamiliar with the latter-day history of America's newest territory. For to them Molokai means leprosy, and very little else; and there is perhaps nothing today that is feared more greatly than this dread disease, which has made itself felt from one end of the earth to the other, and for which no positive cure has as yet been found.

But in Hawaii, where skilled scientists have been combating the malady for nearly half a century, that loathing and fear of leprosy has vanished almost utterly. No longer does the leper, except in most rare instances, hide himself away in some mountain recess and, at the point of a gun, defy the authorities to come and take him. Those days have gone, and, with their passing, science has stepped in with a firm, sure hand to take control of the vestige of the disease now remaining.

In the entire territory today there are a few more than five hundred lepers. A kindly home government sees to it that those who must make their homes at the leper settlements on Molokai have every comfort and consideration. And at Honolulu, capital of the territory, persons who were once lepers are being paroled to go again among their fellow men, science having succeeded in arresting the disease. Time only can tell whether this physical change for the better is to be permanent. No one in the territory has ever claimed that the present method of treatment is a "cure;" but it is claimed, and has been proved, that the treatment will arrest the disease, if applied in the earliest stages, sufficiently to permit the patient to have his freedom.

What is to follow here will in no wise be a treatise upon either lepers or leprosy; but it is necessary to touch briefly upon both subjects in order that the reader may obtain a clear-cut background for the story that is to be told. Hawaii has, perhaps, done more for leprosy and lepers than any other single geographical unit; and today the mention of Molokai means, to the people of the territory, industry in its broadest sense. Its connection with leprosy has ceased, almost, to be a jarring note in the otherwise perfect commercial and industrial harmony. The more important forward steps in the treatment of leprosy have been taken since the annexation of the Hawaiian group to the United States shortly after the close of the Spanish-American war and during the administration of President William McKinley. The old Hawaiian government was equipped but poorly to handle this gigantic problem, and it remained for American scientists, many of them men of note, to bring about an easement of the sufferings of the patients, and to evolve what is held today to be the most effective of all treatments.

It was in 1863 that there first appeared in Hawaii a disease which was believed to be leprosy. The islands were then a kingdom—a monarchy which had become fairly well organized as the result of an influx of and intercourse with foreigners who came to Hawaii to settle permanently in business or in the professions. The case in question was diagnosed as leprosy, and was believed to have been brought in by Chinese who were migrating to the islands in large numbers in those days. An investigation showed that a large number of similar cases were prevalent throughout the group. Having knowledge of the havoc that had been wrought by leprosy in India and other parts of Asia through countless years, the Hawaiian government, in 1865, took its first official action with regard to the disease, and it was decided to set aside for the segregation of lepers the tiny peninsula on the northern coast of the island of Molokai. The first shipment of lepers was made in 1866, and from that time until now the peninsula has been a leper colony, and has become known throughout the world as a refuge for persons so afflicted, although it never has been what might be termed a "dumping ground" for these unfortunate folk. It has been peopled solely by island patients.

The island of Molokai, which is long and fairly low-lying, has an area of 261 square miles. It is located between the islands of Maui and Oahu, and is separated from the former by a channel eight miles wide and having no great depth. Its length is about 38 miles from east to west, the average width being about seven miles. It is quite probable that, in its original volcanic formation, it was considerably larger, with a much greater width and with its highest mountains in the central and eastern portions, forming an irregular ridge running east and west along the middle. In the western part these mountains probably ran more toward the north, save that near the extremity they curved southward again.

In the opinion of geologists and other observers, the ridge or backbone was split by some great volcanic or subterranean upheaval, the northern part being thrown off and submerged in the ocean depths. It has been called a "great displacement" or "dislocation," and "a fault scarp of magnificent size." However, there remains a line of majestic cliffs and noble headlands which, for unique grandeur, can hardly be surpassed. The Pacific Ocean throbs and beats at the bases of these towering cliffs, save where a few valleys or gulches form open places, and where the cliffs recede, forming a line around the head of each.

The somewhat irregular line of bold mountain face varies in height from about 2,000 feet at midway to 3,500 feet toward the east. Some higher peaks lie further back in the eastern portion, the highest being nearly 5,000 feet. This line of cliffs rises abruptly out of the sea along the northern coast, and then the land slopes gently downward toward the sea on the other side, forming an especially fertile stretch that is well forested along the upper portions.

Time was when the island of Molokai held a notable place in the day-to-day history of the group. That was during the halcyon days of the monarchy, when kings ruled and when chiefs and chiefesses* held sway over the individual portions of the land. A very famous line of island chiefs came from Molokai, as did a famous clan of "Kahunas," or priests, notable among which were those who were declared to have the power

---

* a Polynesian term for a female chief

of "praying" a human being to death. It was there that one of the kings
of the great Kamehameha dynasty established his summer capital, and
swam in an inland pool fed by a spring which today furnishes water for
irrigating thousands of acres of rich agricultural land. Molokai's great
fish ponds, then sacred to the king and the chiefs, have gone down in
island history as a sort of seven-day wonder, and even now a few of them
remain, enclosed in the same stone walls that protected them a century
or two ago.

History says that it was upon the island of Molokai that a crude
form of aviation was practised by the native Hawaiians a century or so
ago. Reckless and daring to an extreme, they manufactured huge "planes"
from woven palm leaves and, seating themselves in the center of them,
were pushed off a high cliff. If the "aviator" was skillful enough, he balanced the contrivance until it landed finally upon the ocean a thousand
or so feet below, where canoes were waiting to pick him up. The unskill-
ful "aviator" was merely flung headlong into the sea after the collapse of
his "plane."

It would seem that, in some ancient day, the northern half of the
island had split off and had fallen into the ocean, leaving a great, massive
perpendicular cliff that extends the length of the remaining half. Or it
may be that this cliff line was the southern lip of a huge volcanic crater,
left to stand alone after some upheaval had cast the remainder into the
sea.

Today the traveler disembarks from an inter-island steamer at the
tiny village of Kaunakakai, on the southern side of the island, which,
although bearing certain earmarks of the olden days, has its hotel and
garage and telephone lines and radio station. From here a road leads
upward toward the north, and during the climb one passes first through
the flourishing homesteads of Hawaiians and part-Hawaiians who
are being aided by the territory under a federal rehabilitation act; then
through the highly cultivated acres of a large ranch, and, lastly, through
a vast stretch of splendid agricultural land, every acre of which is planted
to pineapples, a fruit for which Hawaii has become famous almost over-
night, and which now constitutes the territory's second largest industry.

A few moments after passing through the pineapple fields, one finds himself at the edge of a mighty cliff. Stretching away in front, as far as he can see, is the broad Pacific, sparkling blue and green in the sunlight. Far below is the broad, white line that is the surf which forever is beating against the cliff base. The traveler steps out a few feet further and looks downward to the right. There, nearly 2,000 feet below, lies the tiny peninsula which, since 1866, has been the leper colony of Hawaii. Near by, beginning through a small forest of Kukui trees, is a narrow trail which runs down the face of the cliff and into the settlement. It is the only exit by land, but is no longer guarded by men armed with rifles. The occasional visitor, the superintendent and the mail carrier are the only persons who traverse it.

This little peninsula is the only projection along that vast stretch of coast. It is about two miles wide at the base of the cliffs, and extends a like distance into the sea. In the olden days, when people knew far less about leprosy than they do today, there was no escape from it. At the back the insurmountable cliffs reared their heights against the fugitive, for it was not until lately that the trail was constructed. In the front the ocean surf roared out its defiance along the rocky coast line. Once he was in the settlement, there was little likelihood of the leper escaping; and in those days a fugitive leper became as a wild animal, to be hunted down and shot on sight. But modern practices and methods have changed all that.

The peninsula takes the shape of a horseshoe. At the extreme point the coast line is from 100 to 250 feet high, sloping gradually toward the foot of the cliffs. The western side is known as Kalaupapa, and it is here that the main leper settlement is located—a settlement which today has all of the features of a modern village, with neat homes and well-kept yards, large and modern hospitals, well-stocked stores maintained by the government, churches of many denominations, a school, several institutions or homes, an electric light plant, an ice factory, and an amusement hall where there are dances, theatricals and motion pictures regularly, and a radio set which keeps the patients in touch with the outside world.

On the eastern side, known as Kalawao, is located the Baldwin Home for leper boys, and at which are also accommodated a number of adult men, some of whom are blind. Farther on toward the shore line are the now abandoned buildings of what was intended to be a federal leprosarium, established by the United States government and given up finally as a bad job. It was found it was best to let Hawaii take care of her lepers in her own way. The buildings are still in good condition. The federal government has turned them over to the territory, and a few have been torn down and the lumber taken to Kalaupapa for the erection of additional hospitals and homes there.

The reader will understand, therefore, that only this tiny peninsula on the north coast of the island of Molokai is used as a sanctuary for lepers, and not the island in its entirety. The remainder of the island, being highly productive, is devoted to farms and ranches and dairies, as well as to the cultivation of pineapples and the homesteads maintained by the government.

Due to a general improvement in conditions over a period of more than 25 years, the present inhabitants of the leper settlement are orderly, happy and industrious. The fact that they are separated from the outside world, and probably will be for the remainder of their lives, does not appear to bother them in the least. Many of them have small fortunes in their own right, and practically all of them own livestock and maintain homes that have every convenience. They have their dances, their socials, their entertainments and their societies, and have always been in the front line of contributors to worthy causes—Liberty Bonds, war savings stamps, the Japanese relief, the Near East relief, and the starving children of Europe.

On almost any evening, after dinner is over and the chores around the house have been attended to, the manager of the amusement hall—himself a leper—walks out of his front gate and calls to the neighbors.

"Come on down to the hall, folks," he says in liquid Hawaiian, "I'm going to tune up the radio set and maybe we'll pick up Los Angeles tonight." It is pertinent to say something here with regard to the treatment of leprosy now in vogue in Hawaii. For many years Hawaii, like other countries in which the disease prevailed, used chaulmoogra oil in combating the scourge. The plain oil was either given internally or injected intravenously, and while the general effects were not unsatisfactory, there was not sufficient response on the part of the patient which would guarantee a notable improvement within a reasonable length of time.

Finally Dr. J. T. McDonald and Dr. Harry T. Hollmann, both of Honolulu, and Dr. Arthur L. Dean, then president of the College (now University) of Hawaii, perfected a specific which consisted entirely of the element in the chaulmoogra oil which possessed the remedial power. After a long series of laboratory experiments they succeeded in isolating the beneficial element and separating it from the remainder of the oil. This pure element was administered to lepers in Hawaii, with the result that a large number were paroled from confinement, the germ of the disease having been arrested. Practically all of these patients have been granted paroles at the receiving hospital at Honolulu, where persons having the disease in its earliest stages are first sent.

Paroles from the leper settlement at Kalaupapa have been few and far between, and the reason is that, out of the 500 or more patients there, only a few are taking this new treatment, or any treatment at all. There is no law compelling these patients to be treated, other than the ordinary dictates of sanitation, and they are not amenable to treatment *because they are afraid that they will be cured and compelled to leave the settlement, which is the only real home they have ever known.* Leprosy or no leprosy, they desire to remain where they are, and where their homes and loved ones and friends are. Cast out upon the world to shift for themselves, they would undoubtedly soon become public charges, and would be taken from a life of contentment and placed into one of poverty and misery.

# *A Penance Is Chosen*
## 1886

Back in those dark days when the Kingdom of Hawaii was confronted by a battle against a dread disease, the Civil War was occupying the attention of all America, and one year later it was concluded and the North and the South united by bonds that were never to be broken.

Hawaii, busy with her own affairs, paid but passing attention to the conflict. At that time there was no cable to flash the day-by-day reports of this battle and that, and the news of the war reached Honolulu through ships that were few and far between, so that all information was many days, often weeks old by the time it arrived.

In the Quartermaster Department of the Northern forces was a young first lieutenant, Ira B. Dutton, then in his early twenties, who had been drawn into the conflict by the stirring patriotic spirit which swept the country when the war clouds first loomed, and who rose rapidly from a private in the ranks to a commissioned officer. A native of Vermont, and of good stock that had migrated from England, young Dutton had, perhaps, never heard of the Hawaiian Islands, then still known as the Sandwich Islands, nor had any premonition of the strange chain of circumstances which, within a very few years, would land him upon the shores of Hawaii upon one of the strangest missions ever undertaken on behalf of suffering humanity.

By 1864 the spread of leprosy in Hawaii had become alarming. On January 3, 1865, during the reign of King Kamehameha V, the Legislature, sensing the necessity for immediate action, passed "An act to prevent the spread of leprosy," the enforcement of the measure being placed in the hands of the Board of Health. During the years 1865 and 1866 it was reported officially that 274 persons living in the islands were lepers.

As the result of the action of the Legislature, the work of segregating the lepers was begun, and plans were made for the erection of a hospital in some outlying district in which the lepers could be housed and cared for. The government purchased land in the Palolo Valley, now one of the flourishing suburbs of Honolulu, and when this became known in the immediate neighborhood, a flood of objections caused the government to abandon the project.

A site was then obtained in the Kalihi district, another suburb of Honolulu which was at the time well removed from other habitations, and in November, 1865, the hospital was constructed. This institution was, primarily, for the purpose of detaining and examining persons believed to be lepers, and for the medical treatment of actual lepers and suspects. The hospital did successful and satisfactory work in view of its small size, but the need was felt for a larger and more permanent settlement, considerably isolated, for persons declared to be lepers, this to be operated in connection with the smaller institution at Kalihi. It was proposed to continue the latter hospital so that it might go ahead with its endeavors to effect cures in the early stages of the disease.

The search for a suitable site for the enlarged settlement, or asylum, was directed finally to the peninsula on Molokai, which was well protected, and which would not permit the escape of a patient, once he had been placed there. In the face of wholesome trade winds from the Northeast, a place better adapted could hardly have been found. The Board of Health assumed authority over the peninsula on June 6, 1866, and made immediate preparations for the erection of the necessary buildings there.

The president of the Board of Health at this time was Dr. F. W. Hutchinson. R. W. Meyer, whose home was near the top of the pali, or cliff, on the other side of the island, was the Board of Health agent on Molokai, and was prominent in the organization of the settlement. He continued as agent and as business manager of the settlement until his death on June 12, 1897.

At about this time a commissioner of King Kamehameha, being ready to embark upon a visit to various foreign countries upon public business, was instructed to make inquiries as to the various methods employed in the care and treatment of persons afflilicted with leprosy.

The physician in charge of the Kalihi Hospital reported on March 2, 1866, that the institution had received 158 lepers, that 57 had been sent to the Molokai settlement, and that 101 were being retained at the hospital for treatment. In sending lepers to Molokai, considerable difficulty was experienced in separating them from relatives at Honolulu, and many very pathetic scenes were enacted at the wharf when patients, after saying goodbye to their loved ones, sailed away from them probably forever. In order to overcome this condition, a few non-leper relatives were permitted to enter the settlement as "kokuas" or helpers, and this custom is still in vogue. At the settlement today there are many leper husbands living with non-leper wives, and vice versa. The government also undertook to furnish the settlement with livestock, and many cattle and sheep and pigs were sent to the peninsula. The expense account for Kalihi Hospital and the Molokai Settlement in 1866 was $10,012.48; but it should be borne in mind that there were practically no modern conveniences there at that time. The buildings were not of the best, sanitary conditions were imperfect in the extreme, and there was little or no outlook in so far as the future of the patients was concerned.

However, things went along quite well at first, but after a while there developed among the patients an ugly spirit. Drunken and lewd conduct prevailed. A complete change seemed to have come over the ordinarily easy-going, good-natured people. All of this was reported by the president of the Board of Health at some length, but by 1868 it was noted in the official reports that certain changes for the better had been brought about. Some improvements had been made at the settlement, including the erection of a hospital, and a schoolmaster, magistrate and nurse, in addition to the government physician, were employed.

By 1867 the annual cost of maintaining the Kalihi Hospital and the Molokai Settlement had jumped to $24,803, and stronger efforts were being made to render the segregation and treatment of the lepers more effective. Many difficulties were met and overcome. To keep good order in these early years was always difficult.

Throughout the islands the lepers were increasing in number. Practically all of those sent to the Molokai Settlement were located at Kalawao, the site of the present boys' home, on the eastern side of the peninsula. As a matter of fact the settlement was almost entirely at Kalawao, and so continued for many years. In 1890 a better supply of water was brought from Waikolu Valley, and the pipe line soon after was extended to Kalaupapa, where the steamer landing was located. A reservoir was constructed midway on the ridge between Kalawao and Kalaupapa.

Previous to that time, a pipe was laid from a small reservoir in Waileia Valley, between the Waikolu Valley and Kalawao, and extended but partly through Kalawao. At Kalaupapa, two miles distant, the people brought their water from Waihanau Valley in containers upon the backs of horses and mules. The people at Kalaupapa were chiefly non-lepers who had lived there before "settlement times." Their holdings had not yet been obtained, but this was done by the government in 1894, as, after the water pipe was laid to Kalaupapa, the people had began to drift gradually that way. The public buildings at Kalaupapa also went, one by one, including offices and shops. Therefore it was determined that in the interests of good order, as well as convenience, the government should own and control the entire peninsula and all of its approaches. This was done, and the non-lepers were compelled to leave.

Official records show that the number of lepers at the Molokai settlement during the years 1866 to 1873 was as follows:

1866 . . . . . . . . . . . . . . . . . . . . . . . 105
1867 . . . . . . . . . . . . . . . . . . . . . . . 143
1868 . . . . . . . . . . . . . . . . . . . . . . . 228
1869 . . . . . . . . . . . . . . . . . . . . . . . 284
1870 . . . . . . . . . . . . . . . . . . . . . . . 279
1871 . . . . . . . . . . . . . . . . . . . . . . . 402
1872 . . . . . . . . . . . . . . . . . . . . . . . 439
1873 . . . . . . . . . . . . . . . . . . . . . . . 749

Up to and including the year 1871 a Catholic priest visited the leper settlement occasionally from the islands of Oahu or Maui. The Rev. Father Raymond went there and stayed for several weeks during the years 1871 and 1872, and the Rev. Father Aubert made frequent visits and even offered to remain there permanently.

Thus the Catholics engaged in the first real religious activities at the leper settlement, and the courage and devotion displayed by the priests and the brothers is to be marveled at, for in those days, as today, no one knew in what manner the dread disease might be contracted. This problem baffled scientists then as it does now. With the aid of the lepers, the priests erected grass huts which they used as chapels. On May 30, 1872, a chapel that had been erected at Kalawao by one of the Catholic brothers, probably Brother Bertram, was blessed by the Rev. Father Raymond, and dedicated to St. Philomena.

On May 4, 1873, Bishop Maigret and a number of priests went to Maui for the purpose of dedicating a church at Wailuku. After the ceremony, the bishop expressed a desire to journey to Molokai, but a short distance away, and visit the lepers. He asked that one of the fathers accompany him, and the Rev. Father Damien De Veuster, a young native of Belgium, offered his services, which were accepted.

They arrived at Kalaupapa on May 10, 1873. It was proposed that Father Damien remain with the lepers for two or three weeks, and then return to his district on one of the other islands. But during the bishop's visit, which lasted only a few hours, the lepers petitioned for a resident priest. The matter was not decided then, and Father Damien wrote to the provincial, offering to remain permanently. The bishop consented.

Thus there came to Molokai a man whose name has gone down in history as a martyr in the cause of humanity. Father Damien remained among the lepers, and for weeks his only shelter was a pandanus tree near the beach, under which he ate, slept, held services and ministered to the sick. He not only devoted the best part of his short life to the lepers, but died one of them, having contracted the disease in 1876.

It was on July 29, 1886, that an inter-island steamer dropped her anchor off Kalaupapa. A ship's boat was rowed to the tiny wharf and a comparatively young man, robust in health and of pleasing appearance, stepped from it. A little distance from the wharf, in a rig drawn by a white horse, sat Father Damien. The stranger saw him and walked up to him.

"You are Father Damien ?" he asked.

"Yes," was the reply.

"I am Joseph Dutton, a lay brother," the stranger continued, "and I have come here to help you carry on your good work."

Father Damien looked at the stranger for a moment, at the frank look in his eyes, at the clean-cut, smiling countenance. Then he said:

"I need you. Jump up here alongside of me and we will ride over to the settlement."

Thus Brother Joseph Dutton came to Molokai—to do penance for past sins by spending the remainder of his life as God's servant among unfortunate lepers.

*New England gave Brother Dutton to the world.*
*The town of Stowe, Vermont, birth place of Joseph Dutton.*

# From Boyhood To War
## 1843–1865

Ira B. Dutton was born at Stowe, Vermont, on April 27, 1843. The middle initial was added by himself in later years, being taken from his mother's family name, which was Barnes. His father was Ezra Dutton, a descendant of three Duttons who, braving the perils of the Atlantic and the dangers which still lurked in that strange and comparatively new land, came to the Americas from England early in the 17th century, and settled in what later became the states of Vermont and Connecticut.

Near the close of the year 1847 the Dutton family removed from Vermont to Wisconsin, and located on the Rock River at Janesville, which was then a new town. In fact, Wisconsin was only just then preparing to become a state, being admitted the following year. Ira was the oldest child of the family, and is the only member now living. The years of his early youth were normal and unexciting, as there were but few forms of amusement—things to do and places to go—in that more or less unsettled country during that period. As a boy, he received his education from his mother at home, she having been a school-teacher in Vermont. As he grew older, and for several years before he reached his eighteenth birthday, he attended the "Old Academy" at Janesville, the Milton Academy, which was some eight miles from Janesville, and, finally, Milton College.

In all, Ira spent about six years in these institutions. In his leisure hours he worked in James Sutherland's bookstore at Janesville, and came to be known to friends and acquaintances as the "Bookstore Boy." As he recollects it, he began doing odd jobs around the bookstore when little more than six years old. Sutherland, a kindly man, took an intense liking

*Main hall at Milton College, Wis., where Joseph Dutton was educated.*

to the youngster, and there were times when the little money he was able to earn was sorely needed at home, for there was many a period of "hard times" in those days when the country was being settled and built up, the land cleared and tilled, and the forerunners of the great manufacturing and other industrial enterprises started. Consequently, as he grew older, Ira found it impossible to attend school continuously. When compelled by necessity to work in the bookstore, he studied during his leisure moments, and at night his mother assisted him at home. Thus he was able to assist his father and mother financially, and at the same time obtain a fairly sound education.

While a clerk in the bookstore, Ira became interested in and soon mastered the art of bookbinding, as well as a smattering of printing. The coming of the first newspaper to Janesville was a red-letter day in the history of the little town. The editor was Joseph Baker, a close friend of Ira's father, and the youngster took such a keen interest in the enterprise that he was given finally the honorary title of "assistant editor." His "connection" with the paper, which was a small weekly, consisted mainly of clipping jokes from exchanges. Then, each week, after the paper had been printed, Ira would attend to the folding, for which he received a small silver coin. He was about eight years old at the time, and continued his association with Editor Baker for about a year.

Several years later, while still attending school, Ira became active in church and Sunday school work. He also took an interest in athletics of various kinds, and same into possession of a small gymnasium which he conducted for a considerable period, and which he turned over to friends—he gave it away without thought of recompense—at the time he went into the army.

Credit for the success he was able to accomplish in his youth, Dutton today attributes to his mother, who was an admirable woman of very high character, and withal kindly and considerate. Before her marriage to Ezra Dutton, she had been a teacher, and it was her experience along this line which assisted her oldest son materially during the trying times when he could not devote all of his hours to obtaining an education in the institutions provided for that purpose. She had the utmost confi-

dence in her son, as he did in her, and it was unquestionably due to the
confidence that, in later years, she became a Catholic a year after Dutton's
conversion to that faith. She was a descendant of the sturdy and extensive
Barnes family of Vermont, which, in the beginning, was composed largely
of farmers but which, in later years, produced many notable public men.
They were sturdy, hard-working, honest, old-fashioned New Englanders,
and all of their fine traits were inherited by Dutton's mother Abigail.

*"She who taught me the ways of love and led me along the paths of righteousness."*
*Joseph Dutton's most treasured possession—a photograph of his mother*
*Abigail Barnes Dutton, taken at Janesville, Wis., in 1890.*

Like all youths of that period, young Dutton took a keen interest
in things military, and was one of the first boys to become a member of
the Janesville City Zouave Corps, which was organized at the time when

the famous Chicago Zouaves, captained by the intrepid Col. Elmer E. Ellsworth, was in the very flower of its existence. Ellsworth's name will be linked forever with American military history, his career having been terminated abruptly by his death at the beginning of the Civil War.

Concerning that period of his youth prior to taking part in the Civil War, Dutton once wrote:

> "I was not apparently such an awful bad boy just then, but beyond a doubt much more than made up for it by being 'plenty' bad later on. There will not be time for me to write in these brief notes all about my badness. There was ever so much too much of it. But I couldn't feel quite honest to make such a sketch, noting some things supposed to be good, without at least referring occasionally to some of the bad parts. They will come in, mostly, from just after the war; to, say, 1876. Looking aright, there is little room for pride, but ample for shame over misdeeds of the past. I should not, however, cause suspicion of something horrible. There is no murder or robbery; no serious wrong that I know of toward anyone save myself."

In the summer of 1861 the little company of Zouaves at Janesville voted to join and become a part of a volunteer regiment which was then being organized there. War had been declared between the North and the South, and the country was afire with a patriotic spirit that penetrated into every little hamlet and town. Men and youths by the thousands were heeding the scream of the bugle and the rattle of the drums, and flocking to the nearest points where companies and regiments of volunteers were being formed.

The Janesville Zouave cadets were enrolled in a body as Company B of the volunteer regiment, which later was to become known as the 13th Wisconsin Volunteer Infantry. Later on, in 1864, it became known as the Veteran Volunteer Infantry, and in December, 1865, was mustered out of service, Dutton, who had in the meantime risen from the ranks and obtained a commission, returning from special duty in January, 1866.

The regiment of which Dutton was a member served in Kansas, Kentucky, Tennessee, Alabama, Louisiana and Texas, and, while participating in a number of minor battles, was never called upon to aid in any of the major engagements which were factors in bringing about a termination of the great conflict. Dutton, however, recalls that what the regiment lacked in the way of actual fighting, it made up many times over by marches, long ones and short ones. On one occasion, while at Lawrence, Kansas, the regiment lost some 200 soldiers as a result of disease.

To digress briefly, Dutton, upon becoming a member of the regiment, was a private in the ranks for but a few hours. He was appointed regimental quartermaster sergeant at the outset. The regiment then went into the field, and the first vacancy in the commissioned personnel was filled by the sergeant major, the only non-commissioned officer ranking Dutton. Another vacancy in the commissioned personnel occurred soon, and Dutton was appointed second lieutenant of Company I, and then first lieutenant in the same unit. With the appointment as first lieutenant, Dutton was detailed as regimental quartermaster, and later on was appointed brigade quartermaster under Gen. R. S. Granger.

When the Northern forces took possession of the Tennessee River from Bridgeport down, holding it as an advanced line, Dutton was appointed post quartermaster, with headquarters at Decatur, Alabama. He was also quartermaster for the district of North Alabama at the time of General Hood's raid on Nashville. His chief work as post quartermaster was at Decatur, where considerable supplies had been assembled on the south bank of the Tennessee River. Here also were repair shops, warehouses and corrals, and a large number of sawmills scattered throughout the district.

> "It was always a busy time there, and it was necessary for me to go to Nashville about every two months to obtain supplies, and money with which to pay the men. General Forrest paid us a great deal of attention, raiding

along our two lines of railway. On one occasion he captured one of my trains. Personally, on one trip down from
Nashville, I had a busy time keeping out of his hands. I
had on my person $22,000 which I was taking down to
pay employees, and which represented two months' wag-
es, and succeeded finally in eluding Forrest and getting
the money safely to Decatur. Strange to say, during my
14 years' residence in Memphis after the war, I came to
know considerably more of Forrest, his staff officers and
his men.

In the summer of 1865, the war was over. The Confed-
erate forces on our front had surrendered. I had received
their wagon trains and other quartermaster property, and
had disposed of it along with the greater portion of my
other supplies, animals, trains, steamboats, etc., and was
ready to close out. Thus far I had seen four years of service, and all of it in the field.

Knowing that there would be some months yet to
serve, I wanted to rejoin my regiment, which at the time
was with General Stanley at San Antonio, Texas. I filed
this request, the understanding being that I should enter
the regular army as a first lieutenant upon being mustered out as a volunteer. Instead of orders for Texas, I was
surprised to be informed by the headquarters of General
Thomas that I had been selected to take one of the depot
offices at Nashville. This meant that I would be required
to discharge certain duties in connection with the Army
of the Cumberland, assuming control of the government
and contract steamboats, barges, etc., in use on the Cumberland River, and of the depot transportation in Nashville, comprising some 2000 teams, and approximately
4000 men. The officer formerly in charge of the depot
work was going out of service.

*The only photograph in existence showing Ira B. (later Joseph) Dutton*
*in the uniform of a lieutenant of the 13th Wisconsin Infantry*
*during the Civil War. He was 20 years old at the time, and*
*before the end of the war was promoted to captain.*

It was a duty for a full captain and A.Q.M. (Assistant Quartermaster), but there was none unassigned. It had for some time been understood that an appointment was to be issued from Washington to myself as a captain and A. Q. M., U. S. Volunteers, the recommendation having been made by Majors General Thomas, Donaldson and Rousseau, and Brig.-Gen. Granger. But I myself gave the matter no attention, and in the rush incident to the close of the war, the muster out of troops, etc., I never received the appointment. However, I am not sure that it was never made. My regiment in Texas had official information regarding it, and for this reason my captaincy then due in the regiment was passed over."

And so, although for about two years his duties had been those of a captain, Dutton remained a first lieutenant and regimental quartermaster on special detail. Within a short time orders came from General Thomas' chief quartermaster, Maj.-Gen. Donaldson, for Dutton to close up his quartermaster affairs at Decatur in order that he would be available to take over his new duties at Nashville. While closing up his affairs, Dutton received a telegram from Maj.-Gen. Donaldson for him to go to Nashville immediately. Upon reporting at Maj.-Gen. Donaldson's headquarters, Dutton was informed by him, and by his assistant, General (then Colonel) John F. Rushing, that Capt. E. B. Kirk, afterwards major, had arrived unexpectedly from the Army of the Potomac for assignment to duty, and that there was nothing to give him but the duty in question.

"I dwell upon this, somewhat in a lingering and softening memory of the two years of field service in that army, having had at all times such pleasant relations with all of the officers in the department with whom I was associated : The chief, General Donaldson; his assistant, Col. Rushing; Capt. Charles Wing, in charge of funds; Capt. C. H. Irvin, in charge of means of transportation;

Capt. W. A. Wainwright, in charge of quartermaster
stores; Capt. F. J. Cox, and many others. When I recall
these, and the advantages I then had, a meditative mood
comes over me. Those officers were all my senior in rank
and in years. I was hardly more than a boy—22 years old.
These others were men of experience. Yet is was a general
wish among them—I understood—that I should come
into one of the depot duties."

It is questionable whether any other young man of the same age as
Dutton then was, obtained in the army a like responsibility.

Naturally, Dutton had been summoned to Nashville by his chief
and assistant in order that they might tell him personally that they could
not assign him to the depot post which he had been promised, and that
they were sorry.

This gave to Dutton the opportunity to rejoin his regiment, and
shortly after, under proper orders, he left for New Orleans and San Antonio, carrying letters to General Stanley, commanding the 4th Army
Corps, and to General Sheridan's staff officers, then at New Orleans.
After presenting his letters to General Sheridan's headquarters, Dutton
learned that he would have to wait there a few days for a steamer to take
him and his two saddle horses to San Antonio via Galveston. While thus
waiting, orders came for a mustering out of a part of the 4th Army Corps,
and he found that his old regiment was included. General Sheridan assigned him to duty in New Orleans, in the old Jackson railroad building,
as assistant to the chief quartermaster general, to await the regiment.

"I remember, that the 13th Wisconsin had a good run
of luck just then, and went up the river on the flagship,
as I may call it, the 'Ruth,' the finest on the great river. I
shall never forget the hearty reception I had from every
officer and man of the old regiment in these closing-up-
the-river days of 1865, near the close of our last year 'in
the field.'"

## The Runaway Pontoon
## An Incident Of The Civil War

*(A sketch written by Joseph Dutton.)*

When we at Decatur knew General Hood had broken away at Atlanta and was heading for Tuscumbia and Florence, where Southern authorities—civil and military —were gathering supplies from along the Tuscumbia Valley, west of us, our mounted force was on the alert.

It seemed Hood was avoiding Decatur, probably in the belief that a considerable force was there. There had been, but just then the force was small, as those mounted were off scouting. He had passed some distance south of us, probably going around General Wheeler's large plantation south of Trinity Station.

As extensive movement might be expected, I ran up to Nashville, the department headquarters and supply base, for replenishing, so as to have full supplies for the 25,000 troops in the field.

General J. L. Donaldson was chief quartermaster of the department, and while in town I was a good deal about his office. One time there, when he went to headquarters in High Street to see General Thomas, he quickly came rushing back and said that a message had just been received that Hood had invested Decatur. He had informed Thomas that the Decatur quartermaster was at his office, and said that I was to go at once to General Thomas.

The general questioned me as to the situation in and about Decatur, and his remarks gave me an inkling of his thoughts. Indeed it was evident that a withdrawal by Hood from Decatur was highly desirable. If an actual engagement should take place, our force at Decatur would not be sufficient to withstand it successfully.

A general concentration at and near Nashville of all available troops, including the old regiment General Sherman was returning from Atlanta, was regarded as the one safe prospect. As Hood's plan for crossing the Tennessee River at Tuscumbia and Florence, below Mussel Shoals, had become known to us, this was accepted as meaning a march in force against General Thomas at Nashville.

It was presumed, when Hood seemed to avoid Decatur, that he was unaware that we had the best pontoon bridge on the river there. Being above the shoals, it was a long one, and it was swung by cables from the fine piers of the otherwise destroyed railroad bridge—destroyed, as I recall it, by General O. M. Mitchell in about the first raid through that district.

From nearly the first I had there the armored transport Stone River, the largest vessel above the shoals. It not only had work at Decatur, but had frequently to make trips all along the river, as far as Caperton's Ferry, gathering forage, etc., and keeping the river clear of flat boats and the like. Its range of travel at this time was probably about one hundred and fifty miles.

But Hood lost his chance at Decatur. A dash of two cavalry regiments would have gained him and held our pontoon bridge. And he could have easily been before Nashville in five days, with railway rolling stock and coal to help him.

Hood had with him a pontoon bridge thought to be capable of getting his army across the river at a point below Mussel Shoals where it was narrow. But it was a poor affair, I believe, and, as I recall it, his final crossing in the movement toward Nashville was done mostly at Brown's Ferry, and required about thirty days in all.

General Thomas could not have had all of his forces

gathered together within that time; even after the thirty days he had none too many. Yet I am not saying that General Thomas would have been defeated. The army had such confidence in him that defeat under any circumstances was hardly to be thought of.

Why did Hood subsequently withdraw from Decatur? Because of a "bluff" perpetrated by Lieut. Col. W. F. Prosser of a Tennessee Mounted Infantry Regiment. There were barely six thousand men for duty at the post when Hood's forces suddenly appeared. Colonel Prosser, at the moment in command of the post, at once placed six hundred enlisted men, together with my quartermaster employees, who were quickly armed, on an advanced line, mostly deployed as skirmishers, and supported by a small reserve force.

This seemed to act as a check to the enemy. Hood probably concluded that the information to the effect that there was a large force in Decatur was correct, especially in view of the fact that a small detachment, sent by him down a ravine to attempt a survey, was captured. Shortly thereafter the enemy withdrew. All this happened while I was at Nashville.

Anyway, General Thomas was resolved for the present to withdraw from North Alabama in order that he might concentrate at Nashville to meet Hood's forces, and so I was kept busy transporting troops and property, making it a special point to get the pontoon bridge at Decatur out of use and dismantled as quickly as possible.

I feared that Hood might yet find out the true state of things, and turn back for his supplies at Tuscumbia, and all of his prospects by that route were as nothing when compared with the use of that bridge in getting to Nashville quickly.

Our Decatur troops were ordered to gather along the

N. C. St. L. R'y below Nashville. Our N. & D. and M. & C. railway rolling stock could handle that after the troops were across the river. So the bridge could go as soon as I could arrange for the removal of the property. I asked for all of the transport boats at Chattanooga, which were then practically out of use, some of them being actually "laid up." General Thomas communicated with General Granger regarding my request, and it was decided finally to let me have the vessels.

The transports, eight in number, were sent to me at Decatur. The Stone River was there already, and so this gave me nine vessels. Knowing the condition of the boats from Chattanooga very well, I was sure that I could help Capt. Thomas J. Carlisle, assistant quartermaster in charge, to get them off quickly; and Captain Grant, I think it was, in command of the Tennessee River gunboat fleet, waited there for me to go down with him on the flagship.

Everything was hustled. The transports were loaded and dispatched one by one, with some of the gunboats acting as convoys. I telegraphed my general superintendent to let the bridge swing in sections to the north bank as soon as it was evident that the men could get off by the boats with the remainder of the supplies.

That was done, and the boats gotten off. One of the boats, through overloading, became in a sinking condition when not far away, and about half of her cargo had to be dumped into the river. Some of the machinery could not be moved, and had to be burned with the buildings, at a loss of about one hundred thousand dollars.

When it came to swinging the sections of the bridge around, some of the men rode on each section until it was made fast under the great trees which overhung that side of the river for miles.

But one section got away, and one of the gunboats steamed after it and tried to catch it. The crew got lines on it several times, but were unable to make them fast. In such a rapid current it was deemed unsafe to go too near to the great Mussel Shoals, and so, finally, attempts at rescue were given up, and this section of the pontoon bridge was allowed to go on its way. Once it got into that fierce torrent, amidst the rocks, it was thought that nothing with the exception of loose planks and timbers could get through into smooth water.

As soon as practicable after the Nashville affair, we reoccupied Northern Alabama. One of my first duties was getting that runaway section of bridge back, and it was done successfully.

But the runaway section of the Decatur bridge had for me no further existence at all, until, long after the war, a writer in the National Tribune (Washington, D. C.) described the escaping remnant of Hood's army—after Nashville—n the stress of freezing weather, searching for every possible means of crossing the Tennessee River, and sending scouting parties up and down the stream looking for any sort of a boat, canoe or flat, or ferry boat.

At last, at a place up the river toward Mussel Shoals, they found that section of the Decatur bridge that had gotten away from us and which had come through the shoals and lodged at a point near Bainbridge.

The escaping Confederates used this section and it was given the credit of enabling them to cross the river. I should say that the river at that particular point, and at that time, could have been hardly more than half the width it was at Decatur. Although Hood did not get our bridge at the beginning, some of his men got it at the end, and it served them well."

*This rare photograph of Ira B. (later Joseph) Dutton was taken at Memphis, Tenn., in 1877, some years before he reached the decision which led him to Molokai and into the service of the lepers.*

## After The War
### 1865–1884

While the other officers and men of the 13th Wisconsin continued on up the river to Cairo, Ill., where they disembarked and took trains for Chicago en route to their home state, Dutton left the steamer at Memphis, and from there went to Decatur, Nashville, Cincinnati and Mount Vernon. He was bent upon revisiting old friends and scenes, apart from having some matters of business to attend to.

> "I was preparing, for a new and strange notch in my career. At Mount Vernon I was to take the step that was to change my whole life. It was a step that was to put a new color onto everything, to bring on a new and unthought of condition. It was a knot that was to do and to undo wonders. Perhaps it was a great blessing; the best help I ever had."

Dutton, by the foregoing, refers to his marriage at Mount Vernon, Ohio, on January 1, 1866.

> "Not having sufficient means (funds) to carry everything through in a manner appropriate, or as would seem to be good, may have been the one thing needful to prevent greater error. The beginning of this feature, that which led to the marriage at Mount Vernon, dates back to Nashville and Decatur times. Whether I had at first any thought of marriage has been a puzzle to me. Have often wondered as to what I really did intend. A friendly

act at the beginning, I should say it was. A 'rescue,' I may call it."

Regarding Dutton's marriage, but little will enter into these memoirs. He explains it best, perhaps, in this statement:

"My marriage . . . was the first serious mistake. Of course, I am not deprecating marriage in general. It is only this particular one I refer to. Going into close particulars could hardly serve any good end. So I merely say it was a mistake; a very foolish act on my part. No doubt there was a sort of romantic notion. One could even believe that I sought to do great good to another. But every circumstance surrounding the case proved such intent a foolish one. It seemed as if, the restraint of military service and ambition for its responsibilities once over, I had been left free—too free, like an unchained animal gone partly wild.

I met her at Nashville in 1864 or 1865. I was then on duty in North Alabama, having to visit Nashville every month or two for supplies, etc. As to the marriage, I don't claim anything as being really good in my acts. Mostly, they were bad enough. Yet it must be that I had a notion of doing some good, or a hope that some good might come of it. I took her into Alabama, about 20 miles south of our headquarters, to stay with some friends of mine, some excellent people I had become acquainted with while on duty in that region. Then, later, being under orders to go into Louisiana and Texas, I sent her to Ohio to remain near some relatives in an interior town, her other relatives and old home being in Indiana."

Upon leaving New Orleans in December, 1865, with his regiment for muster out at Madison, Wisconsin, Dutton obtained authority to go around about from Memphis, through his former district of North Alabama and on to Ohio via Nashville.

On January 1, 1866, as heretofore stated, the marriage took place. Going on to Wisconsin from Mount Vernon, Dutton was mustered out and, about a month or two later, went with his wife to Alabama, where friends of his wished him to join with them in improving some property which they owned. For a time things pointed toward success, but a little later the situation began to look dark.

> "It seemed best that she should go back to Ohio. But when she did so, I did not dream the 'family' was wrecked, as it afterward proved."

Concerning the divorce which followed, the following excerpt is taken from Dutton's notes :

> "I succeeded in getting my duties and residence changed, made the necessary residence, and the divorce was promptly granted. Was also entertained by the judge and his daughters—somewhat a matter of form. Being at the county seat, the very place where the marriage had occurred, all of the facts were well known.
>
> An uncle of hers, a prominent attorney, attended to it. More evidence than was needed was volunteered. Another uncle (in an adjoining state) at the family home place, offered by telegraph to come and testify—but it was not needed. The case is on record at Mount Vernon, Knox county, Ohio."

At about this time Dutton had become indebted to the extent of about $2200. Some 17 years later he paid this back to the parties, or to their heirs, going over a good portion of the Northern and Eastern states to do so. The actual amount of money which he paid back, including legal interest, was nearly $6000.

For about two years after the war's termination, Dutton remained in the service of the government as a quartermaster agent on cemeterial construction. He attended to disinterments from Columbia, Tennessee, to Decatur, from Decatur to Corinth, Miss., and from Corinth to Columbus, Miss. All of the bodies of soldiers which were disinterred in the course of this work were reinterred in the great cemetery at Corinth.

Suffering under the burden of his unsatisfactory marriage, Dutton, at this stage, began what he termed the downward step. He says:

> "While I was burying the dead, what I had in life was cast adrift. . . . . . And then I drifted. The ambition of former days was taking a rest. The moral foundation, yet mine in judgment and taste, was not adhered to loyally. Conditions that were repugnant I submitted to without resistance, even going of my own will into some of them. The use of intoxicating liquors once acquired, a frequent abuse of the taste therefor naturally followed. This evil was the chief one for several years; four or five, I should say.
>
> In common honesty concerning matters of duty or business, things of the world and its affairs, responsibility, etc., I must have been always considered reliable, for in the darkest and most reckless time of drink and debauchery, I nearly always held a place of responsibility, and have now papers showing a clear settlement of everything.
>
> I had been a moderate drinker before and during the war, but it was in the degenerate decade' that the drinking, chiefly of whisky, was fierce and reckless—even up to July, 1876. Since that time I have been strictly an abstainer."

After the completion of the cemeterial operations, Dutton, while in Louisiana, near New Orleans, received very unexpectedly a letter from a friend of his, a former officer who had been connected with cemetery construction operations in Tennessee, saying that he, together with some other mutual friends, were planning to go into business, and wanted to know whether he, Dutton, cared to join them.

The kind of business was not mentioned in the letter, and Dutton presumed that it had to do with cotton or some other sort of manufacturing. Dutton was glad of the opportunity, and joined his friends immediately. This was about the close of 1868. The enterprise proved to be a manufacturing business, but not the kind which Dutton had been thinking about. The business was the manufacture of high wines, and Dutton was wanted to take charge of the distillery!

"This was, of course, a surprise, although having been used to the finished product for some years, I had never seen the inside of a distillery. In fact, I have not to this day, either the inside or the outside, save that in Kentucky and some other states, passing by rail or carriage road, I have seen some buildings that I presumed were distilleries. And this one almost infernal exception; this making of a deep notch in my life record; this one old distillery amongst the pine hills, pine tops, pine knots; a deep mark, a notch cut as with the wild slash of a knife in a reckless hand; this one old distillery is a burning and biting exception.

Yet I do not actually regret, not as with a worrying sorrow. It was detestable, but has not good come of it? I believe so, and hope for more. I am willing to tell of it. I am almost the only left who could, in fact. I had been off the sound track since muster out from the army; off the sensible, fair track, anyway. And more was needed for my lesson. I had it there, more and more. If I can now do anything to please God, surely I ought, if merely in justice. Never could I do more faithful work for Him than I did there for Satan. Worthy ambition for the moment had

left me. The strength was expended in a grim eagerness
for work, work. Never stopping, hardly, at the high-water
mark (amongst the high wines) of physical strength and
endurance; making the night run, doing the yeasting and
the mashing; by day attending to the business; sleeping
hardly more than an hour at a time; taking a medium
drink of whisky every hour."

This continued for two years, and at the end of that time Dutton
had not only become a proficient distiller, but was practically in sole
charge of the establishment; at least, he was doing the major part of the
work.

The business of the distillery was prospering under Dutton's management when the owners became involved suddenly in politics. Some
sharply contested conditions brought fierce enmity against the owners,
and everything was lost finally in a series of revenue cases. It was at first
thought that Dutton was a part owner of the business, but that was
quickly found to be incorrect. Knowing that all was lost, Dutton did not
even ask for the money which was then due him as salary, knowing that
such a request would avail nothing.

Dutton then went to Memphis—this was about the close of the
year 1870—and another new life began. It was his plan to remain there
but a few months and then go on to New Orleans. As a matter of fact, he
remained there about 14 years, or until the fall of 1884, the year which
marked the notable change in his career, and led him into a work of
self-sacrifice unique in the latter-day history of America.

Not all of these 14 years were spent actually in the city of Memphis. Duties in connection with his employments took Dutton over the
country from time to time. But Memphis was practically his headquarters, save during one year, about 1882, when he had his headquarters in
Ohio, at Mount Vernon, with a field which covered Southern Ohio and
Northern Kentucky.

Dutton spent these 14 years in two employments, six years with
the L. & N. Railroad Company, and eight years with the American war

department as a special agent, making investigations concerning claims, and attending to other business over a field which covered practically the entire United States.

Fortunately, Dutton's own written account of his period of service with the railroad—an experience which, by the way, was something entirely new to him—has been preserved, and is intensely interesting for the reason that it sets down many personal observations, notes friendships formed, and gives some idea of circumstances which led up to the great decision which he was to arrive at eight years later. This account, exactly as Dutton wrote it many years later, is as follows:

> "The close of the year 1870 was rather a blue time for the "Boy in Blue," and yet a very interesting time. I found work at once with the Memphis division of the L. & N. Railroad in the freight department, Memphis, and continued so until about 1876.
>
> This period of about six years was a special sort of "notch" in the record : taking work of a certain strangeness—a sort of work I had never thought of doing. However, I had confidence in myself. Also, it was only for a short while, I thought; just so as to be able to go on to New Orleans. But the New Orleans idea was merely an idea. I did not have any definite plan, and as the work in Memphis became familiar and pleasing, the New Orleans idea faded away.
>
> I may be pardoned for noting here, as it comes to mind, why I had this confidence in myself. There was one trait which I always had, even in boyhood, and that was thoroughness. Sometimes, I think, it was almost overdone. This, it may be, gave me the confidence. An element of stubborness, also, may have helped. Every help was needed at the beginning of this six-year notch. During the war period I had had more or less of railroad matters to look after at times, but it was all in military fashion.

Here at Memphis, taking the employment offered, I had to join up, as it were, with men who had grown into the work, and who possessed rapidity, quickness in discernment, in judgment and in execution; in brief, men with the railway spirit. The work at first was not very important, yet it required these faculties. At the beginning I checked freight into the warehouses and onto the platforms from incoming trains. I was given the fast freight detail, which consisted of the most expert of the fast freight line clerks, who were very rapid, and very popular with the crews of handlers and truck men—old railroaders all—of whom I had to take control. It was work that required the most intense attention even for an old hand. It was not easy at first, when I knew nothing of the duty, but I learned quickly the really important points, and, as I had actual charge of these crews, I had something to stand on, as it were.

Occasionally, at the very first, all hands had to wait a little for me, causing some amused looks and observations, although not particularly bad-natured. A railroad man is rather addicted to raillery in a good-natured way, and however great the tax on his thinking machinery the work may be, it is not good taste to show it; rather, it is better to pass everything in a breezy sort of way, like "This is nothing!!"

The thorough-going railroad man, however, has his thoughts right close by. They are not wandering much, no matter how jaunty he may seem to be. He dreads having an error traced back to him. He is far more serious-minded than he looks. He is bound to be smart, and is almost always a good fellow, and, more than half of the time, one whom you can trust with your life, or your honor, without fear. And once you have his support, it is always a strong support.

These observations have gone on to include all first-class railroad men. At the beginning, I was thinking chiefly of those in the business department. I like very much to testify regarding all, for though I was in business departments during those six railroading years, I eventually had dealings with nearly all the departments, and among all of the friends of a rather 'diversified life,' some of the most highly valued are those into whose ranks I came, a wanderer, crowding my way upon the bottom step—those days after the high wines, after the mash, after the smash!

My way was made clear through, first, about three years of extremely hard work, then in more easy places in some respects. A certain attachment grew up. Even before the first hard times were over I concluded to keep on. Railroad men took their drinks in those times. My own habit of drink, then fully acquired, was not changed, save that drinks were not anywhere near so frequent as when operating the distillery, unless at times when with the people of the night.

The present-day excellent methods of the railroad companies in the employment and retention of men, operating with decision against drinking men, had not then come into practise. But some of my best friends of that time were never drinking men.

These personal habits of the period in question were somewhat restricted as to the field of action, this whole six years being for me a sort of hidden life. Acquaintances were restricted to railroad men and their friends. At first it was entirely so. In the latter part of that six-year period, a few families became known to me through associates whose people were of good, old-time Southern stock, and with a social status wholly unquestioned. Yet my relations were not of the "society" tone, but rather more intimate, as of family nature, a fact that I valued very highly.

They know to some extent my reasons for living this, as I term it, hidden life, and know also of my habits. Considering this, I look upon some of those friendships as being among my sweetest memories. At this time I had no thought of being closer to fashionable society than I was. These good friends knew that, and appreciated my feelings. There was one feature of it, however, that was of rare quality. That was to know of—by hearsay—all of the best people, as to their social traits, etc., coming to me thus as to one behind the scenes. And I would like to state that there was never anything unpleasant in this; never uncharitable words about so and so, or so and so, but always a well-ordered good will, a friendly feeling and a generous expression. All of this gave me, partly hidden as I was, a very high opinion of the social qualities of those people, an opinion which has never been lowered, but rather increased, if possible; for I may as well assert here, before its proper space, that later on I knew all of these good people, and that is why I have stated the foregoing facts so carefully. In the latter part I was treated by all of them far better than I deserved.

But I have not said much about the railroad work, except as to the very beginning. Concerning that first freight work in the wards, I got through it all right. I learned how to handle the crews, and the fast freight people seemed to mark me OK. And when the one who first noted my early awkwardness was married, I was best man.

Many other kinds of work came on. There was a constant handling of cotton, of machinery, of agricultural implements, of live stock, of goods of every sort, night and day. In the busy season, after a full day's work, one or more of us always had to be out with our crews to work through a good part of the night. This would continue for months. Finally I was given the regular night work, which continued for a few years. When there was an unusual press of business, one or two of the gangs might work after supper for a while, two hours or so, but my force kept on all night, and, of course, slept during the daytime. It was a little difficult, and working in rough weather in the winter reminded me somewhat of the hard winters I had experienced during the war.

At about the middle of the six-year period I was given a place in the office as chief bill clerk. This brought me gradually into relation with nearly all of the business departments. I was in line for promotion. I felt that I had become a fixture, and was so regarded generally.

In July, 1876, I think it was, after a "spree" that tried the patience of everyone about me, I figured it out that in fifteen years I had drunk fifteen barrels of whisky. I thought it was fully my share, perhaps a little over, and that I was not entitled to any more. And no more it has been until this day. I might add, also, that I stopped smoking. Neither of these stoppers has caused me a moment of regret or desire. The nerves are all right, and there must be something left in the jug of good will."

# *The Step Is Taken*
## 1883–1886

Dutton's last service with the United States government was in the year 1884. On April 27, 1883, the occasion being his 40th birthday, he was received into the Catholic church of St. Peter's, at Memphis, Tennessee.

Previously, Dutton had been an Episcopalian, and had in fact been reared in this faith. In making the change, however, he had a definite goal in view. Because of what he refers to today as his "wild" life, his indulgence in liquor, and certain associations which he prefers to keep locked in memory, he had determined to give himself up to a life of penance. He was determined to atone, during the remaining period of his lifetime, for that which had occurred in the past, and he felt that by embracing the Catholic faith the best opportunity to effect this atonement would be accorded him.

The sacred doctrines of the Catholic church appealed to him, and inspired him more fully than the doctrines of any other faith were able to do. He had never really considered the priesthood, although this was to come later on. At this point there should be corrected a mistaken impression, which appears to prevail wherever the life work of Dutton is known, that he is a priest. He is not, nor has he ever been. He is a lay worker with the title "Brother."

It was probably during this period, when he was preparing to receive instructions so that he might enter the Catholic church, that Dutton was first possessed with the desire to do penance for what he chooses to call the "sins" of his past life. The desire grew upon him daily, and when, finally, he was baptised and admitted regularly to the Catholic faith, he had made up his mind that at the first opportunity he would seek out and adopt some form of penance.

> "I lived for some years a wild life, and felt that I should make some sort of reparation for it. I have explained that throughout my life I was a firm believer in thoroughness in everything, and so I decided that my penance should be thorough; in other words, that the remainder of my life should be devoted to that, and to nothing else."

How well Dutton's mind was made up was illustrated by what happened early in the year following his entrance into the Catholic church. He went immediately to Gethsemani, Kentucky, where he entered the Trappist Monastery, for the purpose, as he puts it, of "adjusting" himself. He wanted to see whether he could bear up under such a radical change in his method of everyday life. It was the test which would, eventually, tell the tale. It would determine whether he was fitted for the self-sacrifices of a life of penance, or whether it would be best to give up the proposal entirely.

Dutton was accepted in the Trappist Monastery as a layman. The Trappists form one of the orders of the Catholic church, probably the most severe and exacting of them all. The abbot of the monastery is in absolute control, and the bishop does not assume supervision here as in the remainder of the diocese, except, of course, in extraordinary cases. Complete silence is maintained. There is hard work to be done, and plenty of it, and the hours are long. Dutton was quartered in a "cell" in which was a single "cot," which was really nothing more than a shelf about three feet wide. His cell was about six feet square.

While steeling himself to this life of solitude and work and meditation, Dutton, looking into the future, cast about for a method by which he could do penance. What he had in mind, really, was some sort of humanitarian work. He desired to spend the remainder of his life in the service of his fellow man, and the idea of self-secrifice was at the bottom of this desire. It was required at the Trappist Monastery that novitiates take simple vows at the end of the first two years of their retirement, and solemn vows at the end of five years. Dutton remained at the monastery for 20 months, and left without taking vows of any kind. The reason for his leaving was that he did not think this particular order offered the opportunity to perform the pennance which he desired, and that it would be necessary for him to make another search.

> "I think, perhaps, that I would have remained at the monastery, and given up my life to that particular order, if a broader scope for future activities of helpfulness had been offered. As a matter of fact, before I went into the monastery, I had decided that no matter what my life work for my fellow man was to be, I would not accept compensation in any form. I was square with the world. I did not owe a single cent. My debts had been settled after much effort on my part; but they were settled. I wanted to serve some useful purpose during the rest of my life without any hope of monetary or other reward. The desire grew upon me with a forcefulness that is difficult to explain. The idea of leading a penitential life became almost an obsession, and I was determined to see it through."

And so, realizing that the Trappist Order did not offer the sort of opportunity which he desired, Dutton left the monastery. Of his own accord he had dispensed with the name "Ira," and had taken the name "Joseph," after Saint Joseph. Ever afterward he was known as Brother Joseph Dutton. He had been well liked at the monastery, and especially by the abbot, who wept when he departed, and himself carried Dutton's trunk to the entrance. Dutton was not without money, having some $70 on deposit in the prior's office.

This small amount of money Dutton refused to take. He had a number of United States treasury bonds, and from time to time thereafter he converted these into cash as he happened to need it. He recalls having sold one in Louisville, another in St. Louis, and another in New Orleans.

Shortly after leaving the monastery at Gethsemani, Dutton went to St. Louis for the purpose of making observations with regard to the work that was being done by the various religious orders. It was his plan to enter one of these, provided it offered the opportunity which he was seeking, and remain with it. Here he became acquainted with the provincial of the Redemptionist Order, who was on his way to New Orleans to attend a conference.

To the provincial Dutton explained his resolve to do penance for the remainder of his life, and the official invited him to go along with him to New Orleans, explaining that the conference to be held there might enlighten him as regards what form this life of penitence should be. Dutton made the trip with the provincial, and was housed at a convent at New Orleans while there.

One day, while in the reading room of the convent, Dutton was glancing through a Catholic publication and ran across a brief item telling of the work which the Rev. Father Damien was doing among the lepers on the island of Molokai, in the Hawaiian Islands. Immediately a great light dawned upon Dutton.

"There," he exclaimed to himself, "is the very work that I have been looking for!"

At once Dutton began questioning the convent officials regarding Molokai, the leper colony, and the work of Father Damien. They had but meager information, although they were able to inform Dutton of the whereabouts of a man who did know—Charles Warren Stoddard, the author and lecturer who had written one of the first exhaustive accounts of Molokai. Stoddard at that time was professor of history at Notre Dame university, Indiana, near South Bend.

Dutton had made up his mind that he would go to Molokai and work among the lepers during the remainder of his life. He had a hazy sort of recollection where the Hawaiian Islands were, but he knew absolutely nothing concerning conditions there, much less those at the leper colony. Not-withstanding this, his decision was made, and was not to be recalled.

He took a steamer up the Mississippi river and disembarked at Cairo, and from there went by railroad to Notre Dame to interview

Stoddard. He saw Stoddard, explained his desire to go to Molokai and work among the lepers, and asked whether he could make himself useful there. Stoddard was emphatic in his reply that he could, and immediately Dutton began making plans for his long pilgrimage to Hawaii— into an unknown land where he was to arrive unannounced, and among strangers.

Dutton made arrangements, with the assistance of Father Hudson of Notre Dame, to go to San Francisco on an emigrant train, and obtained special permission to make the trip from the head of the railroad division. Upon arriving at San Francisco after a long and tiresome trip across the country—railway accommodations in that period were not as luxurious as they are today—Dutton cast about to find the poorest vessel in service, and which would be going soon to the Hawaiian Islands. He had a reason for this. He desired to make his journey as nearly akin to a pilgrimage as possible, and therefore comfort played no part in his scheme of things. He wanted nothing that was high class.

He finally found that the bark Eureka, Captain Lee, was about to sail for the Islands, and upon this vessel Dutton arranged for passage. It was a long and dreary voyage which lasted some 30 days. The weather, however, was calm; too calm at times, in fact, for on various occasions there was barely enough wind for steerage way. Dutton spent most of his waking hours reading. There were a few books aboard the ship, and one of them, Dutton recalls—he has forgotten the name—was a discourse upon the attributes of Almighty God. He and the captain read this book together.

The Eureka arrived at Honolulu on July 22, 1886—a Honolulu vastly different from the modern metropolis, with its miles of concrete and steel wharves, of today. Dutton went ashore a little after dark, and, after inquiring the way, went directly to the Catholic Cathedral of Our Lady of Peace, in Fort Street. It was in this cathedral yard that the first Algaroba tree was planted—a tree which today thrives in profusion on all of the islands of the Hawaiian group.

Dutton interviewed several of the fathers, who greeted him cordially, and who referred him to Bishop Hermann. He saw the Bishop, introduced himself, and explained in detail the reason for his coming to the islands. That night he slept at a hotel, and on the following morning went again to the cathedral to arrange for accommodations while awaiting the departure of the next ship for Molokai. He obtained a room at the end of a bungalow which was later the old Monsarrat place, in Union street, and there he lived for a week.

His next visit of importance was upon Walter Murray Gibson, then minister of foreign affairs and president of the board of health during the reign of King David Kalakaua, last male ruler of Hawaii.

"I have come here," Dutton said, "to go to Molokai and spend the remainder of my life in work among the lepers."

Gibson received him with every kindness and courtesy. He asked for a brief history of Dutton's past life, which the latter gave him, at the same time presenting the credentials he had brought along. Gibson looked Dutton over and appeared to be satisfied that the man was in earnest in everything he said, and that, physically and otherwise, he was in condition to take up the work which he had chosen.

Yes, Gibson would give him a permit to enter the settlement, he said. Gibson mentioned also the matter of pay, and Dutton explained that he had resolved to accept no pay whatever for his services, whatever they might be. This was agreeable to Gibson, but he added that it would be a simple matter to arrange pay for Dutton at any time the latter felt he was in need of it. But Dutton was firm. Pay, he declared, was entirely out of the question.

It was arranged that Dutton sail for Molokai on the ship Mokolii, a tiny inter-island craft, and the only vessel then touching at that island. Gibson offered to pay Dutton's passage, but the latter had already purchased his ticket. At that time Samuel G. Wilder was head of the Wilder Steamship Co., now the Inter-Island Steam Navigation Co., and he ordered that the Mokolii stop at Kalaupapa, the only landing at the leper colony, to let Dutton off. Dutton recalls that the captain of the Mokolii was considerably disappointed at this order, for his stopping at Kalaupapa caused him to miss a "luau," or native feast, which was held at McGregor's landing.

Brother Joseph Dutton arrived at Kalaupapa on July 29, 1886, going ashore from the Mokolii in a small boat. As has been related already, Dutton had not even communicated with Father Damien, nor anyone else at the leper settlement—nor in Hawaii, for that matter—to say that he was coming, or to inquire whether his services were needed or could be made use of.

He arrived at this strange place, among strange people and strange surroundings, entirely unannounced. Some distance from the landing he saw a man sitting in a buggy drawn by a white horse. Dutton recognized him as a priest, and knew that this must be Damien. In a few simple words Dutton explained the purpose of his mission, and Father Damien accepted him instantly for what he was.

Thus did the pilgrimage of Brother Joseph Dutton end, and thus was the end of the long trail reached. He had found a life work that appealed to him—a service of humanity in the interests of his fellow men. Little did he realize, perhaps, that 44 years later, in 1930, he would be in the same place, alive and in remarkable health, still carrying on the work, and still doing penance for his past "life of sin." The next day Brother Dutton went to work.

*Brother Dutton and Father Damien meet*
*Panel from Blessed Sacrament Church in Stowe VT*

*Reproduction of an old photograph, taken about 1886, showing the original
Father Damien church at Kalawao, Molokai, as it appeared in the year Joseph
Dutton began his work among the lepers there. The church was begun by a Catholic
Brother who preceded Father Damien to Molokai, and the latter completed it.*

# The Task Is Begun
## 1886–1889

When Brother Dutton arrived at the leper settlement, Father Damien had been there for 13 years, and 10 years previously had discovered that he, too, was a leper. He had accomplished a great deal and, in spite of the constantly growing population, had, with the assistance of the government, succeeded in making the lepers fairly comfortable, and improved conditions until they were far better than when the settlement was first established.

At this time, as has been noted already, the main settlement was at Kalawao, and here lived approximately 500 lepers. There had just been discovered the so-called Japanese "treatment" for leprosy, which consisted of pills, a medicated tea, and a bathing medicine. Father Damien had heard of this "treatment" and had gone to Honolulu and obtained a supply from a Doctor Goto, who had brought it to the island capital from Japan.

This supply was taken to the settlement three days before the arrival of Brother Dutton, and in the meantime Father Damien had himself taken the treatment, but was as yet undetermined whether it was relieving him in any way. He had, however, made use only of the bathing medicine. The other items were made use of by him later on, but failed to show any material effect.

With the lepers, however, the "treatment" became immensely popular, and especially the bathing medicine. The natives bathed in anything they could find—in tubs and in water-tight boxes which they built out of old lumber. Bathing became almost a mania among the patients, and this led to the necessity for building a large bathhouse. Brother Dutton took charge of the construction work, and this was one of the first tasks assigned to him. After it was completed, Father Damien took his baths there.

Prior to the arrival of Brother Dutton, Father Damien had not been alone in his work at the settlement. In 1874 Father Andrew began giving assistance from time to time, and in the early part of 1876 he established a residence at Kalaupapa, and remained there until the close of July, 1880. In September, 1882, Father Albert went to Kalawao as a helper, and remained until the close of March, 1885.

The first party of Franciscan sisters arrived at the Kakaako branch hospital, near Honolulu, the Rev. Mother Marianne and six sisters coming on November 9, 1883. The reverend mother and three of the sisters remained there, the other three sisters going to the Malulani Hospital, Wailuku, island of Maui. Other sisters came later. Mother Marianne made a visit to the leper settlement in October, 1888, and on November 15 of the same year, she went to Kalaupapa, in company with Sisters Leopoldina and Vincentia, and established the Bishop Home for leper girls. By this time the settlement was spreading gradually to Kalaupapa, and soon there was to be nothing left at Kalawao but the Baldwin Home for boys, and, later, the federal leprosarium, soon abandoned.

On May 6, 1889, Sisters Crescentia and Irene went to Kalaupapa, while Sisters Renata and Elizabeth went there about March, 1890. On May 15, 1890, Sisters Crescentia, Renata and Vincentia went to Kalawao, and later on Sister Renata went to the Kalihi Hospital, Honolulu, and Sister Irene to Kalawao. Records of long service are preserved in the archives of the settlement, cared for by Brother Dutton, as follows:

The Rev. Father Damien:
   Born January 3, 1840, in Belgium.
   Arrived at Honolulu March 19, 1864.
   Arrived at the leper settlement May 10, 1873.
   Died April 15, 1889.

The Rev. Mother Marianne:
  Born January 23, 1838, in Germany.
  Died August 9, 1918, at the leper settlement.

The Rev. Father Conrardy:
  Arrived at the leper settlement May 17, 1888.
  Left December 27, 1895.

The Rev. Father Wendelin:
  Arrived at the leper settlement November 1, 1888.
  Left September 23, 1902.

James Sinnott: (lay worker)
  Arrived at the leper settlement November 27, 1888.
  Left July 15, 1889.

Emil Van Lil: (lay worker)
  Arrived at the leper settlement July 25, 1895.
  Left Kalawao December 3, 1902.

*The living and the dead: Catholic Brothers on duty at the Baldwin*
*Home for leper boys and men, Kalawao, Molokai, standing beside*
*the graves of other Brothers who died in service there.*

The first Catholic brothers went to the Baldwin Home on November 30, 1895. Since that date brothers have always been on duty at the institution.

As has been stated, conditions at the settlement were fairly good at the time of the arrival of Brother Dutton. He recalls now that one of the things which impressed him then, and has continued to impress him ever since, was the grandeur of the scenery surrounding that tiny space in which there was so much misery and suffering, and which was shunned by all clean people with the exception of those ministering to the lepers. Indeed, the scenery one beholds from any part of that small peninsula is among the most beautiful in the Hawaiian Islands, and today many of the inter-island steamers pass by it so that tourists may view its wonders.

One of Brother Dutton's first duties was to assist in caring for the sick; that is, lepers who were in need of daily attention, and who had terrible sores on the hands, the face and other parts of the body which had to be dressed. Prior to the arrival of Brother Dutton, practically all of this work was done by Father Damien.

The government physician at the settlement at the time was Dr. A. Mauritz, a talented man who later on wrote an illuminating book describing early-day conditions at the settlement. He remained at the settlement for several years after Father Damien died. Now, while Dr. Mauritz was a competent physician and surgeon, he was also a white man, and the Hawaiian patients would have little or nothing to do with him, although they subjected themselves to the ministrations of Father Damien and, later, of Brother Dutton. No doubt they looked upon Dr. Mauritz as a "kahuna" who would work some evil against them. However, it became necessary for Dr. Mauritz secretly to instruct Brother Dutton in the dressing of their sores, in order that he could take a portion of this work from Father Damien.

"The Hawaiian patients," Brother Dutton says, "had the utmost confidence in the Catholic Mission. They had none in doctors. This is probably why they permitted Father Damien and myself to dress their sores."

In those days there were very few persons other than Hawaiians who were patients at the settlement. It is known that a large number of non-Hawaiian patients went to Dr. Mauritz, and in this way he was kept fairly busy. Other government physicians at the settlement after Dr. Mauritz left were Drs. Peterson, Black, Swift and Oliver. The late Dr. W. J. Goodhue remained there for 20 years, and at all times had the confidence of the patients irrespective of their nationality. The day of prejudice against doctors ended many years ago.

Apart from his duties in caring for the sick and dressing sores, Brother Dutton was given considerable other work to do. There were church offices to perform, some in the church at Kalawao, and others in the church at Kalaupapa, where he journeyed with Father Damien twice a week. He was handy with tools and something of a carpenter, and shortly after his arrival he set about to complete the Damien church at Kalawao.

Now Father Damien had taken a fancy to Brother Dutton and, from the very first, had addressed him by the title "Brother." Ever after, and to this day, he was known as Brother Joseph. "I have always believed," Brother Dutton says, "that Father Damien desired to have a brother at the settlement to help him, but could not get one."

While Brother Dutton and Father Damien administered to the sick men and boys, the girl patients, who were housed in buildings on the side of the peninsula towards the mountains, were in charge of a Hawaiian woman who was not a leper.

"Conditions in those years were not as bad as one might imagine. We had become organized somewhat after the American fashion as a result of the influence exerted by the missionaries, and the board of health was not by any means lax in looking after things.

Strangely enough, I never once regretted having taken the step which brought me to Molokai. I took an interest in the work from the start, and that interest has never lagged. Today, even, I cannot think of any better mission that I might have performed. I sought a service of self-sacrifice which would benefit my fellow men. I found it at Molokai.

I recall now that my mother took my going to the leper settlement beautifully. She had good judgment, and fortitude almost beyond belief. I had been away from home since 1861, except for occasional visits; but she never worried. She was in every way balanced, and had, even before becoming a Catholic, after my conversion, the most implicit trust in Divine Providence."

It may be that Brother Dutton, looking today over his 44 years of active service, is inclined to be optimistic. But however one views the situation, those first years must have been bitter ones—filled with hard work, fraught with danger.

Brother Dutton often personally dressed the sores of Father Damien, although not a great deal of dressing was needed until some months before his death. Brother Dutton refers to Father Damien's ailment as a very pronounced tubercular type of leprosy, although there is no doubt in his mind that it was leprosy, and not tuberculosis, which killed him finally.

The Kalawao settlement, known as the Damien Home, was maintained solely by the board of health, which, Brother Dutton says, was fairly generous in the matter of supplying food, medicine and all other necessities.

The so-called Japanese "treatment" remained in use for many years, even after the establishment of the Baldwin Home at Kalawao, but was finally discontinued about the year 1896. The next "treatment" to be used was Gurjun oil, which was sent to the settlement by Edward Clifford, an Englishman, who had visited the settlement and, while there, painted Father Damien's portrait. This "treatment" was sent by Clifford from India, after Father Damien's death. It was used only a short time, and was abandoned after it had been proved to be a complete failure. Thereafter many so-called "cures" were administered, the most important of these being the "anti-leprol," which was a derivative of the famous chaulmoogra oil, now used in practically all parts of the world in the treatment of leprosy. This came into use after Brother Dutton had given up the actual care of patients, such as sore dressing, this work having been taken over by the Catholic brothers in 1898. The first actual chaulmoogra oil was then introduced, and this was used up to a few years ago, when the new specific, perfected in the laboratories of the University of Hawaii, at Honolulu, took its place.

When Brother Dutton first arrived at the settlement, Father Damien had about completed his church. With the church completed, Brother Dutton turned his attention to the erection of some twelve large buildings for lepers, and a shop. There was some talk of enlarging the Damien church, and Brother Dutton proposed a new church on the highlands near Kalawao, but Father Damien desired to leave the structure as it was.

This structure contained a single long room, with an altar at one end which Father Damien had fashioned with his own hands, and with whatever material happened to be handy. Finally, after considerable discussion and planning, Father Damien and Brother Dutton began building the present wooden portion toward the sea and over the transept of the old church. In its original form, the first Damien church was of wood, but later there was added a portion built of lava blocks cemented over. The walls of this portion were completed, and the roof being put on, when Father Damien died.

Father Damien took an intense interest in these additions to his church. On one occasion he went to Honolulu to consult builders in order to find out how to strengthen the tops of the walls so that they would support the roof, and brought back with him a lot of two-inch planking with which to make a "cap" over the top of each wall. The rafters rested upon this cap. The two wings of the original church served as "wings" to the reconstruction edifice, and in these the Damien altar, and the benches which were used in his day, are preserved. A new and splendid altar occupies the sea end of the present building.

*The Rev. Father Damien De Veuster, "Martyr Priest of Molokai,"
from a photograph taken in France circa 1860 before he came to
the Hawaiian Islands for duty with the Catholic Mission.*

# The Death Of Damien
## 1889

Father Damien died at Kalawao, then the main leper settlement, on April 15, 1889, after 16 years of service among the afflicted people, and at the age of 49 years. His death occurred three years after the arrival of Brother Dutton.

He was truly a martyr, for his death was due directly to leprosy, which he contracted three years after his arrival at the settlement to devote the remainder of his life in work among the sufferers from this dread disease. The fact that Damien died a leper has caused certain writers to question his morals, and to charge that he contracted the disease as a result of improper relations with leper women. Dutton declares these charges to be absolutely without foundation in fact, and in this he is sustained by other Catholic workers who knew Damien and who worked with him among the patients up to the time of his death.

Just how or where Damien contracted leprosy will probably never be known. The theory of some experts who have made exhaustive studies of the disease is that leprosy does not make itself visible until after an incubation period of seven years. If this theory is correct, then Damien did not contract it on Molokai, because it began to show upon his person three years after his arrival there. That he contracted it in some manner while upon his missions of mercy on other islands of the Hawaiian group, prior to going to Molokai, is the belief of those who are inclined to revere the memory of this man, and not to question his life deeds, now that he has passed on.

What Damien did on Molokai is known generally to the entire world. Certainly it is well known in Hawaii, and among the Hawaiian people, for whom he gave up everything that he might serve the afflicted ones of this race—persons who knew that, once they went to Molokai, they would never leave.

On March 10, 1889, there came into existence a document, hitherto unpublished, which, it would appear, exonerated Damien of the charges preferred against him after his death. On that day, just one month and five days before he died, he called Brother Dutton to him and asked him to take down a statement which he desired to make concerning phases of his past life, and with special reference to his having contracted leprosy.

At that time Damien was a sick man, and knew, as his associates must also have known, that the end was very near. He was not a pleasant sight to look upon then (as Brother Dutton will testify) for the disease had ravaged his entire body, had broken down that once superb physical strength, and had left but a wreck of a man clinging to life merely by a desire to better prepare himself to meet God. He had endeavored to obtain relief for himself from time to time through the use of a Japanese "remedy" for leprosy, which for some years had been tried out now and again at the settlement, but with no noticeable results, except temporary abatement.

There is some question, also, as to whether Damien actually desired any great amount of relief, much less a complete cure. It is said that when he first discovered he was a leper, he went immediately to his little church and knelt down and thanked God, realizing that, as one who was himself afflicted, he was at last truly in the service of his unfortunate patients.

So, knowing that the end was not far away, he summoned Brother Dutton to him and dictated a long statement. Brother Dutton made notes, and from these wrote out the statement, which Father Damien signed as being correct. This document, together with Brother Dutton's personal observations, and letters of transmittal to the Catholic Mission at Honolulu, follows:

Kalawao, Molokai.
Notes taken March 10, 1889. Tubercular.


Rev. Father J. Damien De Veuster, Catholic priest, native of Belgium; Belgian parents; 49 years of age. All of the members of his family very strong and healthy. No taint of scrofula or syphilis. No relatives on these islands. Served as priest on the island of Hawaii from 1864 until 1873. Occasionally heard confessions of lepers; ministered to them in their cabins sometimes, but had no constant or very personal contact with them until he came here to the leper settlement in 1873, since which time, until now, his contact and association with them have been almost constant.

In 1873 was strong and healthy, with remarkably robust constitution. Has never had any sexual intercourse whatever. Is quite sure that when near to lepers, as at confession or in their cabins—before coming to the leper settlement—he felt on each occasion a peculiar sensation in the face, a sort of itching or burning, and that he felt – the same here at the settlement during the first two or three years; that he also felt it on the legs.

Is confident that the germs were in his system certainly within the first three years of his residence here; can trace it back positively to 1876. Small, dry spots appeared at that time, particularly on the arms, some on the back. On these spots perspiration did not appear as elsewhere. Upon treatment with corrosive sublimate lotion, they would disappear, but return again.

Finally, in 1877 and 1878, they assumed a yellowish color, and became larger. In 1877 he took sarsaparilla, as a blood purifier, when the spots become more refined, still yellow, and would remain until the lotion was applied. This describes the first marks, but earlier still there was a suspicious movement. His feet had a peculiar sensation; made him restless. He could not sleep without first giving them a cold water soak; nor without doing this could he keep them covered at night. This was in 1874 and 1875. He continued to enjoy strength and health. In 1877 he was vaccinated at the time of the smallpox epidemic in Honolulu. The operation was performed by one deputized by the Board of Health, who said the vaccine matter came from America. In some degree the operation was successful. During a few days he had some fever, and there was inflammation at the point of vaccination, on a space about the size of a silver dollar, some matter flowing therefrom.

In connection with this note, it is well to state that the natives, and some others, have a firm belief that leprosy was greatly spread throughout the islands by the process of vaccination at this time, and perhaps at other times.

In the autumn of 1881 he began to be badly troubled with severe pains in the feet, especially in the left one, and, in 1882, sciatic nerve trouble came on, clearly defined, all along the left leg. At the close of 1882, or early in 1883, entire insensibility of one side of the left foot took place, and so remains until this day; the outside portion of the foot, Father Damien being able to draw a line marking division of the sensible from the insensible portion of his foot. This is the only part of his body that has been so attacked. The pain of sciatic nerve and of the inside (big toe side) portion of the foot was intense and almost constant, accompanied by formation of nodes in the left groin.

All of these pains disappeared, at once, about June, 1885. Then the right ear became swollen, with tubercular enlargements, making the whole thing an immense affair. At the same time began the disfigurement of his person in a general and marked manner. The eyebrows began to fall out, the other ear became enlarged, and tubercular swellings took possession of face, hands, etc. The knuckles and knees are in hard, enlarged knobs, becoming suppurating sores. Many sores on hands and wrists, some about the neck, eyes weak and at times very much inflamed. His nose greatly obstructed, causing much distress, during the past two years appearing as catarrh*. The bridge of nose much sunken. The foot that was partly insensible was, for a long time, exceedingly weak. Now, since the disease has spread over the body, it becomes strong again.

Correct:

(Signed) J. Damien De Veuster,

Catholic priest.

The above is a full copy of the notes proper. This copy is made (Oct. 6, 1903) to agree with two other copies that I had sent to the mission—to Bishop Hermann, and which have been brought back to me (yesterday, Oct. 5, 1903), by Bishop Libert, that I may add some remarks, and make affidavit covering the whole matter now, while I am able. The earliest of the two copies was sent to Bishop Hermann, with the following letter written upon the last page, at the bottom, by me:

Kalawao, Molokai,
June 9, 1890.

To His Lordship, Bishop Hermann,
Honolulu, H. I.

Dear Bishop:
This copy came to me by the last mail from Dr. P. A. Morrow of New York, for whom I made the original notes. After making slight corrections with the pen, as you see, (the notes were typewritten) I recognize it as a true copy of the original as signed by Father Damien. I made the notes from his own lips, using as near as possible his very words, and read the statement all over to him before he signed it. His last illness had then just begun. The declaration as to non-intercourse sexual—was his own, voluntarily given. When I wrote for you the 'statement'—February last—regarding Father Damien, which you had called for, I had forgotten this declaration that he made, though I remember it very well now. This paper might be added as supplemental to that statement.

Very truly and respectfully yours,
(Signed) Joseph Dutton."

---

* catarrh : excessive discharge or buildup of mucus in the nose or throat, associated with an infection and/or inflammation of the mucous membrane.

The other copy sent to Bishop Hermann (also typewritten) had the following letter added to it by me—in writing:

To His Lordship,
Bishop Hermann,
Honolulu.

Dear Bishop:

The copy of these notes heretofore sent you has some slight alterations—some that I made on its receipt from New York, where the original is, in the hands of Dr. Morrow. I notified Dr. Morrow of the alterations and he has had some new, clean copies made and sent me. This is one of them. Will send one to Mr. Meyer and give one to Father Wendelin. They are strictly accurate. You will remember I made the original, for Dr. Morrow, from Father Damien's own words, about one month before his death. I read the notes over to him. He said they were entirely correct, and signed the paper at my request. You may like to have this other copy.

Very truly and respectfully yours,
(Signed) Joseph Dutton.
Kalawao, Molokai,
August 28, 1890.

Leper Settlement,
Kalawao, Molokai,
Oct. 12, 1903.

To Whom It May Concern:

The "notes" I made for Dr. P. A. Morrow, 66 W. 40th St., N. York City, were requested by him upon the conclusion of his visit here in the early part of March, 1889, just before Father Damien's death, April 15, 1889. I made notes in a number of cases, some 15, if I remember correctly. These "notes" concerning Father Damien being one set of the lot. This set is dated March 10, immediately, I think, after Dr. Morrow's departure for New York. Very likely all of the sets bear the same date. Am not sure, and it is not important. I sent them all to N. Y. for Dr. Morrow soon after completion. These typewritten copies were afterward made and sent me by Dr. Morrow, or by his direction. The sets of notes were all made up in about the same form, but the set relating to Father Damien was the only one signed, as I now remember.

The "old-timers" are now passing away, so the Catholic mission thinks it a good idea, and quite opportune, for me to make oath to some, or all, of these things, which I cheerfully do, and would have it to embrace all that is set forth in two copies of notes and in the memoranda, for I am now going through them very thoroughly so as to detect any error heretofore overlooked (as the year of vaccination, on second page of notes, corrected in red ink). Shall make oath to the two papers as to the best of my knowledge and belief.

In this connection it may not be out of place for me to put upon record what my own impression has always been concerning Father Damien's chastity, partly because of the pertinent declarations he makes in the notes, and partly because of the question having been brought up—soon after his death—in the public prints, and which might possibly at some time occur again. It is a question one can never speak upon positively without having positive proof for support, therefore I can state only of impressions and belief.

Upon April 15, 1893 (4th anniversary of Father Damien's death) I forwarded a copy of the "notes" to the Damien Institute, Louvain, Belgium, with the following verification and remarks:

> "The above paper constitutes a true copy of 'notes' made by me, from Father Damien's own words, a little over a month before he died. The 'notes' being read over to him by me, he said they were correct, and signed the paper. The original was sent to Dr. P. A. Morrow, New York, at whose request I made the notes.
>
> Regarding the remark that he 'never had any sexual intercourse whatever,' I would state that Father Damien

made it of his own motion, not from any question or remark of mine so far as I know. There was not anyone present save Father Damien and myself. Why he made this statement (the absolute truth of which I, of course, never doubted) was not exactly apparent to me. Idle remarks had been made against Father Damien's chastity, but I never knew of any responsible source whatever or that anyone well acquainted with Father Damien had any belief in the tale. "It might be that he suspected someone would take it up and make use of it, after his death, which, in fact, did occur. In verifying these 'notes' I make the above explanation in respect to Father Damien's memory. I was very intimately associated with him from July, 1886, up to his death on April 15, 1889.

Very respectfully,
(Signed) Joseph Dutton."

Earlier still, that is, on February 12, 1890, I made a statement to Bishop Hermann, at his request, some thirty pages, giving my ideas concerning Father Damien, his virtues and characteristics, his relations with the work at the leper settlement, and with the officials of the Hawaiian government, etc. Shall here quote some of that statement as relating to the subject herein, beginning at Page 18 of the original statement:

"The question of his purity has been brought up in the public prints. In this I can merely state my firm belief that he was wholly devoid of sensuality during the time I knew him.

Will introduce here something repugnant but apropos. Leprosy in its course shows some curious freaks in this regard. I have taken some pains to investigate the same for the information of a well known medical gentleman in New York. The effects upon sensual passions appear differently in different forms of the disease, and again differently in the various stages. Without going into particulars, I will state that what Father Damien told me about himself, in that regard, seems to hold good in many cases of his type. And what he said was this: That for several years (of the latter part of his life) he felt no tendency towards sensual excitement. He volunteered this, and his conversation led me to infer that in the earlier years here on the islands, he had to resist such movements.

In going about, in the country districts, it was sometimes necessary to stop over night with some native family. He told me that one night, when in one of these huts, a young native woman being about to sleep near him, he left the hut and stayed outdoors. It never occurred to me to question his lifelong adherence to virtue, in this regard, at least. He seemed, while I knew him, to have no thought for such things, no thoughts tending toward sensuality. And this condition, in my opinion, was the cause of there being certain idle reports, or gossip, indulged in by some people.

The charges on this point, published since his death, are not new ones. I heard the same things, at least some of them, here while he was living. That is, I was informed of them, but the parties so informing—intelligent men—always asserted their belief that Father Damien was innocent of the charge; except insofar as he gave (apparently unwittingly) ground for suspicion, by his want of caution, in allowing women to be about his house, etc., being apparently blind to what might seem to be evil in the eyes of others.

These things I myself could not help seeing. Yet I never saw what would cause me to suspect that there was anything wrong, unless in appearance.

Coupled with the charges as published was one to the effect that he was unclean in his personal habits. Of this I cannot say so much in denial. When visitors were here, he used to keep in presentable appearance; but ordinarily he paid very little attention to the cleanliness of his person or his dress. Did not pretend to neatness in his personal belongings. Has told me that he considered this a defect. Was very simple in his bodily wants, and was quite able to subsist upon the closest fare."

I was intending to make some remarks from memory, but now that these old records are copied or quoted from, the points seem to be covered, and I have still the same belief as then. Will merely add that I did not know anything personally concerning Father Damien previous to July, 1886. But from that time until his death, April 15, 1889, I lived and worked in the same small yard where he lived, had meals with him a good part of the time, and we went to Kalaupapa together twice a week. Will also note here that he had a number of enemies, mainly caused, so far as I know, by his harsh manner and self-assertion.

I make oath to the things related or referred to, in this paper, as to the best of my knowledge and belief. Two copies signed and sworn to before Thos. K. Nathaniel, notary public, with seal, October 15, 1903. This I keep as memorandum.

(Signed) Joseph Dutton.

Damien died while the roof on the famous Damien church, just across the road from the present Baldwin Home at Kalawao, was being completed, with Brother Dutton superintending, and lepers doing the carpentry work. He was laid to rest in the churchyard, over which the Catholic Mission at Honolulu later erected a handsome monument. Some years later a monument to Father Damien was erected at Kalaupapa by the people of England.

Brother Dutton was appointed executor of his estate, and shortly after his death went to Kalaupapa to attend to the shipping of his effects to Honolulu, from where many of them were sent back to his native land, Belgium.

In 1921, George J. Donahue of Meriden, Conn., wrote:

"But it is growing late. The moon is riding high, and the stars are glinting chill and cold. There is not a single light back in the leper settlement. Every native has retired and sleeps the heavy, restless sleep of sorrow and grief. The eternal crooning of the sea along the beach alone keeps company with our sad vigil by the grave of Damien. Let us say farewell to our Father and our Friend by whose last resting place we have lingered, striving to learn the secret of his greatness and praying for grace to imitate something of his charity. Our farewell might fitly appropriate the words of a brother poet-priest :

"O God, the cleanest offering
     Of tainted earth below,
Unblushing to Thy feet, we bring
     A leper white as snow.'"

*The Baldwin Home campus at Kalawaoe*

*The house of Frank Leighton Gibson and Emma Warren Gibson on the grounds of the United States Leprosy Investigation Station (U.S.L.I.S.) which was a very short distance from the Baldwin Home.*

# The Baldwin Home
## 1894–1936

It was only a few years after the death of Father Damien that Brother Dutton realized the necessity of making enlargements and improvements at Kalawao. More lepers were coming to the settlement, and there was a large influx of boys and girls, and of young men and women, and the idea of segregation—that is, one institution for boys and another for girls—occurred to Brother Dutton as perhaps the most feasible solution of the problem.

At Kalawao, from early in 1886 to 1888, the settlement consisted merely of a cluster of cabins, and in the latter year two large buildings were erected, and many of the poorest of the cabins destroyed, their occupants being moved to the new structures. On January 1, 1889, the Damien Home, as it was then called, was accepted by the board of health and operated as a home. Father Damien was the manager, and received from the board of health a salary of $25 a month.

On July 1, 1889, shortly after Father Damien's death, Mother Marianne was placed in charge of the home. She asked Brother Dutton to take charge of and operate the institution until such time as sufficient Catholic sisters could be spared to assist her. Brother Dutton took over the management, and for a time was assisted by John Gaiser. On May 15, 1890, three Catholic sisters arrived—Sister Crescentia, in charge; and Sisters Renata and Vincentia. Later Sister Renata returned to Honolulu and her place was taken by Sister Irene.

*The late Hon. H. P. Baldwin, financier and philanthropist of Hawaii, and founder of one of its best-known families, who gave the funds for the establishment of the Baldwin Home for leper boys and men at Kalawao, Molokai.*

With the sisters in charge, Brother Dutton continued with the work he had done previously, which consisted of keeping the accounts, attending to the correspondence and the general business affairs, attending to the sick and handling the sore dressing. In May and June, 1894, following the completion of what is now known as the Baldwin Home for Boys, the patients were moved into the new buildings, and on December 1, 1895, the Catholic sisters were relieved of duty at the home, their places being taken by four Catholic brothers of the Picpus order, under the direction of Brother Dutton.

Brother Dutton first discussed his plans for a home for boys at Kalawao with William O. Smith, then president of the Board of Health, and at present an attorney at Honolulu. Smith visited the leper settlement on several occasions and he and Brother Dutton became very friendly. They discussed a variety of subjects, but the one in which they were most interested concerned what could be done toward further assisting the lepers, making them comfortable, providing means for recreation, and helping them to make the most out of a life which at that time was anything but optimistic.

They discussed at considerable length Brother Dutton's plans for a home, and Smith seemed to take kindly to the proposal. Previously, Brother Dutton had sketched his scheme to the late Henry P. Baldwin of Maui, father of Harry Baldwin, former delegate to Congress from Hawaii. With Smith interested, Brother Dutton took up the matter again with Baldwin, and finally an understanding was reached among Brother Dutton, Smith and Baldwin that a home would be built at Kalawao, and that Brother Dutton would take over the management of it.

That is how the Baldwin Home came to be built. It cost in the neighborhood of $6,000 and, while Baldwin contributed the initial outlay of money for the construction, the Board of Health assisted in a number of ways, and today maintains the institution. Frequent contributions are made to the home by the Baldwin family.

While the institution was primarily for the housing and care of leper boys, regulations were passed later on by the Board of Health which permitted the entrance, when there was room, of other patients who desired to live there, although only male patients were to be received. At first the home housed only boys under 18, but today there are many men there, practically all of them being men who are helpless, such as blind and lame.

Brother Dutton was in full charge thereafter. With the coming of the Picpus brothers, he was soon relieved of many of his more arduous duties, such as manual labor and sore dressing, these labors having been taken over by the brothers. He still attended to the accounts, however, and the general business transactions, making out all of the requisitions for supplies, and handling the correspondence.

By the time the Baldwin Home was completed, a general movement of patients toward Kalaupapa had begun. This was a slow process, however, and it was not until after the Hawaiian Islands had been annexed to the United States that Kalaupapa began to be settled in any definite degree. As Brother Dutton recalls it, it was probably not until 1902 that all of the patients at Kalawao, with the exception of those in the Baldwin Home, had moved to the other end of the peninsula.

The home consisted, as originally constructed, of 45 buildings, the majority of these being dormitories for the patients. Since then some of the buildings have been torn down, and others erected in their place. As soon as the institution had been completed, Brother Dutton undertook extensive improvements to the site, laying out lawns, building stone walls and planting trees and shrubs. At the rear of the home, and along the base of the cliff, he planted 50 young coconut trees which he obtained from Samoa. These trees obtained their full growth many years ago, and from the nuts scores of other coconuts are now growing. He also planted 5,000 eucalyptus trees. After the arrival of the Picpus brothers, Brother Dutton conceived the idea of a modern sewer system to take the place of the insanitary cesspools, and completed this project with the assistance of Brother Louis, which has been at the Baldwin Home for 19 years.

In the meantime the Damien church had been completed just across the road from the Baldwin Home. The stone portion of the edifice had been erected under the direction of Brother Dutton, and what was the original Damien church is now preserved in the form of two wings

*A photograph of the Baldwin Home campus for leper boys
and men at Kalawao, Molokai, taken about 1910.*

of the main church, one of these housing the first altar which Father
Damien fashioned with his own hands from such material as was handy.
For years the Damien church has been a Mecca for such sight-seers and
others fortunate enough to obtain permission to visit the leper settlement. It is still in use today, and Brother Dutton has worshipped in it
for 38 years.

All of the chandeliers in the Damien church were sent to Brother
Dutton by George W. Woods, now dead, and at one time medical director in the United States Navy. He died at San Francisco in 1902, and
Brother Dutton had his naval record printed and sent to scores of his
friends. He was retired from active duty in 1900.

Following is the record of the Catholic brothers who have been
at the Baldwin Home from time to time since the first contingent of
brothers arrived there:

Brother Dominick (Victor H.) Lappe.
  Arrived November 30, 1895.
  Left December 21, 1898.

Brother Aloysius (Louis) Liesen.
  Arrived November 30, 1898.
  For 20 years at the Baldwin Home.
  Now at Honolulu.

Brother Severin Baltes.
  Arrived November 30, 1895.
  Died at the home September 19, 1921.

Brother Sylvester Van Volsen.
  Arrived November 30, 1895.
  Left November 30, 1904.

Brother Serapion Van Hoof.
  Arrived November 30, 1895.
  Died at the home May 12, 1910.

The foregoing, with the exception of Brother Louis, are the four brothers of the Picpus Order who first went to the Baldwin Home.

Brother Victor Schumpf.
  Arrived July 1, 1899.
  Died February 20, 1900, at the home.

Brother Laurent Bergmans.
  Arrived April 1, 1902.
  Left August 25, 1903.

Brother Rochus Rech.
  Arrived October 21, 1902.
  Drowned November 10, 1902, at the home.

Brother Severianus Springer.
  Arrived November 18, 1902.
  Left January 27, 1903.

Brother Willibrord Slaats.
  Arrived August 25, 1903.
  Left November 10, 1903.

Brother Silvester Barbe.
  Arrived November 24, 1903.
  Left May 6, 1920.

The Catholic fathers who have been or who are still at the home are:

The Rev. Fr. Emmersan Schultz.
  Arrived April 25, 1907.
  Died August 14, 1912.

The Rev. Fr. L. L. Conrardy.
  Arrived May 17, 1888.
  Left December 27, 1895.
  Died August 24, 1914.

The Rev. Fr. Philip Blom.
  Arrived August 21, 1912.
  Left March 1, 1915.
  Now at the Catholic Mission, Honolulu.

The Rev. Fr. Engelbert de Vriese.
  Arrived March 11, 1915.
  Left October 1, 1918.

The Rev. Fr. Athanasius Bous.
  Arrived September 26, 1918.
  Left August 7, 1919.

The Rev. Fr. Bruno Bens.
  Arrived June 28, 1919.
  Left July 15, 1919.

The Rev. Fr. Martin Dornbusch.
  Arrived July 31, 1919, from Germany.

*The Baldwin Home campus for leper boys and men at Kalawao, Molokai,
as it appeared in 1913, showing the abandoned
U. S. Leprosarium buildings along the beach at the left.*

The establishment of the federal leprosarium at Kalawao, some
distance removed from the Baldwin Home, came about as the result
of the passage by Congress of a bill providing that the territory cede
to the United States government a tract of land a mile square for the
establishment "of a hospital station and laboratory of the Public Health
and Marine Hospital Service of the United States for the study of the
methods of transmission, cause and treatment of leprosy."

The bill carried an appropriation of $100,000 for the erection of
the buildings, and $50,000 for maintenance and pay of officers and em-
ployees during the fiscal year ending June 30, 1906. The tract was visited
and inspected twice by Surgeon General Wyman of the United States

Health Service, and also on various occasions by officials of the Board of Health at Honolulu, who held their meetings and conferences in Brother Dutton's office.

An elaborate group of buildings was erected upon a high cliff along the seashore, and the understanding was that patients would be supplied from both Kalaupapa and Kalawao. But things went wrong from the very beginning. Lepers, satisfied with their conditions of living, declined to move to the new institution. There was difficulty encountered in obtaining competent medical directors and employees. There was also considerable criticism to the effect that those in charge of the institution stood in fear of lepers and leprosy, and that consequently the few patients who consented finally to go to the leprosarium were not receiving the proper treatment.

In about 1913 the entire project collapsed, the institution was abandoned, and the federal employees moved out bag and baggage. Even today, in the once well-equipped laboratories, bottles, instruments, retorts, gas burners and other articles of equipment are strewn about the tables. The more valuable portions of the equipment were removed during the general exodus. The timbers in the buildings, however, are in a fair state of preservation. A few of the structures have been torn down and the lumber taken to Kalaupapa, where to be used for the erection of additional buildings. In 1923 the United States government turned the land and the buildings over to the territorial government.

~

A good many years ago Brother Dutton made some notes regarding his "emigrant" trip to San Francisco and thence to Honolulu, and his interview with Walter Murray Gibson, then minister of foreign affairs under King David Kalakaua, and president of the Board of Health. He wrote, in part, as follows:

> "The bishop (the late Bishop Hermann of the Catholic Mission at Honolulu) was very much pleased with this plan to give the far end of my life in helping Father Damien and the lepers. I think he was also pleased that I

had made that 'emigrant' trip to San Francisco and then coming to Honolulu by sailing vessel, registered as a servant, and all without speaking to anyone about it.

But we had to consult the Honolulu Board of Health. He went first to see Mr. Gibson, the president of the Board of Health. Mr. Gibson wished to see me. Taking a bundle of papers—my three army commissions, various appointments, complimentary letters, certificates of non-indebtedness for my various responsibilities, etc.,—I went to his house near the Palace. The legislature was in session, the members having just returned from an official visit to the leper settlement.

There was quite a flurry of business around Mr. Gibson's house, but he took me to his den for a talk, glanced over my bundle of papers and then handed it back, and seemed to be very favorably impressed with my idea of going to work for the lepers. He gave the necessary authority and induced Mr. Wilder to send the steamer Mokolii around to the settlement with me. This weekly trip was to have extended only to the southern side of the island, going around to the settlement the next week.

Before I left Honolulu, Mr. Gibson introduced me to Mr. Hayselden, then secretary of the Board of Health, and to his clerk, Mr. Hendry. Mr. Gibson wanted me to see the latter because we were born in the same state. He sent Mr. Hendry to get me an outfit of dishes, provisions, etc.

In all of the changes since then in the make-up of the Board of Health, I have never seen the time when I did not consider each officer and member my personal friend. Nor, in the duties I have had to perform, have they ever refused anything I asked for. They have even indulged my fancy for work without pay—a favor never granted to anyone else, so far as I know, except to Mr. Van Lil. Mr. Van Lil was one whom I knew at Gethsemani, and who had written to me asking if he might come to the settlement. (Note: Mr. Van Lil went to the settlement. He is still there today as a patient.)

I must not omit mention of the sisters of St. Francis who had been at Honolulu since 1883 at the branch hospital for lepers, which they were carrying on very successfully. In 1889 some of them came to the leper settlement.

In July, 1886, I reached Honolulu, and arrived at the leper settlement July 29. Father Damien had but recently returned from Honolulu, having gone there to test the Japanese treatment. He came back to the settlement with the members of the legislature on the official visit of the latter.

To tell you the joy I felt upon arrival, after seeing Father Damien; upon getting to work; the enjoyment of nature's wonders; sympathy for the lepers; the weird and strange conditions; and to give any detailed account of the life here, would be quite beyond my opportunities, if not beyond my powers.

You have seen a great deal in print regarding the settlement, and many accounts have been published by persons more able than I am. One question often asked is how long Father Damien was afflicted when here, and whether I had the entire care of him after he grew very ill. As to the first part, I refer to a copy of the 'Notes' in Father Damien's case that I made from his own words a few weeks before his death.

Regarding the care of him, I should say that I had the main care for a long time, but a great part of this time he was able to be about some. After he became very ill indeed, others helped, particularly Mr. James Sinnott, a lay worker who was here for some months. During the latter part, he had no other duty. I was then alone in looking after the sick at the home, and attending to the other work. The home, as a government institution, was just started.

Upon landing at Kalaupapa on July 29, 1886, I went first to the church there to give thanks for safe arrival, accompanied by Father Damien and quite a crowd of natives. Shortly after, Father Damien and I started, at nightfall, for Kalawao, the father's headquarters. This was also the headquarters of the leper settlement. Kalaupapa had then no water supply, but a limited number of people lived there, and it had the only steamer landing. The people there had to bring water on horses and donkeys from a neighboring gulch. Since the bringing of water to Kalaupapa by pipes some years ago, that side of the settlement has gradually become the main part, chiefly on account of the steamer landing. That leaves our home at Kalawao more in quiet than before—a good result.

But I was coming with Father Damien to Kalawao. Reaching his house there, close by the church, I found a little gathering of natives, men and boys, some only about 20 years old, who occupied a group of cabins in the same yard. That was the forerunner of the home. There was no organization as yet. The numbers increased, one by one, and steps were taken looking to organization. A few months before Father Damien's death it was a regular institution under government management, and with nearly a hundred inmates.

The Bishop Home for women and girls was started shortly at Kalaupapa. This one at Kalawao was known in those days as the boys' home. Now we have the Baldwin Home, capacity 144 lepers, although there are only 128 just now, because of the lingering cases that died during the recent severe weather (am writing now in January, 1900) and newly-found lepers not being sent here lately.

The Bishop Home is nearly the same in numbers, etc. Mother Marianne and four sisters remain there ordinarily. The mother provincial from Syracuse, N. Y., and two new sisters she has brought on to teach in a Catholic school at Hilo (island of Hawaii) are now visiting there. There are also five Franciscan Sisters at Wailuku (island of Maui) operating the hospital there. This is a hospital for general patients. Three are at Honolulu attending to the Kapiolani Home for non-leper girls, the daughters of leper parents. Three of the sisters were located here at Kalawao for several years prior to December, 1895. They were at the boys' home and in charge of Mother Marianne of the Bishop Home, represented by men in business matters here.

About June, 1895, a different arrangement was made. The three sisters at the boys' home, being needed elsewhere, were to be replaced by some new brothers from Europe, the bishop at Honolulu to obtain them from a convent for work at the home under my management. This I first learned from the Honolulu papers, having had no intimation previously.

A quandary came up here. The new brothers would be young, would not be able to speak English or Hawaiian and would not be used to the work. The question was: How should they be 'given a lift' at the beginning?

Just then came a letter from Oregon, signed by Emil Van Lil. At first I could not remember him, but, coming finally to the mention of Gethsemani, I remembered. He was a novice there, but did not make vows. What had become of him in the lapse of 10 years I knew not—until the letter. It was surely providential (as everything is), for here was a Belgian speaking English, and a good gardener accustomed to general work. He wanted to come to the settlement. If he came at once, he would get about five months' experience while the sisters remained, and he would be exceedingly useful in getting the new brothers started, assisting them with their English, etc.

At my request, the Board of Health provided money to bring him on and authorized me to send for him. He came, and worked without pay, the same as I was doing. He has been very useful in general work, developing a good garden and helping to get the brothers started after their arrival on November 30, 1895. Four brothers came then, two Germans, a Belgian and a Hollander. They have succeeded very well in their duties, which include attending to the food and clothing departments. I still attend to the sick, doing the sore dressing, etc., as from the beginning, and also the business and the general work.

I have never left the leper settlement grounds since my arrival in July, 1886. When Father Damien was able to attend to the duties at Kalaupapa, I was there with him on Fridays and Sundays. I remember being at Kalaupapa but three times since his death; once in about 1891 to meet the authorities regarding a proposed removal of the boys' home to Kalaupapa, and two days in 1893 attending to the shipping of Father Damien's effects to Louvain, Belgium.

Shortly before his death, Father Damien had asked me to attend personally to the disposition of all of his effects, and to settle his money accounts. He asked the priest remaining here, who had lately arrived, to let me settle all of the accounts. I was also the executor of his will. One time it seemed as if I should have to go to Honolulu on that business, but the authorities, at my request, arranged so as to avoid that. Later there was another time. I wanted to transfer my father's estate in Wisconsin, but again avoided going to Honolulu through the kindness of the American minister."

*A picture of Brother Dutton from ~1921, center, with a group of Catholic Brothers
on duty at the Baldwin Home, Kalawao, Molokai.
At the left in the front row is Brother Louis, who served nearly 20 years
at the home and who is now at the Kalihi Orphanage, Honolulu..*

*Brother Dutton with some children of the settlement*

*The Old Bay View Home at Kalaupapa*

*Father Damien's Church*

# Side Lights On Settlement History
## 1905

*(Note: The following is composed mainly of excerpts taken from a manuscript written by Brother Dutton about 1905, shortly after the establishment of the Baldwin Home for boys at Kalawao, and the Bishop Home for girls at Kalaupapa. It contains many interesting and enlightening references to leper settlement history of that period.)*

Rather heavy breakers are coming in. It would appear, from a distance, that the beach slopes almost to the sea, whereas the cliff there is about 50 feet high, having part of the way—just in front of the Home—a ledge of lava rock below the cliff proper and running out a considerable distance into the sea, the other edge being from 10 to 20 feet above the sea.

The surface of this ledge is very rough, having many depressions into which the sea water comes from time to time, several of these making fine bathing places for our people in the summer season, a change from the fresh water of the bath houses. When the breakers are heavy, the uprising waters along this ledge at times—not very frequent—surround the whole cliff, as much, I should say, as 70 feet in all, and the spray is then carried over our grounds, even to the pali (cliff), withering the leaves of plants, shrubs and trees so that they drop off. But new and brighter ones come out quickly with a "Here we are again!"

Looking westward, to the left, the sea cliff becomes higher and higher, until a half-way point is reached, where the cliff must be from 150 to 200 feet high. This is the part that is the most advanced into the sea, and opposite the crater (a dead volcanic crater with a well at the bottom which connects underneath with the sea). At this point, opposite the crater, where the sea cliffs are not only honeycombed with but abounding in well-like holes, caverns and wonderful lava formations where the breakers and heavy rollers sometimes fill everything with snow-like, irritable waters, coming in with a crash and going out with a splash—through all there is a moaning underneath, almost as a wail from the tomb; a resounding rush with a sudden vibration from time to time, a hissing through small apertures, the foaming and frothy sea rising and falling in the well-like places; the places that one suddenly and unexpectedly comes upon in going with long, jumping steps over these water-worn, rounded rocks. The slimy, spidery, crab-like, curious specimens of southern sea life crawl and climb through these water rushes. But one should not look too closely, nor linger in these times of angry seas; those rocks are smooth and slippery with the mad, dashing waters.

And they are treacherous. If a body slips into one of those wells which, over the rough surface, are hardly seen until one is quite upon them, then his chances for enjoying the surface again are very slim, even if a companion is along who does not fall in. If no one knew of his going there, it would simply be a mysterious disappearance. The waters would never tell. Nearly 19 years ago it was when I went there alone, knowing nothing of the place. Twice a week I used to go with Father Damien to Kalaupapa, and in returning, during the first few months, I made the three sight-seeing trips, far away from the occupied parts of the leper settlement peninsula, each time walking: To the head of the gulch of Waihanau, to the crater, and to this one around the sea cliff. I have never made any other. The whole scene in this locality is so grand that one teems with it, and wonders how anyone can doubt the existence of Almighty God.

The gulch and the crater are worthy of description, especially the gulch, but we cannot visit them now. We have stopped so long to talk over this interesting spot on the sea coast; and now I have forgotten the one thing I started out to say—about the silence. The gulch and the crater has its own kind of silence for the visitor, especially if no one else is along. It is like the silence of the grave. Of human sounds there is none. It is smothering. Out on the sea cliff, when the sea is smooth, the silence is something different and wonderful. It is something one never forgets. Save occasional angry mutterings of the sea, no sound comes there, not even of bird or animal. If man and all of his tumult were millions of miles away, they could not be more completely absent. It is a condition that is weird and awesome, as I felt it all in 1886, having never visited any of those places again. Were I to do so, things might seem different. I might not be so impressed. The heart was full then of the glories of God's creation in this—to me—new, strange and sorrowing colony.

Now let us go on towards Kalaupapa. The cliff becomes lower and lower until Kalaupapa is reached. Finally it becomes less in height than it is at Kalawao. This circuit, or rather half circuit, is about three miles on its somewhat zigzag and rounding course, but the road from Kalawao to Kalaupapa—the "Damien Road"—is about two miles long, running close to the pali (cliff) until near Kalaupapa, when it branches in various directions, as Kalaupapa spreads out more than Kalawao.

The houses at Kalawao are all near the road. Kalawao was formerly the leper settlement proper, having the offices, shops, etc., and also a small fresh water system. Kalaupapa then had some lepers, including a few who worked at the landing, for it had then, as it has now, the only freight warehouse, and the only small wharf for the boats from the inter-island steamers. But there was no fresh water there, except that which was brought, usually on horses, for about a mile from the head of Waihanau gulch, and for this reason the lepers there were not numerous.

But after some years the water pipes were extended from Kalawao on to Kalaupapa. The Board of Health offices and shops were then moved there one by one. Gradually a good portion of the Kalawao people followed, and now our Baldwin Home—the largest family—has usually about half of the Kalawao population. The number has fluctuated in the home between 100 and 150. Our ordinary capacity is 144.

To the left are scattering houses along the road, while others are to the right. To the right of the church, in the large pasture lot, are the wash houses, drying houses and the cart house. The old home used to be over there; two, in fact. The first group of cabins, and then the first regular houses—the large ones—were built under the direction of Father

Damien, assisted by me. Those old buildings served their purpose well enough, but finally the present ones were built by me, and occupied about 10 years ago. This is doubtless my last effort at construction.

The church (the Damien church) is about 70 feet long. To the right of it stands Father Damien's house. This was at one time a two-story structure, but the lower story was cut out, the top part dropped down upon sills, and moved to where it now stands, being used as a singing house, and for other purposes. It used to stand on the other side of the church, about half way between the church and the present house of the priest.

Just beyond the priest's house is the Calvinist church with a white fence in front. The Catholic church and house have large yards and are surrounded by stone walls. We now come to the home proper, beginning at the rear, which is our immediate front. That bushy mass back of the garden and all around the sides, wide and thick, consists of countless plants, now small trees of the Croton family, with leaves doubly uncountable, and no two alike, variegated in one of nature's wildest frolics, in colors bright and flaming, almost a twin to the Flag unfurled. Off to sea they say it looks like the home was set in a big, red bouquet. These trees are more than ornamental. When five or six years old the wood becomes hard and supplies a good deal of fuel, growing again from the stump with great rapidity.

I have two kinds of these trees in my cabin yard. Still another kind, the brightest red of all, but much smaller in size, is growing around the dormitories—some 300 of them. When a Kona (south wind storm) comes along, all hands turn out with knives and hatchets and cut such things all down close to the ground to prevent them from being up-rooted. Then they grow out again quickly, in new styles and fresh colors. Not costly, these trees. They grow amongst the stones in the back and side parts not yet fully cleared and graded.

The cultivated part in front is the garden, with a little ash house and a fine date palm near the center. Just within the circle of red trees we have about 2000 bananas. That garden, near the pali (cliff), has some rich earth, but there was a great number of big and smaller rocks over it.

We dug long trenches about 15 feet wide and 15 feet deep and buried the rocks, leaving about three feet of earth on top.

The home buildings on both sides of the road number about 55, but some are small, as the ash house and the oil house. The house occupied by the Catholic brothers (formerly occupied by the sisters) is the best constructed of them all. This residence has a fine yard in the front, on the road nearly opposite the singing house. At the edge of the garden is the recreation hall, which contains also a schoolroom and a band room. It is 60 by 34 feet, including the veranda. The dormitories, each 20 by 36 feet, are to the right and left of the hall.

There is also a tailor shop where Brother Severin is the chief artist. One of the brothers cooks for the brothers' mess, and Brother Aloysius and another brother attend to the general work, such as the housekeeping and the dining room. Brother Aloysius and Brother Severin have a part of the work which I did for about 17 years—the care of the sick, the sore-dressing, etc.

But let us go back to the hall and go down the other side of the yard. There are six more dormitories that way. The mattress house, standing the other way, like the tailor shop, is behind the row of dormitories on this, the western side of the yard. In the corner near the garden is a cute little cottage with a cute little yard, on a terraced sort of place. A white leper used to live there. It is now occupied by two natives. There is another with just the same history below the dormitories. Just beyond the mattress house is quite a large shed for lumber, etc., connecting with the tool house, carpenter shop and paint shop. This paint shop is the cottage Father Damien built for me, adjoining the church. I had it moved across the road and over here. As first built, it opened by a little passageway into the sacristy of the old church. The present church was built over that part of the old one. Where the cottage, or cabin, stood, the Father Damien pandanus—the palm under which he slept before his own cottage was built—swept the roof.

Father Damien's grave is just in front of where it stood. The pandanus became decayed. It is all cleared away now. Only the square rock that was at the front of the tree—Father Damien's first table—is left standing by his grave, as Father Joseph has fixed it lately.

In the dormitories the smaller boys are at the lower end on the right side in front of the tailor shop. Going up the hill, they increase in age and size to the hall; and on the other side, being full grown men, they go down the gentle slopes, in the sunny afternoon of life, to the grave, eventually. The two lower dormitories house the old and helpless patients. Some remain there a long time, however, before being removed to the house for the dead. This house for the dead is near the church, just below the singing house. Those who are taken to that house have finished their life of pain and trouble.

The home was established for orphan boys. Then helpless cases were admitted, including the blind, persons who prefer the home to being housed elsewhere, those without families—all male. For the women and girls, the Franciscan sisters from Syracuse, N. Y., have a well-cared-for home at Kalaupapa. Father Maxim is the chaplain.

These homes, and all in the settlement outside the homes, are under the general control of the Board of Health at Honolulu, whose officials attend to the business matters of the settlement, and with whom we of the homes keep a good understanding.

In the homes our special aim is not only to do what we can for the bodies of these afflicted ones, but, and very specially, to maintain a good moral condition through all. Keeping this standard has good results not only in the homes, but the influence is spread more or less outside.

This home for men and boys is called the Baldwin Home, after the Hon. H. P. Baldwin of Maui and Honolulu, who furnished the means for its establishment, and who makes a standing offer to help in instances of special need.

The home for women and girls at Kalaupapa was established by the Hon. Charles R. Bishop, formerly a banker of Honolulu and now of San Francisco. (Mr. Bishop and his wife, Bernice Pauahi Bishop, founder of the Kamehameha Schools for Hawaiian boys and girls at Honolulu, have long since died.)

This memo has wandered away from the actual description, so let us go back to the row of coconut trees along the garden wire fence, and extending all along the eastern side, back of the dormitories and tailor shop. There are some 30 in all. We got these, through a gentleman in Honolulu, from Samoa. They are growing finely, and within a few years will be highly ornamental and useful. We have some 45 Japanese plum trees, about 50 eucalyptus trees, and about 50 alligator pear (avocado) trees, all fairly large. We also have a dozen or more date palms, partly grown; and for smaller things, quite a number of hibiscus, pomegranate, etc.

In the very center of the playground is a plant that I admire very much, and had it put there for that reason. It is a lauhala (in Hawaiian) of the screw pine family, as is the pandanus. The lauhala is a noble plant. The leaves, which are from three to six feet long, droop over the outside, making a handsome figure, regular and shapely, something like a bee hive, but large enough for bees the size of eagles. If one presses through these leaves, he finds the interior surprising. The numerous strong branches, of screw pine fashion, make space for, say, 50 boys to perch on.

Just below the two dormitories for old and helpless patients is the office. The office contains the drug stock, and the back room is a storage place for drugs, surplus small material, tools, etc., and opens into the shoe shop, saddle room, and my bath room. The bath house and the sore dressing rooms are connected with the office by verandas 10 feet wide. These verandas, with long benches at the edge, make the place for floor games, picture and other papers, magazines, books, and various musical instruments. And here, from the office door, I give a phonograph concert Sunday night.

What I call the machinery department is in front of the office, but with an open way of about 50 feet from the front of the office right down to the front gate, opposite the church, the machinery buildings being ranged along both sides of this open way. The poi house, the boiler house, the beef room, the pantry and the banana room are all under one roof. Then there is a dining room, a kitchen, a woodshed and coal room, a lime and cement room and a slop house. The storage house, for provisions and housekeeping articles in general, fronts on the road, and is arranged so that the carts hauling provisions have a convenient place for turning.

I have seldom mentioned interior matters here, save sometimes a little description of the scenery, of the family, or the like. I did not really come here to write, and in early years had little occasion or reason for writing. Of late years, however, many old friends have dropped in through the mail. This paper may please them, and I am hoping that it may be free of all evil.

As for a description of the lepers, and the details of the work here, it has not seemed to me that they were nice subjects for description. Some inquire about Father Damien. The coming here of Father Damien was something unique, it seems to me, and something good. It was from a noble motive, we must believe; and although he has been painted as being rough and uncouth, is it not quite possible that his coming to this unusual service was through a special action of Divine Providence? A special vocation? Well fitted for the work here as it was in those rough and difficult times, he came to it with eagerness, and with firm resolve. He was earnest and determined. So intent upon what he thought should be done, he was occasionally in "hot water" with the authorities. Yet, with this, and considering also his nature, he was still really fitted for the work at that time. He accomplished, I think, much good; a good far greater than was apparent.

It was a sort of object lesson for the world—a source of information. The general public over the world hardly knew of the presence of leprosy before Father Damien came here. It was known only in isolated localities—outside of India, at least—and little mention was made of it over the world. In fact, such information was not general for years after Father Damien came here; not even when I came, in 1886, a few weeks after the first mention I had seen of Molokai, or of present-day leper asylums.

Father Damien's death in 1889 brought the subject before the world distinctly, as by some great, mutual upheaval. This information was added to, and special interest in it developed as the disease began to spread in various countries—just as if Father Damien and Molokai were thrown up as a warning signal.

If his history here had never been made, would the world know as much about leprosy as it does today—and would so many scientific steps in its study have been taken? We know not. Some other means might have been used. Some other priest might have come; all of the priests of Father Damien's congregation would seem to be about as well qualified. So why Father Damien? I am prepared to believe he was the right one.

For the rest of us, however, is there any reason for special mention save, perhaps, among our friends? Hardly, I think. We are but imitators.

*Joseph Dutton at the grave of Father Damien, the "Martyr of Molokai," at Kalawao. The grave is in the yard of the coral stone church which Father Damien built.*

*Copyright, R. K. Bonine.*

*Memorial to a lifetime of devotion to the suffering: Monument erected at Kalaupapa leper settlement to the memory of the Rev. Mother Marianne, who headed the first group of Catholic Sisters to minister to lepers on Molokai.*

*Tribute to the "martyr priest." Monument to Father Damien, which was erected at the Kalaupapa leper settlement by the people of England.*

*The Catholic church at Kalaupapa, Molokai, showing the boat-landing at the left.*

*Interior of the Catholic church at Kalaupapa, Molokai, as it appears today.*

*The Great White Fleet Visit of 1908*
https://sanpedrobayhistoricalsociety.com/windows-into-the-past-1-the-great-white-fleet-visit-of-1908/

*USS Connecticut (BB-18), the Flagship of the Great White Fleet*
https://upload.wikimedia.org/wikipedia/commons/
thumb/3/3a/USS_Connecticut_-_NH_73318.jpg

# A Mighty Fleet Passes By
## 1908

*Note: President Theodore Roosevelt's "Great White Fleet,"*
*a force of sixteen battleships bristling with guns and painted sparkling*
*white, steamed out of Hampton Roads, Virginia to begin its 43,000-mile,*
*14-month circumnavigation of the globe "to demonstrate to the world*
*America's naval prowess."*
*The four-mile-long armada's world tour included 20 port calls*
*on six continents, and is widely considered one of the greatest*
*peacetime achievements of the U.S. Navy. The hulls were painted*
*white, the Navy's peacetime color scheme, and decorated with gilded*
*scrollwork with a red, white, and blue banner on their bows.*

It was in 1908 that the United States Atlantic fleet, cruising in Hawaiian waters, swerved out of its course and steamed by the tiny peninsula on Molokai so that the unfortunate lepers might view those mighty steel fighting craft.

And it was Brother Dutton who conceived the idea of asking that the fleet make the detour from the direct navigator's course to Honolulu; and his request for it, on behalf of the people of the leper settlement, was urged in the spirit of his life devotion to those to whom he is giving the undivided service of a lifetime.

That the people of the settlement appreciated the pageant of the passing fleet, and the good will and the sentiment which prompted it, is evident from a letter sent to Rear Admiral Charles Stillman Sperry, in command of the vessels, which was written by Brother Dutton on the day the fleet passed the settlement, and transmitted through Governor Walter F. Frear, now president of the Bishop Trust Co. at Honolulu.

The letter is touching in its direct sincerity. It reads as follows:

My dear Sir:

That splendid fleet of United States battleships coming from San Francisco to Honolulu, turning from the big road, coming down the lane, passing in parade in our front yard along the full extent of the Molokai leper settlement, under the towering rear wall over two thousand feet high, which is flanked by majestic headlands and backed by a reserve of mountains that are much higher!

Thus precisely on time and in exact order, with grave and serious movement, not like the cute little steamer that clicks its heels and scatters the dust, but like a powerful warrior in battle array, came the sixteen-this 'around the world' patrol that Mr. Roosevelt is sending in the name of Uncle Sam. These sixteen battleships that have the full confidence of America came down the lane with a friendly nod and passed on, so dignified and beautiful, this early July morning.

The weather is favorable—everything is—for this wonderful visit; this visit so exceedingly wonderful as to make the blood tingle and the heart grow warm. It helps to bring our inherent patriotism to the surface. It makes us love our whole Navy—every officer, every sailor. It makes us salute Uncle Sam very affectionately. It makes us better Americans. It is an object lesson to all, Americans or otherwise. And may God bless every one who has had even a little to do with bringing about this great pleasure.

The writer had that good fortune to think of, and to suggest, the possibility of such a visit. You have been, however, as our discreet governor, the most active in obtaining it. Surgeon General Walter Wyman has helped, also the Hon. W. O. Smith, and the territorial secretary, E. A. Mott-Smith. Without this good recommendation the proposition would hardly have succeeded. The interior department and the secretary of the navy have been very nice in forwarding the matter, for, for final action, Rear Admiral Sperry, in command of the fleet, has given prompt attention.

In all this I am speaking for the people of the leper settlement. Mr. Waimau, representing the Board of Health in the absence of Mr. McVeigh, has asked me to extend thanks to all concerned in the name of every one here; of all in the leper asylum, a place having in it some suffering, it cannot be denied, but it is the home of sensible and contented people whose lot has become, after many years of labor and improvement, a condition not so very difficult to bear, having patience as head nurse. A people also becoming better acquainted with our Uncle Sam, and better satisfied to be Americans.

Thus do I express their most hearty thanks. Personally, it is a gratitude almost beyond expression. As thinking of myself, 'Did ever one deserve so little and get so much?' There has been everywhere in the settlement, so far as I have any knowledge, the greatest possible praise. If anything is lacking, it is a new dictionary to supply words for this.

Our abode has been called 'Molokai the Blest.' It has surely been so this day. And the artistic temperament is not the least amongst the things benefited. Such a conjunction of wonders, both of Creation as seen in nature's boundless museum, and in the works that man has brought to such perfection, could hardly anywhere in the world have more impressive exposition that in the unique grandeur of the mountains of Molokai and the silent, stately movement of that column of sixteen noble battleships as they came in such precise formation down the lane to the leper settlement.

Very gratefully,
Joseph Dutton.

In reply to the foregoing letter, Ernest A. Mott-Smith, then secretary of the territory, wrote to Brother Dutton as follows:

Dear Brother:

I received your very kindly letter of July 18 together with the photographs to be distributed among the admirals and captains of the Atlantic fleet. There have been some changes in the roster, and in such cases, where you have named the captains, I added a little personal note to the effect that you were not aware of the changes, and though the picture was addressed to the former captain of the battleship, it was intended for the present captain, and I hoped it would be accepted as such. I enclose herewith a roster issued as of July 20, 1908, which gives the complete list.

Your letter addressed to Governor Frear, and marked for Admiral Sperry, has been sent to him together with a little personal letter from myself asking Admiral Sperry if he would not allow the letter to be published. I told Admiral Sperry that though you did not seek to put yourself into print under ordinary circumstances, that, all things considered, I thought it altogether fitting that your splendid letter, breathing such true American spirit and enthusiasm, should go to the press. And Admiral acceded to my request; I hope that the matter will not embarrass you in any way. Furthermore, I wish to congratulate you upon your letter to Admiral Sperry and to assure you that it was exceedingly pleasing to him. I have also asked him to send you an autographed photograph of himself.

This brings us to the point of my own photograph, which I am unable to send by this mail, as I have none on hand, but will have some printed and send one at the earliest opportunity. I shall feel proud to have myself included among the others which you already have.

No more grateful thing could have been done, or things which would be more appreciated, than your remembering the admirals and captains of the Atlantic fleet by sending them the splendid photographs, together with your signature and a personal note in each case.

I re-enclosed the photographs separately in large blue envelopes of my office and addressed the same. And when I took the envelopes down to Captain Grant, the chief of staff, and explained the matter of the contents, and who the sender was, he at once ordered a boat and told the officer to immediately distribute the envelopes not only throughout the vessels in the harbor, but those lying outside the harbor.

I am sincerely glad that your efforts to have the fleet pass close to Molokai, in order to give the people there an opportunity to see it, have been successful. Very little credit for this is due to any of us here. It is all due to you.

Aboard the U. S. S. Connecticut, flagship of the fleet, Admiral Sperry, on July 22, 1908, wrote the following letter to Brother Dutton :

Dear Sir:

It gives me great pleasure to receive your letter of 'gratitude and good will' expressing your appreciation of the visit of the United States Atlantic fleet.

Anticipating the interest and pleasure of the people

of the leper settlement in witnessing the unusual spectacle of a fleet of this magnitude parading before them, your suggestion was regarded as a most happy one and there was never any doubt that it would be carried out, if circumstances permitted.

On behalf of the officers and men of the fleet I extend to you and those with you in your splendid work, and to the people of the settlement, my best wishes for the prosperity of all.

The island and settlement were a beautiful sight as we steamed by almost under the shadow of the mountains, and I thank you for the photographs of the scenery and of yourself.

It gives me great pleasure to send you herewith a photograph of the commander-in-chief as a token of respect and regard.

On July 23, 1908, Governor Walter F. Frear sent the following letter to Brother Dutton :

My dear Brother Dutton :

Your letter of the 17th instant with that for Admiral Sperry, and the photographs, were put into separate packages and delivered to his chief of staff, who immediately handed them to an orderly with instructions to take a launch and distribute them to all the captains inside and outside the harbor.

Your letter to the admiral was published in the papers, with the admiral's warm approval. The admiral was very pleased with your letter and has spoken to me about it several times.

When I dined with him the other evening, he had the photographs you sent him spread out on the desk in his cabin and called attention to them with a great deal of satisfaction.

I understand that he has sent to Mr. Mott-Smith a letter to be transmitted to you with his photograph. He said that he was only too glad to have the ships go by the settlement and that there was no difficulty at all in having that done. The mere suggestion was sufficient. I infer from your letters that the settlement fully appreciated having the fleet pass near it and it is certainly a gratification to me that it was possible to bring this about.

The original letters are now in the possession of the Wisconsin State Historical Society, together with the letters of acknowledgement from the ten captains of the fleet. The fleet was formed into two columns in front of the American flag flying at Kalawao, one column steaming eastward and passing around the island of Maui before heading for Honolulu; the other column passing on at once to Honolulu.

The captains who sent letters of acknowledgment to Brother Dutton were:

Capt. H. Osterhaus of the Connecticut,
Capt. K. Niles of the Louisiana,
Capt. C. E. Vreeland of the Kansas,
Capt. W. P. Potter of the Vermont,
Capt. Alex Sharp of the Virginia,
Capt. Hamilton Hutchins of the Kearsarge,
Capt. J. B. Murdock of the Rhode Island,
Capt. T. B. Howard of the Ohio,
Capt. John Hubbard of the Minnesota, and
Capt. W. H. H. Southerland of the New Jersey.

Similar honors were bestowed upon Brother Dutton in the spring of 1925, when the United States battle fleet, holding maneuvers in Hawaiian waters, passed in review before Kalawao and the scene of his labors.

*American Battleships Salute Brother Dutton*
*Panel from Blessed Sacrament Church in Stowe VT*

*Brother Dutton and the residents saluting the flag*

# *The Patriotism Of Dutton*

## C.1913–1923

Brother Dutton himself seems to be the best answer to the question of whether a man can isolate himself from the country of his birth, and yet remain a staunch and loyal citizen of that country. For Brother Dutton, born an American, is even a more patriotic American citizen today than he was, perhaps, when he shouldered a musket and marched away to the Civil War.

In those rollicking days when, to the uninitiated, war was a sort of sporting proposition, Dutton was a beardless youth. But today, living his life of isolation on Molokai—isolated from America and from the whole world, for that matter—he looks back upon the Civil War as but child's play when compared with conflicts that have since come to pass. He saw the Spanish-American war come and go, and he knew that America was in the right. Then, after a long era of peace, he felt the World War shake the earth; and he knew again that America was in the right.

On October 18, 1923, in response to a letter, Brother Dutton wrote to the National Economics League as follows:

> "All problems relating to our country, great as some of them are, have, it seems to me, a fundamental cause rather general or common to them all. This grandfather problem might be designated as the need for all people to become truly sober, just normal. The present feverish anxiety to excel in everything, the dangerous inventions, the nerve-straining ways of life, excessive frivolity, plays and pictures of evil suggestion—all of these indicate decay.

May our lives become more calm and ever useful. May God bless all we do.

The immediate grandson problem, I should say, must be firm enforcement of laws, greater respect for law and order under our Constitution, and a good-natured settling down to sober citizenship as reasonable Americans, each one working for the interests of all."

The patriotism of Dutton dates back several hundred years; in fact, to the 17th century when three pioneers, bearing his name, migrated from England and settled in America. Thus from his father's side, and from his mother's side as well, he inherited those sterling New England qualities which have done much for the national good, and which have brought forth some of the strongest, if not the strongest, patriots in the country.

Today he cherishes among his possessions a copy of an excerpt from an address delivered at New York in 1916 by Cardinal Gibbons, in which that noted Catholic official said:

"You live in a Republic where there is liberty without license, and authority without despotism; and where the civil rulers hold over you the aegis of its protection without interfering with the God-given rights of conscience. In view of the signal blessing you enjoy, it is your duty to take an active personal, vital interest in the welfare of your country. You should glory in her prosperity, and be concerned at every adversity that may befall her. You should hold up the arms of those who are charged with the administration of public affairs, as the children of Israel held up the hands of Moses while he interceded for them before the Lord. The inspired word of God enjoins this loyalty to country and reverence to its fealty. The religion you profess demands this fealty.

But, my friends, if the Republic is to endure, it must rest on the eternal principles of truth and justice and righteousness, and downright honesty in our relations with foreign nations. It must rely on our firm belief in an overruling Providence, who created all things by His power, governs all things by His wisdom, and who controls the affairs of nations as well as of men."

During the past several years Brother Dutton has distributed a large number of pen copies of this excerpt among his friends. Recently, in order that the advice of the noted Cardinal might be further broadcast, he had typewritten copies made.

As far back as he can remember, Brother Dutton has had a flag pole near his cottage at the leper settlement. And from the top of that pole has been displayed the Stars and Stripes. He has quite a collection of flags, some of them comparatively new, others torn and stained by the elements. Every morning the flag is run to the top of the pole, the halyards in the hands of Brother Dutton; and every evening, at sunset, it is lowered, folded and placed away until the morrow. Even when Molokai was a part of the Kingdom of Hawaii, Brother Dutton's American flag flew over Kalawao, and was, perhaps, the first standard of its kind to be raised there.

This daily flag ceremony was as much a part of Brother Dutton's routine as his meals, or his bathing, or his office duties. In very stormy weather the standard was hauled down.

For many years past it has been a custom with the Grand Army of the Republic, at its annual encampments, to vote some word of greeting to Brother Dutton, an active member of the organization, and an American flag. The result was an accumulation of flags, and Brother Dutton, being unable to use so many, began giving them away, one by one, to schools and other institutions in need of them.

The following excerpt is from the journal of the 47th encampment of the G. A. R. at Chattanooga, Tenn., September 18 and 19, 1913:

Comrade Hamilton of Tennessee: Comrades, I ask your attention for a moment as I desire to speak to you regarding an absent brother, Comrade Dutton, who is in charge of the leper colony in Kalawao, Hawaii. At Milwaukee the Encampment of that year sent Comrade Dutton a flag in token of their love and their appreciation of the work which he is doing. From time to time the newspapers have reported the death of Comrade Dutton from the disease which he contracted there. That is all a mistake. I have a message from Comrade Dutton, dated August 20. I offer this simple resolution:

Resolved: That this Forty-seventh Annual Encampment of the Grand Army of the Republic, assembled at Chattanooga, Tenn., acknowledge this greeting of "Aloha" from the far Pacific of Brother Joseph Dutton, in charge of the leper settlement at Kalawao, Hawaii, and return his greeting and extend to him this tribute of our love and esteem, hoping the Great Commander may continue him on his special detail for many years, and the Adjutant-General be instructed to send him a copy of this resolution, accompanied by an official badge of this encampment.

Commander-in-Chief: The resolution will be referred to the committee on resolutions without action here.

Comrade W. M. Scott of Georgia and South Carolina: Commander-in-chief and comrades, I desire to say that I served in the 13th Wisconsin four years and a half with that same Joseph Dutton, who has been mentioned, and who has given up his life and services to the leper settlement, and cannot leave it. And I move you, sir, that this encampment send him a flag to fly over the leper settlement.

The motion was duly seconded.

Commander-in-Chief: If there is no objection, the motion will be put upon its passage without reference to committee. All in favor of the motion will signify by saying "Aye."

The motion was adopted unanimously. Later on the resolution was adopted, also unanimously, and a copy sent to Brother Dutton, signed by Henry J. Seeley, Post Adjutant General.

Under date of October 8, 1923, Gaylord M. Saltzgaber, commander-in-chief of the Grand Army of the Republic, residing at Van Wert, Ohio, sent the following letter to Brother Dutton:

My dear Comrade:

The 57th National Encampment of the Grand Army of the Republic passed a resolution that the commander-in-chief should write you a letter, and an amendment thereto was adopted that a United States flag should be sent to you.

I wrote to Comrade Cola D. R. Stowitz, quartermaster general, to purchase and send you a flag, and he informs me that on the 4th day of October he sent you a silk United States flag, 4 ⅓ by 5 ½, which I hope will come to you safely.

The Comrades bear you in very grateful remembrance, and this is not the first instance in which they have expressed their great appreciation of your wonderful service in behalf of humanity. You are certainly complying with the Great Commandment to love God and your neighbor. Such supreme sacrifice of one's social surroundings, your altruism, your devotion to the unfortunate members of the leper colony, entitles you to the praise of all good men, and the comrades who admire your great work thus bear signal witness to your devotion.

We hope that you may find a satisfaction and happiness in your work, and that all the blessings that may come to anyone may come to you.

The demobilization of two flags of St. Peter's church, Memphis, Tennessee, one a service flag and the other the Stars and Stripes, on Sunday evening, February 22, 1920, has always been of intense interest to Brother Dutton, for it was at St. Peter's, on his 40th birthday, that he was received into the Catholic church.

On his 80th birthday, April 27, 1923, Brother Dutton prepared a brief sketch of the demobilization, which he sent to many of his friends. This sketch follows:

"If there was, in the Great War period, any incident of a patriotic nature, associated with any church, that was more inspiring, I am not aware of it. Surely it was highly edifying to every true Christian of our country who knew about it.

The earnest young men of the parish who were in the Great War had a record in the chancel of dear old St. Peter's—each one a blue star on the service flag. The United States flag was close by—the flag of our country and people. One was sent from Molokai, suspended from the right hand of our crucified Lord—about life-size—against a large column near the communion rail. And this was a place of private devotion for hundreds of people-parents, brothers, sisters and friends of those gone overseas as soldiers in a great cause. The old-time standard newspaper of Memphis—still coming here to Molokai—several times mentioned this beautiful devotion. One dropping in at St. Peter's at almost any time was likely to see groups of the faithful at prayer by the base of this great crucifix, with its starry emblem as a shroud.

The demobilization of the two flags on Sunday evening, February 22, 1920, was a ceremony that brought this private devotion into full bloom, carried out in a solemn and intensely patriotic manner under the direction of two Dominican fathers who had both served as army chaplains during the war, Father Pastorelli and Father Moore. In the general arrangements they had been assisted by committees of the people, men and women. Members of religious and patriotic organizations attended in a body. There were representatives also of the national, state and city governments; delegations from the United States Army, Navy, Marine and Aerial Corps; of the Red Cross in uniform, and of the Knights of Columbus in regalia acting as ushers. The great church space was a mass of people. The newspapers said that fully 500 were turned away, there being no more room. All gathered to honor Washington's birthday and to join in the demobilization ceremony.

After a processional hymn and solemn vespers, "The Star-Spangled Banner" was sung by the sanctuary boys, choir and congregation. The choir was augmented by special instruments which gave a military character to some parts of the ceremony. Then came the oration, ably delivered by Father Pastorelli, the subject being The Dogma of Patriotism. This was followed by a salute to the colors and the lowering of the flags by officers. These officers very reverently folded the flags—now cherished relics of the war—and placed them in the sacristy.

Solemn benediction of the Blessed Sacrament closed the service that was very generally declared to be the greatest Catholic demonstration ever held in the city.

The local press noted through the great concourse deep attention and much suppressed emotion.

My first writing of the above was in memorandum form as the facts came to hand in letters, etc. Later, Mrs. J. M. Semmes of Memphis has written and sent me a better account. She and Mrs. Luke E. Wright were joint chairmen of the patriotic societies. Mrs. Semmes' four sons were in the Great War service. She is a grandmother. Her mother-in-law, Mrs. B. J. Semmes, was present at this flag ceremony. She is now past 94 years, and is my godmother. I was received into the church at this same St. Peter's, Memphis, on my 40th birthday, and that was just 40 years ago today."

The patriotism of Brother Dutton embraces not only love of and loyalty to country, but love of and loyalty to his chosen life-work—the work of a life of penance—and love of and loyalty to his friends. For 44 consecutive years he has attended to the duties which caused him to give up the world and retire into isolation so that he might minister to suffering lepers. From every part of the world letters have come to him from persons desiring to express their appreciation of his untiring labors on behalf of humanity.

An inkling of the man's character, and an expression of his devotion to this, his life work, has crept into a letter which he wrote in 1905 to the Rev. Father Francis of Syracuse, New York, who at one time visited the leper settlement, and who later wrote in praise of the work done by Brother Dutton following Father Damien's death. This letter follows:

"Your good letter has interested me. Your praise for the work now done among the lepers is appreciated.

The record of Father Damien has set a standard for praise that is world-wide, and the expression of it even now I recognize as voicing the world's approval of his life here, unique in being the first, and as admiration for his lowly death. This death struck a note in the world's melody of things fair and good that reached the hearts of everyone.

Some personal friends speak of us, the imitators (as we truly are), but the world in general, thinking or speaking of this leper settlement or of lepers anywhere, has Father Damien chiefly in view. His death, so tragic yet humble, has placed him high in the world's affection. We are not able to measure the good thus done, but surely it is great and very pleasing to God. We ought to rejoice for having the chance to aid in this by keeping up the work, and the work ought to occupy us quite fully.

It is good to correspond with our personal friends, to state the facts that are good for them to know, but we cannot have any vain thoughts concerning these facts, nor as to our relations thereto. Our feeling should be chiefly of gratitude, and I think this sentiment fills us all who are in the work; and that it binds us not only to the work, but to each other, that everything may go on in unity, peace and concord, under the will of God.

Thus we will help to perpetuate Father Damien's work, and the light in which it will ever be considered, I take it, over the world. Had he never begun it, we should hardly have been here—may never, indeed, have heard of the place.

It has often been stated that Father Damien was rough, lacking in culture, etc. He fitted, however, the early times and the work well. I doubt if there were many who could have effected all the good he did. Things have changed, advances have been made, and are still being made. The settlement is not what it was 20 years ago.

Some of these thoughts I have had in mind recently, intending to express the substance in a little 'souvenir' of our home and briefly of the work in general. That our

work is better than the work of others we cannot believe.
Yours, I hope, is fully as good. Your intentions and desires
may have been better than ours.

But I do not lack in appreciation of the peculiar conditions and qualities of this work. Indeed, its special fit-
ness for my own spiritual needs has been a strong incentive to coming here, and in staying 'home.' My love for
the work has never decreased. Everything in your letter
has inspired me with good thoughts. I thank you very
much and sympathize with you in the afflictions of your
advancing years. We can meditate well upon the Eternal
Life now so near.

It is well for us to be humble, but we must not be
proud of our humility."

The "souvenir" about which Brother Dutton speaks in the foregoing letter was never written. There had been no time, owing to the duties
which keep him busy throughout the hours of the day, and often long
into the night. But in his actions, Brother Dutton carries with him today the same spirit of unselfishness, and the same degree of love for his
especial calling, as he did 25 years ago, when he wrote the letter.

# Brother Dutton Answers Some Questions
## c.1899

Throughout his 44 years of continuous service among the lepers of Molokai, Brother Dutton, 87 years old as this is written, has received letters from persons in many parts of the world who desire to know: "Why did you do it?" It is, perhaps, not simply morbid curiosity that has prompted them to ask the question; probably, in many cases, a sincere desire to ascertain why the man placed the world behind him, as it were, to devote the remainder of his life in ministering to lepers, and under conditions which, in the early years, were little short of revolting.

Even today, the fear of contracting leprosy is sufficient to cause even the strongest man, or woman, to shrink from work among the unfortunate sufferers, unless, of course, they are acquainted with the results of modern scientific research regarding the disease, and with the splendid sanitary conditions prevailing at present, and for many years past, at the settlement.

The fear of contracting leprosy has, apparently, never bothered Brother Dutton; and this in spite of the fact that the noted Damien became himself a patient, and died from it in the midst of his labors, with Brother Dutton, who had been his right-hand helper, among those at the bedside.

Concerning the question: "Why did you do it?" some unusually interesting side lights are thrown upon it in a document, in Brother Dutton's own handwriting, which is a copy of a letter which, many years ago, he sent to personal and intimate friends, explaining why he did do it. It is one of several documents, still intact, which reveal the character and the characteristics of the man, and which are expressive of his early-formed views regarding the Catholic church. The document in question forms a valuable portion of the Dutton memoirs, and is given herewith, a few facts and figures contained therein having appeared in previous chapters:

## Question No.1:
## What was the date of your reception into the Church?

"April 27, 1883. Baptised at Memphis, Tennessee, in St. Peter's Dominican church. The Rev. Father Kelly, godfather. This was my 40th birthday.

Born at Stowe, Vermont, April 27, 1843."

## Question No. 2:
## What priest instructed and received you?

"The very Rev. Father J. A. Kelly, O.P. (now dead). Was named Joseph by Father Kelly. The former name was Ira B. Dutton. A change of use was then out of the question on account of business and official relations. A lifetime use could not be changed at once. Besides being an investigating agent of the War Department, Q. M. D., I was also United States commissioner in Western Tennessee. But all of these relations were closed and the accounts settled before I started for Molokai.

With the approval of Bishop Hermann (deceased) the old name was dropped, and I thenceforward used the proper Catholic name, as I very much desired to do. I felt very grateful to Father Kelly for giving me the name of Joseph. At the very start Father Damien called me Brother Joseph. He never used any other name for me—his own baptismal name, also.

The old name, Ira B., never had to be used afterwards but once. My father died before I came to Molokai. I was the oldest child; the only one living, in fact. But having no use for the estate, unless to give it away, I left it in use by my mother in Janesville, Wis., the family having moved there from Vermont about 1848, just as the territory of Wisconsin was being formed into a state. I was about five years old at the time.

Then, later, after I came to Molokai, mother and I agreed to give the property away—at least, the most of it—and I wished to convey my rights to my mother so that she could act. This was done through the State Department, and I had to use the old name for the occasion.

But to return to the occasion of my baptism. I will note here that I insisted upon making a public renunciation of error. It was done at the High Altar, St. Peter's, a Dominican nun on each side to make some responses. In the matter of names, two have been added, although I never write the name other than Joseph Dutton. In confirmation, 1884 or 1885, at Gethsemani, Bishop McCloskey added the name Maria. I was admitted to the third order of St. Francis by the very Rev. Father Francis, provincial from Syracuse, New York, on his official visit here to the Sisters (at Molokai) on March 20, 1892. He named me Francis, in the order Joseph, Maria, Francis. If only I were even half worthy to be the bearer of three such names—so honorable, so holy, so noble!"

## Question No. 3:
## Why did you turn from the Anglican Communion?
## In what way did Anglicanism fail to satisfy you?

"Anglicanism was very satisfying so long as my chief aim was to be simply respectable; highly respectable. Even now recollections come of people, of places, of churches associated with Anglicanism that have in them many sources of pleasure—some that I would not, perhaps, find anywhere else.

But I accept these—all the pleasure resulting from such transient thoughts—with another, an added plea-sure in being given the grace to do without them, and to never desire them; willing and happy to cling stoutly to Our Faith so generously given me, and to let the af-fections dwell, so far as weak human nature will permit, on things that relate wholly to the soul's welfare, aiming for everything deeper, yet higher and better than those things that simply please the senses; that relate to this world and its pleasures. I have in thought principally the pleasures of personal associations, of agreeing tastes, etc.

I do not forget, nor do you, the many really pious and good, sincerely devout followers of Anglicanism, but in looking for Holy Church, one cannot be governed in any large degree by this. Devout people are found in all religious societies; nowhere in greater proportion than in the Catholic church.

In the early times, I could not myself be classed as particularly devout. The first suspicion acquaintances had of that condition must, I imagine, have been not very long before you (a friend to whom the letter was sent) knew of me.

To what extent the incidents of my past life influ-enced the actions of that time, and later, none of us can tell. I shall note some of them later. Anyway, at the time I refer to, my thoughts had a really serious turn, tend-ing toward religion. Just how it came about that I was somewhat intimate with so many Anglican ministers, particularly in Tennessee, I am unable to state. I do not remember clearly, but think it all came from social rela-tions, combined with a growing soberness within myself.

It soon became the understanding that I should prepare for Holy Orders. An old army friend of mine was doing this in Pennsylvania and in New York. (At the time this was written, the friend in question was located at Grace Church, New York City.) I was getting into shape for it, doing some reading, etc. A bishop, who was a really interested friend, authorized me to act as lay reader in Tennessee. I conducted a service at Somerville. The bishop then suggested that I help Dean Kline to occupy the official residence adjoining St. Mary's cathedral, Memphis.

The Anglican Sisters of St. Mary were conducting a school adjoining the cathedral on the other side. Col. Snowden's sister, Sister Hughetta, was then at the head of this fascinating work. I shall insert here that it would be difficult to find any sisters, Catholic or otherwise, of more sisterly deportment than these. And, so far as one could judge, they were sincere and believed themselves Catholics. A Dominican nun told me after my conversion, that these sisters made them, the Dominicans, ashamed.

The bishop's official residence was given him years before by the people, but he actually lived at Sewanee. In the house at Memphis there was always spare room. A son of Bishop Pierce of Arkansas was there. As my quarters had to be partly an office, I used the former's parlor and we divided expenses. At this time I was still investigating agent for the War Department, as well as United States commissioner.

It is quite needless to state here how ritualistic everything was there. It was, in fact, of the most pronounced type. "Priests" of that cut, in passing through the city, were pretty sure to come out there. It was in that way that I met Father Betts of St. Louis. All of that suited me finely. My budding devotion seemed to be wholly in line with it. I clung to that wonderful theory of the "Branches" —caught in the branches, as it were. It was all exceedingly comforting, and nice and respectable.

But I am leaving Dr. Gray out. He came in at the very beginning, I may say, in my exploits in becoming an active Christian. He was the first to propose a preparation for Holy Orders, and encouraged every step. While he was at Bolivar, and later at Nashville, I saw much of him and of his family. When I was in other sections, on my duty, we exchanged lengthy letters, and I will say that in his writing there was much good thinking and loving exhortation.

Dr. Gray was more hurt, in feelings, by my conversion, probably than anyone else. In his estimation, I had taken the wrong branch. Taking up the reading recommended, with zeal and deep interest, I began to lose confidence in the "branch" theory. I began to investigate along lines different from what was intended. It all began to have an interest almost tragic. Soon I became dominated by the idea, and very properly so, that my eternal happiness depended upon knowing the one Church, and in being a faithful member thereof; that if the Catholic church was what it claimed to be, then I must know it.

But in order to make sure, I had to take the necessary time. I changed my habitation and devoted a year to the study of the question: The validity of Catholic claims. There is no doubt that I was sincere in wanting to find the Church. There is no doubt that the reward is far beyond what I deserved. The study was good, but God's grace, with prayer, was necessary. The great essential—a visible head, effective authority—in church militant, seemed the most decisive single point. That opposing Christian bodies all originated in rebellion seemed also a strong point."

## Question No. 4:
## Did you have any difficulty in accepting the whole "Deposit of Faith" as taught by the Roman church?

> "Certainly not. There was no chance for difficulty. I accepted everything held by the church; everything that I could and ought to understand; and, in matters of faith, everything that I could not or need not understand. The matter was settled. I gave the controversial books away. I do not know of one person converted by them.
>
> Controversy has held no attraction for me since that day. I waste no time on it, in paper or in magazine. Life is so short, and there is so much to work for. Why stop by the wayside to dispute?"

The reminiscences which follow here include a number of incidents up until the time of Brother Dutton's arrival at Gethsemani, and his entrance into the Trappist Monastery:

> The aim to be "highly respectable," as mentioned before, might have further mention. This respectability certainly was my aim, or one of my aims, and you very likely had no doubt that I was respectable, or worthy or respect, and others had the same idea, I am sure.
>
> This must have been about 1880 or 1881. Yet in my heart I felt unworthy, because of blemishes in the past, in particular, say, 1865 to 1875, inclusive. That was certainly a degenerate time with me; in a considerable measure, outwardly, but for the most part it was within. And it is not only in the past I could have located the blemishes, but in that present time, and to this day.
>
> Blemish is a very soft term; sinfulness is better. But this in a general way applies to all of us. What I am referring particularly to now is conduct of a disreputable

nature, especially from 1865 to 1875, inclusive, and not to any secret, hidden sins.

There is one comfort, however—I can believe that the chief injury was done to myself. In being a bad example was, perhaps, the most serious injury done to others. Am thinking of the degenerate decade referred to. Another point: Being a sort of social highwayman, to be noted further on. This latter came years after, principally in 1880, 1881 and 1882, in the time of highly respectable appearance; because of it, in fact—partly in not disclosing my married state, being reluctant to break with those respectable and delightful associations.

In common honesty concerning matters of duty on business things of the world and its affairs, and its responsibilities, I must have been always considered reliable. For in the darkest and most reckless period of drink and debauchery, I nearly always held a place of responsibility, and have papers showing a clean settlement in everything.

I had been a moderate drinker before and during the war, but it was in the "degenerate decade" that the drinking—chiefly of whisky—was fierce and reckless, even up to July, 1876. Since then I have been strictly an abstainer. ... It seemed that the restraints of military service and ambition for its responsibilities, once over, left me free, too free; like an unchained animal gone as yet partly wild. When you have read this batch of notes, you will no more regret that I did not become a priest. You can say: "How fortunate the priesthood was, not to be burdened by such a one."

Though I am surely sorry for my sins—for the actual sin—yet there is no doubt that some of these sins helped in leading to my ultimate good—always agreeing that there must be true sorrow. If none of these very bad things (very bad for the moment, until repented of) had occurred, would I now be a Catholic, and at Molokai? We cannot know."

This sketch contains also reminiscences of Brother Dutton's boyhood at Janesville, portions of which are as follows:

"At my boyhood home, Janesville, Wis., I was looked upon as a tolerably good boy; but, knowing something of the heart, it is perfectly clear to me that I was not one-quarter as good as I "made out" to be, or as I was regarded as being. Being somewhat delicate, I was not kept constantly at school, but grew up partly in a printing establishment and book store.

One of my earliest recollections is of being associate editor of the first home paper, called, if I remember correctly, "The Janesville Gazette." This must have been about 1852, when I was nine years old. Of course it was a joke—my being associate editor—but it was far from being a joke to me. I felt myself to be almost a man. It is interesting to note that I hardly ever had anything to do with children or young people of my own age, but grew up almost wholly among mature people.

This early-time newspaper was established and edited by Joseph Baker, a friend of my father's. A son of his was in my regiment throughout the war, being a member of the band. Baker, senior, took a sort of fancy to me, and introduced me to his "sanctum." I folded the papers, and Baker called me his "associate editor." Although a joke, there was one column in the paper left wholly to my management. Of course, it was made up almost entirely of clippings. The jokes were there—and other things.

Mr. James Sutherland, later Honorable James Sutherland, soon invited me to a place in his book. store, for a business home when not in school. My first regular salary was received there, being $100 for the first year. After the first year, I received $300 a year for about six years, and this, with the time at school added, brings me to the summer of 1861. When enlisting for the regiment began, I joined. The pay of $300 a year is not much at the present time, but in the fifties it was quite a sum—certainly for a young boy.

The book store and everything connected with it suited my tastes. It was a general stock for wholesale and retail trade, and was quite complete, with a wallpaper department and bindery on the second floor, and a printing office on the third floor. I had a thorough acquaintance with the stock. It was often said that I could find any book, or anything else named, in the dark.

Especially, though, I looked out for the wallpaper room, and attended to certain things about the bindery. Mr. G. L. Knox was the head binder, and was a great friend of mine. In fact, we were somewhat "cronies," though he was a man of middle age, and I a boy. His wife was a sister of Frances E. Willard. I am not sure, but it seems to me that this great temperance advocate and I attended at one time the same public school. The girls had a brother, Oscar, who was a student and rather delicate. Their father was Col. O. A. Willard, for many years president of the Rock County Agricultural Society. They lived on a farm about five miles to the west of Janesville, but Frances and Oscar located at Evanston, Ill., near Chicago, at Northwestern University. I am not sure whether the entire family moved there during or after the war. I never returned to Janesville to live after going away with the troops in 1861. After the war, however, I returned several times on visits.

In the Fremont and Dayton campaign, the "Wide

Awakes" cut a large figure. I was then but 13 years old, but was "wide awake," though, and belonged to the Janesville Club, which was a large one. We must have numbered at least 200 in the great Chicago demonstration.

When about 14 years of age, I developed a great interest in gymnastics. I subscribed for a paper then published, called "The Gymnast." I possessed a gymnasium suit and various gymnastic implements. Mr. A. K. Allen, whose son was something of a gymnast, put up a public gymnasium on the second floor of a building nearly opposite the book store. Of course, it was a business proposition, and I was one of the earliest patrons. Every night, as soon as the store had been closed, I hurried to the gymnasium for about two hours of exercise. Finally I was graduated in accordance with the rules of the art.

Some subscribers, enthusiastic at first, began to lost the spirit and dropped out. Before many months had passed the gymnasium, as a business proposition went the way of about three-quarters of all gymnasiums. Some of us who always clung to it organized a gymnastic club, relieved Mr. Allen for his losses, and kept the gymnasium for club purposes. This must have been about 1857. And just about that time a new diversion came up. The fame of that wonderful company, the Chicago Zouaves, Capt. E. E. Ellsworth, was running high. Any of the new cities of that new country that could not organize a Zouave company was suspected of falling "below the mark." Many cities in all parts of the country had these companies.

The "Janesville City Zouave Cadets" did not lag behind. Before many months had passed, it was a very spry company. Capt. E. E. Woodman was the commander. That double E was popular. In Chicago it was Elmer E., and in Janesville, Edwin E. Capt. Woodman later became secretary of a large railroad, with offices at St. Paul, and had a son who served at Porto Rico during the Spanish-American war. Later the son became an assistant engineer with the railroad with which his father was connected. The fate of Capt. Ellsworth, as "Col. Ellsworth of a New York regiment," at the beginning of the Civil war, is well known.

This Zouave company at Janesville was, more or less, an exhibition company, but of course not to be compared, in that respect, at least, with the Chicago company. It was then a sort of local ornament, and in 1861 became something more.

This "new diversion" cut into the gymnastics somewhat. A portion of the club turned Zouave and dropped the former organization, while I clung to both, keeping up my regular gymnastic exercise. Oftentimes, however, the latter was private. Finally, not more than two or three belonged to the gymnasium, so I settled the accounts and moved the fixtures and apparatus to a cheaper place. There I continued taking the exercises until the summer of 1861.

Friends who wanted to take exercise came to me for the key to the building, which at one time had been the assembly hall of the Masonic lodge.

On the second floor of this building were law offices occupied by Eldridge, Pease and Ruger. The latter was Thomas H. Ruger. He was graduated from West Point about 1852, remained in the army for a few years, and then resigned and took up the practice of law. At the outbreak of the Civil War he raised the 3rd Wisconsin Infantry, became a brigadier general and then a major general, and at the close of the conflict was appointed colonel of the 16th (or 18th) United States Infantry. He was also at one time the commandant at West Point. In about the year 1899 he was retired as the second ranking officer in the army. He had three brothers in the 13th Wisconsin, and I dined with them on one occasion at Murfreesboro.

When the war came, and our company of Zouaves voted to go, in the summer of 1861, the gymnasium became an incumbrance. I settled the rent and asked the "stay at home" boys to remove the paraphernalia and divide it among themselves. And so, pau gymnasium, as the Hawaiians would say; finished. But it had done its work with me. It had made me slender, quick and active, and had equipped me with a set of muscles really surprising. When mere activity was in question, of course I was ready, and also in what are termed "feats of strength." I never regretted the training I had received.

The Zouave company had, as I have said, voted to go to war, and so we went away as one of the companies of the 13th Wisconsin Volunteers."

*A characteristic photograph of Joseph Dutton, taken in 1902 by
the Rev. Fr. Joseph Julliotte, who later returned to France.*

*From a snapshot of Joseph Dutton taken at Kalawao, Molokai, about 1911.*

*This snapshot of Joseph Dutton, taken in May, 1920, shows him seated by the stone wall outside his office at Kalawao, Molokai.*

*Brother Louis snapped this excellent likeness of Joseph Dutton as he appeared in September, 1922, in his 79th year.*

*Joseph Dutton seated at his desk in his office at Kalawao, Molokai,*
*reading the original manuscript of his memoirs and reminiscences.*
*Photograph by Brother Louis.*

# A Day With Dutton

## *An Interview by Howard D. Case* ED.
### C.1925

Brother Dutton came down to the main gate of the Baldwin Home to meet me. I saw him swinging along over the close-cropped grass of the lawn, shoulders squared, head up; not at all the slow-moving, frail wisp of a man I had expected to see.

He was dressed in faded blue overalls, held up by a pair of faded suspenders; and a faded blue denim shirt and a pair of faded canvas shoes which at one time or another had been brown. His head, covered with a thick mass of almost white hair, was bared to the cool morning breeze. His white beard had been trimmed to a point. He wore glasses, for, as I found out later, he had lost the sight of one eye completely, and at times sees not at all too perfectly with the other. His faded clothing was clean, and from top to toe he was as neat as a pin.

My first square look at Brother Dutton recalled immediately a famous painting I had once seen. It was of Saint Joseph, he of the flowing hair and beard, and it was quite a coincidence, I thought, that many years ago he was chosen by Brother Dutton as his patron saint. The resemblance between that portrait and Brother Dutton, as the latter appears today, is striking, to say the least.

Brother Dutton shook hands cordially, and with a firm, hearty grip which seemed to tell me that he was glad to see me, and that I was welcome. He then turned to greet "Jack" McVeigh, general superintendent of the entire leper settlement on Molokai, who had driven me to Kalawao from Kalaupapa, where I had landed that morning. "Jack" had

to go back to Kalaupapa to attend to some business, so he left me with
Brother Dutton, who promised he would entertain me as best he could.
A couple of minutes later we were on the best of terms.

I looked at the little man beside me and wondered. Forty-three
years before, then in the prime of manhood, he had come unannounced
to the leper settlement, approached Father Damien, and said simply: "I
have come to help you in your work among the lepers." That was all. He
had been there ever since, with the exception of one visit to Honolulu in
1930 for eye treatment, and it was his desire to die there. He was leading the penitent life which he sought as atonement for his past "sins."
Forty-three years among the lepers! I wondered how many other men
would undertake such a mission today.

We left the road, shaded by magnificent trees through which
peeped the famous old Damien church, and walked up through the yard
of the Baldwin Home, past the kitchen and laundry and storehouses,
until we came to a long, low, white-washed building which is a sort of
a combination amusement hall, reading room, drug store, work room,
shop, general office and what not. Nearby, in another building, were the
showers for the patients, and the room in which Brother Louis—a four-
square man, by the way, and truly one of God's gentlemen—did the sore
dressing.

To the right of the larger building, upon a small plot of land surrounded by a low stone wall, was the little house, shining with fresh
whitewash, which for many years had served as Brother Dutton's home.
In former years it was much smaller than it is today, but some time ago
another room was added when Brother Dutton found need for the extra
space. The left portion of this little building is Brother Dutton's office,
with its crude, homemade desk, homemade table and bookshelves. The
portion at the right is his bedroom and bathroom. That is all. Everything
was bare and plain. There was nothing indicating luxury, and few things
indicating even modern conveniences. It was the plain abode of an unusually plain, unassuming man. For more than 43 years he had known
no home other than this tiny cottage, flanked by a lauhala palm on one
side, and a gorgeous purple bougainvillea on the other.

*This photograph, taken in 1921, shows Joseph Dutton standing in front of the cottage which he occupied for so many years at the Baldwin Home, Kalawao, Molokai. At the left is his study and office and at the right his bedchamber.*

*Joseph Dutton, for nearly 44 years in service among the lepers of Molokai, Hawaii. This photograph shows him seated in the doorway of his cottage at the Baldwin Home, of which he was in charge. Copyright R. K. Bonine.*

*"The Girl and Dancing Bear" on the cliff face above the U.S.
Leprosy Investigation Station. the home of the Gibsons*

Brother Dutton had not been away from Kalawao for more than 37 years. In fact, during that time, he had hardly been out of sight of this tiny three-room house where he works and sleeps. In all of his 44 years at the leper colony, he has only once been to Honolulu, and in the last 38 years he has made but two trips to Kalaupapa, only about two miles distant. One was for the purpose of fumigating and shipping certain of Father Damien's effects to the Catholic Mission at Honolulu, including all of the priestly ornaments which were intended for the Damien Museum in Belgium. The other was to take a steamer to Honolulu to enter a hospital for eye treatment.

From the veranda of his cottage Brother Dutton has an unobstructed view of the broad Pacific Ocean, and also of the lofty mountain crags that rear themselves aloft at the back and to one side of Kalawao. Nowhere else in Hawaii does one find such scenery as this—such ruggedness of cliff and such limitless expanse of turquoise water-and nowhere else in the world, perhaps, will one find a colony of happy and contented, though sorely afflicted people, nestling amidst such a remarkable specimen of God's handicraft.

Brother Dutton told me that he loves those stately cliffs, and that restless ocean which roars and beats beneath the ledges along the seashore; the trade winds rustling the leaves of the palm and eucalyptus trees, the morning mists which sometimes hide the mountain tops, the sometimes none too gentle rains which sweep down from the high places, and the furtive rainbow which shows occasionally across the naked faces of the cliff walls.

"It was hard to believe, when I first came here," he said, "that there could be so much human suffering in such a lovely spot. But later on I came to realize that perhaps the beauties of nature can, to a certain extent, relieve physical and mental suffering. One could hardly conjure up a more beautiful spot than this in which to spend one's life. And so, after 43 years, I have come to know these old mountains quite well. We have come to be splendid friends. After viewing them in all their mightiness and grandeur, one cannot question the power of God."

He pointed toward a spot half way up the side of a cliff rose a sheer 2000 feet into the mist.

"Two other friends of mine," he remarked.

On the almost perpendicular face of the cliff were two objects formed by some freak of nature when that mighty mountain was in the making. They were fashioned from a lava outcropping of a strain darker than the surrounding substance, and hardened to the consistency of granite through the centuries. For a moment I could not make them out. Then finally it dawned upon me that on one side was the figure of a girl, and on the other a figure which resembled an animal reared upon its hind legs. I looked inquiringly at Brother Dutton.

"I call them the Girl and Dancing Bear," he explained. "They have kept me company many a long year."

We walked into Brother Dutton's office and sat down, I at the table and he at his desk. The place was a model of neatness and cleanliness, bare of floor, and containing many articles which I could see were hand-made. His desk was an ordinary flat table, but on one side of it, against the wall, was a box-like affair filled with compartments and pigeon holes stuffed with letters and papers, all neatly folded and tied into bundles. Beneath the table were several drawers, large ones. Brother Dutton pulled these out, one by one, and I saw that they were filled with letters, many in envelopes, many faded and yellowed with age—an accumulation of more than 40 years of correspondence.

"And here," Brother Dutton said, pulling out another large drawer, "are all of my unanswered letters."

He explained that, because of the large number of letters he received from all over the world, he is now about a year and a half behind in his correspondence.

"But I hope to be able to catch up one of these days," he smiled confidently.

Few men, probably, get more personal letters than does Brother Dutton. The story of his work at the leper settlement, and of his life of penance, has gone around the world—and is still going around, for that matter—and people from all parts of the globe write to him; some asking questions about his life and work, some conveying a word of praise, some wanting "jobs" at the leper settlement.

It is quite true that Brother Dutton has received many contributions from persons with whom he is not acquainted personally. But he has not spent one penny of this money upon himself. Every cent of it has gone toward the Baldwin Home, in order that the patients may be made more comfortable and happy, or to some other good cause when the need for funds at the home was not particularly pressing. We sat down in the little office. Brother Dutton said that I could smoke if I wanted to. I lit a pipe, and he remarked that he rather enjoyed the smoke. He then explained that he had given up smoking many years ago.

"But," he added with a smile, "I didn't give it up until after I had colored two meerschaum pipes. I guess that every man who smokes has colored a meerschaum pipe or two in his lifetime."

He also gave up tea and coffee many years ago. His two drinks are milk and water, and he believes that the fact that he drinks a lot of milk is one of the reasons for his present good physical condition.

There are few men who are able to reach the age of 87 years and continue to be unusually active both mentally and physically. Brother

Dutton is one of them. He is possessed of a memory that is little short of amazing, and has a faculty for remembering names, dates, places and incidents which I found to be truly remarkable. Physically, of course, he is not as strong as he was 30 years ago, but he is no weakling by any means. That burden of 87 years appears to rest but lightly on his shoulders. But it is in his face that one may read the story of this burden of the years; but it is ever a smiling, kindly face, and there is something there which denotes perfect peace.

He writes a bold, perfect hand that is without even the semblance of a quiver. In fact, all of his correspondence is done with a pen, and he writes hundreds of letters. His fingers have never touched a typewriter. In fact, when I took one to his office a day or two later, it did not seem to interest him, although he did remark that I seemed to be able to work it fairly fast by the two-finger system known to all newspaperdom.

With the formalities over, and by way of opening the conversation—it wasn't an interview—I touched upon half a dozen current events. To my surprise I found Brother Dutton to be exceedingly well posted upon what is going on in the outside world. He discussed these subjects with ease and readiness.

I looked around the tiny office and made a mental note of some of the things I saw there. There was a large number of books, several well-thumbed encyclopedias, a small statue of Saint Francis, an American flag, a large map of Europe, a "Big Ben" alarm clock ticking away merrily, stacks of letters, a half-filled wastebasket, a box filled with old-fashioned, steel-rimmed spectacles, a box of pen points. Among the books, as I recall them, were

*Fruits of the Hawaiian Islands,* by Gerrit P. Wilder;
*History of Hawaii* by Alexander;
a copy of the Henry P. Baldwin Memorial—it was this Baldwin
   who made the initial subscription toward the founding of the
   Baldwin Home;
a Catholic directory,
*The Americanization of Edward Bok,*

*Two Years in the South Seas*, by Charlotte Cameron;
*Men of Hawaii,*
*Who's Who"*
and the *American Blue Book.*


Many newspapers, and many of the better magazines, reach Brother
Dutton regularly. But, because of his poor eyesight, he is able to do only
a little reading now, and this is confined largely to his correspondence.
Consequently, the bulk of the newspapers and magazines are placed in
the reading room at the home, after being first carefully censored, and all
questionable pictures cut out. The reason for this censorship is explained
elsewhere in these reminiscences.

Brother Dutton then imparted to me the rather surprising information that he has read but one popular fiction book since his arrival
at the settlement. That was *Pigs Is Pigs*, by Ellis Parker Butler, the noted
short story writer. Is there anyone in America who hasn't read it? The
remainder of Brother Dutton's reading is devoted largely to the Catholic
publications, of which he received a large number.

In spite of his isolation, Brother Dutton, so he informed me, is a
member of a large number of organizations and orders in various parts
of the United States, with all of which he is in close contact through
correspondence. First of all, he is a member of the Third Order of St.
Francis, and has been since March 20, 1892. He is also a member of:


the Association of Trappists,
the Holy Name Society,
the Society for Propagation of Faith,
the Holy Land Association,
the Wisconsin Historical Society (honorary),
Wisconsin G. A. R. Headquarters, Grand Army of the Republic,
Mission of Hope,
the Lucius Fairchild Post of the G. A. R. at Madison, Wisconsin
    (honorary), which is now the senior Grand Army post.

Other organizations with which he is associated are:

the National Council of the Economic League
　of the United States at Boston,
the National Association for Constitutional Government
　at Washington, D. C.,
the Academy of Political Science at Columbia University, and
the Anti-Saloon League and Humane Society of Honolulu.


I found that Brother Dutton was quite willing to answer all questions relating to his past life, but I did not care to discuss this subject with him to any great extent. He told me, quite frankly, the reasons why he had gone to Molokai to spend the remainder of his life in service among the lepers. After the Civil War, he explained, he had committed certain sins for which, he concluded later, he could make amends in the eyes of God only through a penitent life. He selected Molokai and service among the lepers as his penance.

There has always been a question in my mind whether these "sins" were of a gravity necessitating the severe task which Brother Dutton set before himself. But I will say, and I do not believe anyone will disagree with me, that he has performed his task in the fullest and ablest manner. His record of 44 consecutive years at Molokai proves that. It is without a blemish. And in the end he will be just as much if not more of a martyr than the famous Damien, for he will die finally in the service of the lepers. He will never leave Molokai permanently. When death summons, he will find his final resting place there.

Our talk covered a wide range of subjects as we sat there in the little office. I noticed that Brother Dutton's penholder was of the common penny type, and that he had wrapped rubber bands around the nib end so that he might obtain a better grip.

I asked him if he wouldn't let me send him a fountain pen upon my return to Honolulu. I had in mind a certain well-advertised make and figured that it would be easy to obtain one with the style of pen point exactly suited to this kindly old man.

"Why, no," he answered me. "It's kind of you, but I don't believe I'd care for a fountain pen. I have used this old one a good many years and have sort of gotten used to it. And, besides, they tell me that fountain pens are in the habit of leaking."

And that was that. I did not mention fountain pens thereafter. He wasn't going to let his old-fashioned pen, a friend of many years standing, be replaced by one of these new-fangled contraptions, and that ended it. So I switched the conversation to other modern things.

Yes, he had seen an airplane once, although rather indistinctly. It had been the first one he had ever seen. This was probably one of the big army or navy planes, stationed in Hawaii, which have been doing considerable flying among the islands lately.

Brother Dutton has never seen a motion picture, and he had never ridden in an automobile until just recently. He has not seen electric lights since coming to the leper settlement, except, of course, in the far distance, when the federal leprosarium was in existence, and on passing steamers. He has never seen at close range, except in illustrations, any of the improved types of electric light bulbs.

On several occasions the late "Jack" McVeigh offered to install electric lights in Brother Dutton's little cottage, but each time the latter has declined. He does a great deal of his writing at night, he says, and his eyes have become so accustomed to the soft glow of a candle that he is afraid the strong beams of an incandescent light might soon make him totally blind; and he desires to preserve what sight he has as long as possible.

I asked Brother Dutton for the reason why he had been able to pass the 87 mark and still be in such vigorous health, both mentally and physically.

"Well," he said, "I think the main reason is simple living. I live an exceedingly simple life here, and always have. I eat simple food and I wear simple clothing. Again, I have not a worry in the world. I ceased worrying years ago. In my opinion, worry will kill a person more quickly than disease will. I do not use tobacco, alcohol, tea or coffee. I gave these up many, many years ago. I get plenty of fresh air, plenty of warm sunshine, and plenty of exercise. I have regular work to do and many good friends to write to and receive letters from."

Brother Dutton could have retired from active service some years ago, and lived in comfort the remainder of his life, as the result of a pension granted him by the Territorial Legislature in recognition of his long period of untiring service. But he declined to accept it, preferring to continue with his work and be won the job" until the day of his death, dying "with his boots on," as it were, in the service of Christ.

I questioned Brother Dutton regarding the "wild life" which he had led for a considerable period after the close of the Civil War, and which caused him to seek the life of penance which brought him finally to Molokai. He smiled, and remarked that "perhaps it wasn't such a wild life after all, but wild enough." Elsewhere in these reminiscences this subject has been gone into more fully, although there are without doubt some secrets locked in the heart of Brother Dutton which will never be revealed. There is no tangible reason why they should be.

"Have you never gotten tired of your work here?" I asked. "Have you never longed to leave Molokai and go out into the world once more and meet people and view the changes that have been wrought in the last 44 years?"

Again that smile, this time accompanied by a slow shaking of the head.

"No, I have never grown tired of my work," he replied. "One never grows tired in Christ's service, you know. The work here fascinated me from the very beginning. It continues to fascinate me today. And as for leaving Molokai, the thought never enters my head. My life work is here on this little peninsula, and among these people, whom I have come to love. The rest of the world has absolutely no attraction for me."

I talked to Brother Dutton then about his boyhood days, and he told me, in a simple way, his life story. His fondest memory is, perhaps, that of his mother, a noble, courageous woman who, during his youth, was his teacher, his mentor, his guiding star. Then he told me of his experiences during and after the Civil War, of his joining the Catholic church, and of his decision to a life of penance.

"I'm kept pretty busy answering letters," he said, fingering a pile of newly arrived communications. "Sometimes I sit up far into the night writing, writing. It seems that I'll never get all of these letters answered. I trust that friends of mine whom I owe letters will be patient just a little while longer. One of these days I hope to be able to catch up."

Then he showed me the index of names of friends—many of whom he has never seen—to whom he sends cards of greeting on the several holidays. There are several hundred on the list, and it is said that only on rare occasions has Brother Dutton missed sending greetings to those persons whose birthday dates he has listed. He obtained my birthday date the latter part of 1923, and a few days before my birthday in 1924 I received a neat card from the old gentleman. He has never since failed to send me a card.

It might be said that Brother Dutton's greatest hobby is writing. He spends hours at it, and obtains a world of enjoyment and satisfaction from it. In fact, it is practically the only thing he has to do now, as he retains only a few simple duties about the home, apart, of course, from keeping a supervisory eye upon things. The kindly Catholic brothers, still young and vigorous, have relieved him of the more arduous tasks, but he still takes care of the general business affairs of the home.

In all of these years Brother Dutton has never received a cent of money as salary, nor monetary remuneration of any kind from the Board of Health or other source. But I will wager that if he should suddenly write to the board and request to be placed on the salary roll, he would be requested to name his own figure.

As has been explained already, his Civil War pension of $50 a month is sent to an institution in the South. When the check comes from Washington he opens the envelope, makes the indorsement, and immediately places the check in another envelope, addresses it, and puts it in the mail. Never once has he deviated from his solemn vow, made nearly 40 years ago, never to accept a cent of money in the service of his fellow men. It is a spirit of unselfishness that has seldom been equaled.

Brother Dutton and I chatted there in his little office during the greater part of the sunshiny morning. Outside the majestic stillness was broken now and then by the songs of birds, or the softly spoken words of leper boys passing by. Once I heard the tap-tap of a stick as a blind leper felt his way along to his cottage. Far away could be heard, dimly, the pounding of the surf on the cliffs at the sea edge.

"We have been patriotic over here at the home," Brother Dutton remarked. "During the World War we did our bit when the call for funds was sent out. Of course, these patients here haven't a great deal of money, but they gave generously of what they did have. Of course, it was the only way in which they could help, and I am thankful for the praise which they received through the press and otherwise."

Brother Dutton gets a wheelbarrow-load of printed matter in every mail. Besides the letters which come from persons whom he does not know personally or intimately, he has about 200 correspondents with whom he exchanges letters regularly.

"And once a year, as regularly as clockwork," he told me, "I get a big fruit cake from my old friend Sam Schloss of Memphis, Tennessee. Let me see: Sam is 89 years old now. And it's wonderful cake!"

Just then the Angelus rang. Brother Dutton arose and excused himself, and went into his little bedroom, where he knelt for a moment before a crucifix. In a little while he was back again.

"We'll wash up a bit, now, and go down and have some luncheon," he said.

## Our luncheon

Brother Laborious, the cook, had set out a splendid luncheon in the little dining-room adjoining the Catholic brothers' quarters. There was steak, boiled potatoes and gravy, bread and butter, a huge lettuce salad swimming in French dressing, sliced canned peaches and coffee and cream. Brother Dutton made a simple meal of bread and milk, and a few of the potatoes.

I found the brothers to be splendid fellows. There were only three of them at the table with us—Louis, Jules and Laborious—and the conversation touched upon many subjects. They told me some interesting things about their work at the home, and then asked me many questions concerning what was going on at Honolulu. The brothers, to all appearances, have their hearts and souls in their work, but are not at all willing to accept any credit for what they are doing. A word of praise brings merely a shrug of the shoulders, but no verbal reply.

## The Afternoon

After luncheon Brother Dutton and I went back to the little office to rest for a while before inspecting the home. It was while we were sitting there that he told me a most amazing story—the story of how, at one time, he probably became a victim of leprosy, but was able, as a result of his vigorous health, to expel it from his system. Brother Dutton explained

"A good many years ago, I had a sudden breakdown which left me in bed several times for short periods. I could see plainly that this had been coming on for a number of years, but I had, probably foolishly, neglected the early warning. Having never been ill before to speak of, I refused to recognize the signs, depending too much upon my strength. A general improvement was brought about as soon as I began taking half way reasonable care of myself.

But at that time there were some signs which suggested to me the possibility that I might have contracted leprosy. It seemed not unreasonable, as I had been so many years with the lepers, and considering especially the first nine years before the helpers came, when I sat among the lepers and shared with them the poor food which they had prepared with their own hands. But later on I came to the conclusion that I did not have leprosy. If there was any attack at all, I presume that my system rejected it. Perhaps I was not a fit subject!

There were never any sores, save one that was caused by an accident and which healed within a few days. Some patches appeared, and a numbness came. But the patches disappeared without any treatment, save the usual regular bathing. The numbness remained with me awhile, with occasional cramps, but nothing troublesome.

I fancy the chief cause was the deviltry of past times. It was the irregularities of those days when nature was in flower. Those times covered a long run of risk and experiments in getting as close as possible to the jumping-off place, and still hanging on by a shrub or a tuft of grass; for I had a strong grip then, that of a long-practised gymnast."

Our after-luncheon rest over, Brother Dutton suggested that we visit the long, whitewashed building just opposite his own cottage, which, among other things, serves as his work room. A long veranda runs across the front of this building, and on it were congregated a number of the leper boys, some reading, some playing games, some waiting to have sores dressed, and others just talking. I will not undertake to describe any of these boys here, for some of them are not pleasant to look at; but they all smiled and spoke to me as we went by. Some of them have no visible signs of the disease; others have, most astoundingly so. And yet they gave me the impression that they were happy, and especially so due to the fact that they had just been served a substantial lunch.

The end of the building toward Brother Dutton's cottage is partitioned off and serves as a reading room for the boys. On tables ranged around the walls were scores of books, magazines and papers. Dozens of pictures, clipped by the boys, were pasted on the walls.

As we entered the other section of the building, Brother Dutton pointed to a phonograph, a gift from a resident of Honolulu.

"We have lots of records, and are getting new ones all the time," he said. "The boys play the phonograph whenever they feel like it."

Upon a shelf back of the phonograph were a number of musical instruments, principally guitars and ukuleles, which belong to the boys, and which are placed there when not in use. Brother Dutton keeps on hand at all times a supply of strings for these instruments.

As we passed on toward the rear of the building, and by sets of shelves filled with books, I noticed a tiny compartment containing what appeared to be a broad shelf set into the wall near the floor. I asked what this was.

"That," Brother Dutton said, with a smile, "was my bedroom before the cottage was built. That shelf was my bed."

Near the entrance of this small room was a large packing box which appeared to be filled with pieces of stone. Brother Dutton explained that this was a collection of Hawaiian relics which he is planning to send back to the museum of the Wisconsin Historical Society. The collection consists largely of old Hawaiian stone implements which Brother Dutton has found or otherwise obtained during his many years at the settlement.

At the back of the building, which looks out upon the row of stately palm trees at the cliff base, is Brother Dutton's workshop. It is here that he does odd repair jobs, wraps up such packages as he has to mail, unwraps and sorts out newspapers and magazines as they are received, and prepares them for distribution in the reading room.

Brother Dutton also calls this his bindery. A certain number of papers, after being taken from their wrappers, and flattened out, are placed one on top of another, and then put beneath a heavy weight, where they remain for several days. This process leaves them absolutely flat and easy to handle. They are then ready for the scissors for Brother Dutton in his official capacity as censor.

This old building is full of memories, for it has been Brother Dutton's workroom ever since the Baldwin Home was established. In one end there used to be a "drug store," but this was abandoned with the establishment of a sore-dressing station, which is near by. Many pictures, some of them faded and yellowed with age, adorn the walls. In one corner is a radio set, not in use at present. Here also is kept the athletic paraphernalia—the football and the baseball outfits—with which the boys occasionally enjoy themselves. Here also is Brother Dutton's safe in which he keeps such papers and documents as are of value to him.

We then left the building and walked down across the yard and over the road to the Damien church. From the outside this structure is not by any means imposing, but it is noteworthy when one considers the effort that was exerted in constructing it—first by Father Damien, and then by Brother Dutton. It is rather weather-beaten, but it is surprising to note how well it has withstood the ravages of the elements during all of these years. Inside the church is strikingly beautiful from an architectural standpoint, and the altar appeared to me to be a work of art—something that had been fashioned and since maintained by loving hands. The ornaments are as fine and as imposing as those in many of the Catholic churches in Honolulu.

*Plaque outside the Philomenia Church at Kalawao
showing its development over the years*

Brother Dutton knelt for a moment before the altar, and then sketched briefly the history of the old church. In my mind I could picture Father Damien laboring with his limited means and resources to construct for himself and his flock a proper place of worship, and the completion of the unfinished task by Brother Dutton after his arrival.

*Here a martyr to duty lies under the tropic skies.*
*The Father Damien church, Kalawao, Molokai, taken many years ago and*
*before the planting of the stately trees which now surround it. The cross over*
*Father Damien's grave is seen just over the wall at the right of the center.*

*A side view of Father Damien's church at Kalawao, Molokai,*
*and showing the cross above his grave in the yard.*

*Left: Interior of
Father Damien's church
at Kalawao, Molokai,
as it appears today.*

*Right: The altar which the
Rev. Father Damien made for
his church at Kalawao, Molokai,
as it appears today (1931)*

It seems that when Brother Dutton was completing the Damien church, he built this crypt with his own hands; a crypt for the special purpose of housing his own body after his death. That was many, many years ago.

After he had told me this I remarked to him:

Adjoining the church is the cemetery in which rest the remains of Father Damien. Over the grave is a monument placed there by the Catholic Mission at Honolulu. Near by are the graves of the four Catholic brothers who died at Kalawao while in the service of the lepers—Brothers Rochus, Victor, Serapion and Severin, martyrs all.

"In my opinion, with your present good health, you will pass the hundred mark."

I saw also the spot where once stood the pandanus tree under which Father Damien slept for a time after first coming to Kalawao. It was not until some time after his arrival that a cottage was erected for him. Also under this pandanus he held religious services, and ministered to the suffering lepers.

After I had seen all of these things, Brother Dutton said that there was one thing more he wished me to see. Pushing open a wooden door which opened onto the ground at the rear of the church, he led me down a flight of stairs and into a small room with a dirt floor and stone-walled on four sides. It was lighted by one tiny, oblong window on a level with the surface of the ground.

"It is here," Brother Dutton explained, "that I will be buried when my time comes."

"Do you really think so ?" he asked, and smiled, rather wistfully, I thought.

Brother Louis is a camera fiend, and I visited his workshop with its hand-made enlarging apparatus, hand-made printing device, and various other hand-made bits of paraphernalia which are of assistance to those photographically inclined. The finest collection of leper settlement pictures in the world is perhaps that owned by Brother Louis. On the way out, I met and chatted for a moment with Father Martin, the Catholic Priest at Kalawao, who has his own cottage.

Brother Dutton and I went back to the office in the little white-washed cottage.

"It may seem strange," he said after we had sat down, "but I pray day and night to Almighty God to give me strength to finish the work which I think that I should finish before I am taken. Some of us get into a lot of mischief, but it often turns out that that very thing is our greatest blessing. Take my own case, for example. I committed a great error during my lifetime—nothing very evil in a worldly sense, however—and it turned out to be my greatest blessing, for it was the cause of my coming here to Molokai."

"Do you not think," I asked, "that by your long service here among the lepers you have made sufficient atonement for that error?"

"That," Brother Dutton replied, "is in the hands of Almighty God. What He wills in my case will be the right thing."

He spoke then of his friends, and of the value of friendship. He told me of those friends of his who, although having intimate knowledge of his past life, have remained loyal to him these many long years. And I wondered whether there wasn't something providential in being able to hold friendships for such a long period through the sole medium of correspondence. But Brother Dutton has done it; the splendid letters he receives from his friends in every mail proves it.

"Of course you know," he said, "that I have been reported dead on several occasions. All of my friends appeared deeply concerned over these reports, and wrote me beautiful letters after they found the reports were unfounded. I tell you, it is half of one's life to have friends like that."

Down the road came the sound of an automobile horn. "Jack" McVeigh was coming to get me. Brother Dutton and I walked slowly down the yard toward the gate.

"Have you now," I asked him, "any outstanding, definite object in life other than the continuance of your work among the lepers?"

Brother Dutton did not answer immediately. Then, finally, he said :

"Why, yes; I am now preparing myself for death and my meeting with God. I look upon it as the happiest moment of my life."

Could there be any higher object than that? I think not.

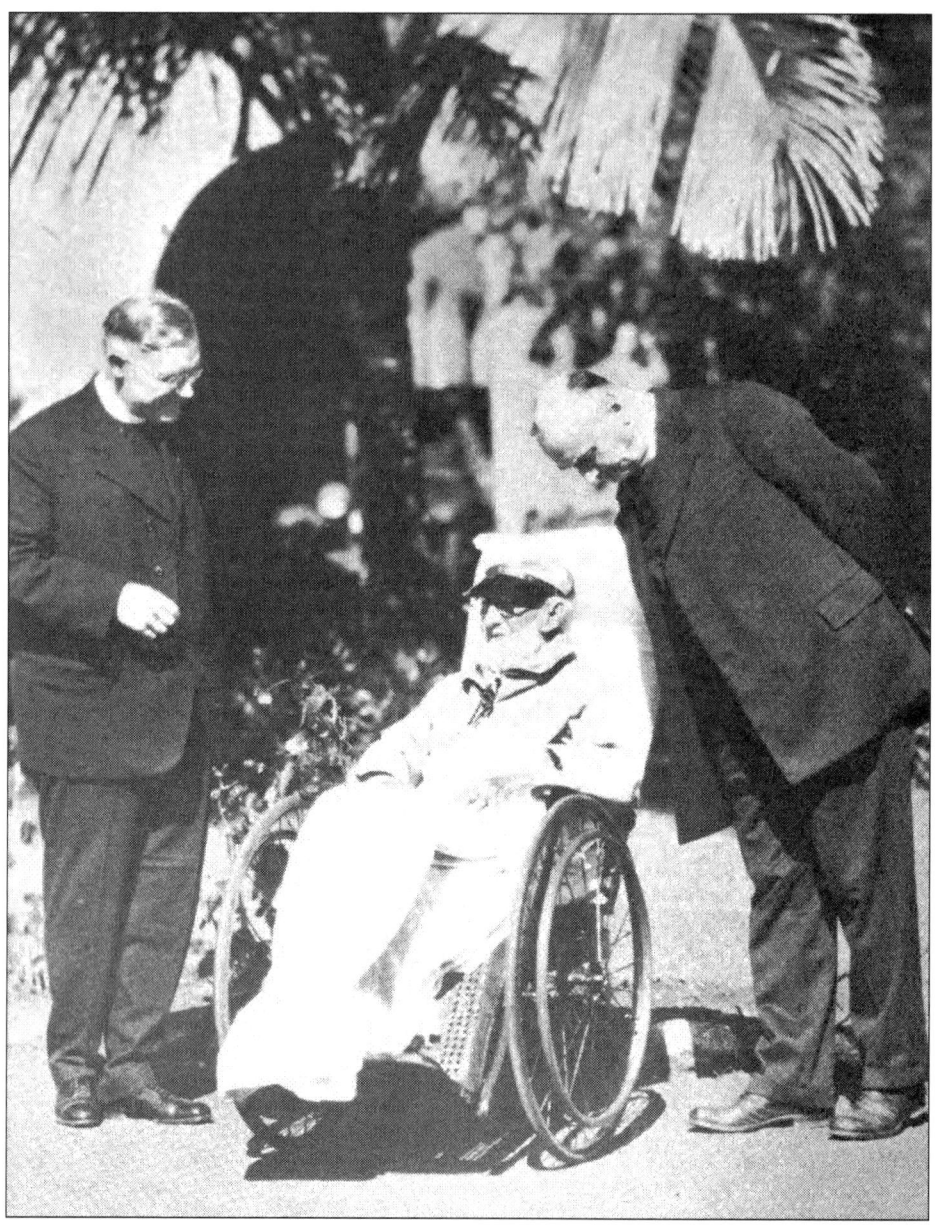

*At the left is the Rev. Joseph E. Hanz of the Brother Dutton School, Beloit,*
*Wis., and at the right the Rev. Charles M. Olson of St. Mary's Church,*
*Janesville, Wis., who in January, 1931, traveled to Hawaii to bring*
*greetings to Joseph Dutton, center, from his friends in Wisconsin.*

# The End Of The Trail
## 1930–1931

Brother Dutton had never intended to leave the leper settlement. On numerous occasions he expressed to friends a desire to die within sight of the mountains which he knew and loved so well, and within sound of the softly murmuring ocean which washes the shores of Kalawao. He wanted to be laid to his final rest, he said, in the little stone crypt beneath the Damien church.

But in June of 1930 Brother Dutton was destined to survey the progress of civilization beyond the boundaries of his isolated home for the first time in 44 years. He had begun to suffer from an eye affliction, and this, coupled with general poor health caused by his advanced age, made it necessary that he be taken to Honolulu for hospital treatment. Plans for his journey were arranged by officials of the Territorial Board of Health.

In April of the same year Brother Dutton had observed his 87th birthday, and that spring he went over to the settlement at Kalaupapa, some three miles from Kalawao, for an eye operation; that occasion being the first time in 35 years that he had journeyed beyond the boundaries of his home.

On the morning of July 5 the steamer Hawaii docked at Honolulu, and a muscular Hawaiian carried the frail little old man down the gangplank. A few moments later Brother Dutton was placed in a waiting automobile, utterly exhausted after a night's voyage from Kalaupapa. He explained afterward that he had stood the trip very well, but that he had become violently seasick as the steamer Hawaii, entering Honolulu harbor, was tossed about by waves caused by an outgoing liner.

Unable to walk alone, he was met at the steamer by a delegation from the Catholic church, a group of old friends, and newspapermen.

"Honolulu! So this is Honolulu again," he murmured as he peered into space, his fading eyesight denying him a picture of the capital city he had not seen for nearly half a century.

He was taken immediately to the St. Francis Hospital, a Catholic institution, and put to bed in a cheerful room. Tender hands ministered to his every want. Old friends surrounded his bedside with flowers. Later an operation was performed. It proved successful and partially restored the aged man's eyesight.

The dawn of 1931 saw Brother Dutton considerably improved in health, and utterly aware that he would never again return to his beloved Kalawao; never again hear the trade wind rustling the fronds of the coconut trees he planted so long ago, nor see the girl and the dancing bear etched upon the mountain side.

"I guess," he said falteringly one bright day in January as he lay with his head propped upon pillows so that he might see dimly the golden Crucifix on the dresser, "that I have come to the end of the trail; that my work is finished. I hope that God approves."

He did not speak then of death, although he must have realized that it could not have been very far off. But he had often remarked that he had no fear of death, as he fully believed he had made reparations in God's service for his so-called sins, and that he was at all times ready to answer the call to begin the long journey into the unknown.

And so this brave old man, his task among his suffering fellow men finished, was content to lie and talk of things which, to his mind, were the high lights of a half century gone by.

"My friends in many far places continue to write to me," he said, "and the sisters here in the hospital have been very kind regarding such a large mass of correspondence. One of the sisters has answered nearly two hundred letters for me. You see, my old eyes won't let me read any more, and these old fingers can't hold a pen. But it is good to hear a phrase here, and one there, from the letters of old friends."

His hair has whitened with the passing of the years, as has his neatly trimmed beard, and he wears a green eyeshade above a pair of very modern horn-rimmed glasses which have taken the place of the steel-rimmed spectacles which he knew on Molokai. His hearing is also failing rapidly.

"But I can hear you if you speak a little loud," he says with a chuckle. "The sight of this right eye is just about gone, but I can see quite well out of my left eye with these new glasses."

His thoughts went winging back to Kalawao for a moment, and he seemed particularly concerned over the fact that some of the lumber from the old federal leprosarium buildings there had been taken to Kalaupapa for new construction projects.

"I told them," he smiled, "that we needed that lumber at Kalawao; that it rightfully belonged to us because our buildings were falling to pieces. They were very kind to me about it, but"—and he chuckled again—"I guess they started taking the lumber over to Kalaupapa right after I left."

Of course he hasn't seen much of Honolulu. One doesn't see much of a city from a hospital bed. But Brother Dutton said he had been amazed beyond all words at the growth of the city in nearly half a century.

"They whizzed me up to the hospital from the dock," he said, "and we went so fast that I probably couldn't have seen much even if my eyes had been all right. Everything goes like a whiz these days. Oh, yes, I have been out riding. Twice. I wanted particularly to see St. Louis College. I thought it was right close. But I found it was miles away. I did not know that Honolulu was so large. Nearly fifty years. That is a long time, isn't it?"

In the spring of 1931, several months after Dutton had entered the St. Francis Hospital, two events occurred which reflected public recognition of the little man's many years of work among the lepers.

Affectionate greetings from many of those in Wisconsin who knew of Dutton's work were brought to Honolulu by the Rev. Joseph E. Hanz., Ph.D., of the Brother Dutton School of St. Jude's Church at Beloit, Wis., and the Rev. Charles M. Olson of St. Mary's Church, Janesville, Wis.

*Top Right:*
*Dutton School, St. Jude's parish, Beloit, Wis.,*
*named after Joseph Dutton.*

*Bottom Right:*
*The raising of the Brother Dutton Flag*
*at the Dutton School, Beloit, December 8, 1928.*

*Left:*
*The Brother Dutton Flag.*

Among the greetings was one from the faculty of the Brother Dutton School, which is administered by the Sisters of St. Agnes. These were signed for the sisters by Sister M. Rosemary, C.S.A., and with them was a spiritual bouquet in the form of a beautifully printed and colored card. The letter made one request:

"That you bequeath the past, present and future teachers and pupils of Brother Dutton School your spirit of self-sacrifice and zeal for the good of humanity."

Another interesting letter, from the L. H. D. Crane Post, G. A. R., Beloit, contained the greetings of Comrade Chesbrough, who spent some of his childhood days with Dutton and served with him in the same regiment during the Civil War—the 13th Wisconsin Infantry. The Beloit Daily News carried an article commenting upon the visit to Hawaii of Fathers Hanz and Olson; paying tribute to Dutton's life and work, and adding that the personal greetings from Rock County, the scene of his youth, and from some of his old-time friends would perhaps be comforting at a time when there might be periods of loneliness in his life.

The second event occurred shortly after the 1931 territorial legislature convened. Officially recognizing, on behalf of all the people of Hawaii, the long service of Dutton on behalf of suffering humanity, the Senate and House of Representatives passed an act granting him a life pension of $300 a month. It was signed immediately by Governor Lawrence M. Judd.

Brother Dutton explains how he had attempted to carry on his work at Kalawao despite the fact that his eyes were giving out, and that the burden of old age was hampering him.

"The Catholic fathers and brothers carried on for me when I finally had to take to my bed," he says. "They were very kind about it. Brother Laborius, the cook, brought me my meals. Two a day was all I needed. A little rolled oats was about all I wanted.

"It may be," he explains, "that God brought all this about. Perhaps it was He who ordered that I should cease my work, and be taken to a place where I might have peace, and quiet, without worry. I have been very comfortable and contented. No, I don't think I shall ever go back. … Everyone has been so kind.…"

Having lived and worked among the lepers of Kalaupapa and Kalawao for nearly a half century, Brother Dutton expresses himself quite emphatically regarding a movement now under consideration by Hawaiian health officials to abandon that portion of Molokai that has been used for so long as a leper settlement, and remove the sufferers to some other part of the territory better suited for carrying on modern methods of treatment and hospitalization.

"I hardly think the plan is a suitable one," he says. "Kalawao and Kalaupapa are the homes of many persons who are lepers. A great many of them have lived there for years. I do not think they would approve of the change. Better to leave them where they are. They have always seemed happy and contented. Perhaps, in the future, leprosy will become a thing of the past in Hawaii and there will be no need for a leper settlement."

Brother Dutton is contented in his new surroundings, but certainly it is a fact that his thoughts are ever winging their way back to the peaceful little mountain-girt settlement, and to the little whitewashed house which was his home for so many years.

"I wonder how it looks after all these months?" he asks wistfully. He recalls that Brother Louis, his right-hand assistant for nearly 20 years, is now at the Kalihi Orphanage at Honolulu; that Father Martin has been to Europe and back and is now at work on the island of Maui; that perhaps by this time electric lights have been installed at Kalawao.

"I used to attend to my routine tasks in the day time," he reminisces, "and my evenings I devoted to writing letters to my friends. Many a time I wrote far into the night. Candles furnished the only light I had. When I got sleepy I would crawl into that little bunk in the room off what I called my office; it was just a shelf upon which I kept a few blankets."

Every morning the Rev. Father Valentin Franckx visits the hospital and assists Brother Dutton in celebration of Holy Communion.

"He has written my will for me," Brother Dutton explains, "and is going to look after everything for me after I am gone."

There had been some talk of the legislature granting a pension to Brother Dutton, as he is without funds; and of providing him with a radio for his entertainment. As to the pension, he says nothing. In all his many years at Molokai he has never accepted remuneration for himself, even sending his Civil War pension to a Catholic seminary in one of the eastern states. As to the radio, he only smiles.

"I probably wouldn't be able to hear it," he says. "I remember once when we had a radio for the boys at Kalawao. The brothers asked me to go up and listen to it. Well, I went along; but I couldn't hear a thing, so I sat there and said my prayers until it was time to go to bed."

Brother Dutton's philosophy of life, as he has often summed it up, is simply service to one's fellow men. That was the goal he sought so many years ago when he set himself for the humanitarian task through which he might atone for his so-called sins.

The gravity of those "sins" may be best judged by the reader, whatever they may have been. Brother Dutton has devoted the best years of a long, busy life to the service of the lepers of Molokai, without having once ceased that service.

And today Brother Dutton's implicit confidence and hope is that God, in whose service he has been so faithfully and conscientiously enlisted, will approve of the manner in which the task of patient devotion and unfaltering love has been accomplished.

A little old man, broken in health, perhaps, but not in spirit, Brother Dutton awaits tranquilly the summons that will terminate what we call life; a career unique in American history. And until the end of time his name will be emblazoned upon the pages of Hawaiian history as one who dared follow to the uttermost the dictates of his conscience and his God.

Such is the life story and personal reminiscences of Joseph Dutton; a story of nearly half a century of labor among the lepers of Molokai. It is best closed with his own words, found written upon a scrap of paper among his notes:

*"Thus we go on striving and progressing,*
*trying and failing,*
*each one advancing in the ways of God, we hope;*
*sometimes missing a step,*
*sometimes many steps,*
*bringing wholesome compunction as our duties come and go,*
*come and go,*
*day by day,*
*under the mighty mountains,*
*verdure-clad,*
*'midst such wondrous creation;*
*while the voices in the waves*
*and in the winds proclaim to us,*
*in Nature's grand oratorio,*
*the power and majesty of God."*

# The Death Of Brother Dutton

### MARCH 26, 1931

A noble life, rich in achievement for humanity, came to its end peacefully and quietly at 1:50 o'clock on the morning of March 26, 1931, when Brother Joseph Dutton passed to his reward.

Death took place at St. Francis Hospital, Honolulu, where the aged lay brother had been given every care and attention that medical science and loving, tender nursing ministrations could suggest.

Hardly had the closing chapter of this book been written and the book itself put on the press, than death wrote "Finis" to the earthly existence of the "Good Samaritan of Molokai."

Immediately, officialdom and those in private life, throughout the territory, joined in tributes of admiration and esteem. Preparations were begun at once for funeral services which would represent the high regard in which this humble worker among the unfortunate was held by all acquainted with his work.

In these funeral plans, Federal and Territorial officials, the dignitaries and members of the Catholic church, the Federal Veterans' Bureau, the American Legion, and other organizations united. As Brother Dutton had been, in Civil War days, Captain Ira Dutton of the 13th Wisconsin Volunteers, plans were made for special military features at the funeral.

The funeral was held on Saturday, March 28. The services began with civilian rites, under the auspices of the Catholic church, at Williams Undertaking establishment on Nuuanu street, Honolulu, at 8:30 in the morning. At 9:30 there was a requiem high Mass at the Catholic cathedral on Fort Street, where more than forty years ago Brother Dutton, just arrived from the mainland, had gone to offer himself as a lay worker among the lepers. A corps of buglers sounded "taps" at the conclusion of the Catholic church services; then the body of Brother Dutton, in a casket covered with patriotic colors, was escorted by a police escort, a detachment of U. S. troops and a firing squad to the Catholic cemetery on King street.

And there, as this is written, the body of the Good Samaritan of Molokai awaits removal to Molokai, where it will be buried among the people he served so faithfully and long.

Father Valentin of the Catholic Mission will accompany Brother Dutton's body to the burial ground on Molokai. The grave on Molokai is on a site chosen by Brother Dutton himself before his last journey to Honolulu.

The U.S.S. Sunnadin, Naval tug, will carry the body to Molokai —a recognition extended by the U. S. Naval Department.

Under the auspices of the Federal Veterans' Bureau a headstone for the grave will be provided by the war department.

Preparations for the funeral were accompanied by plans to provide a permanent memorial for Brother Dutton. The first suggestion came, within a few hours after his death, in the territorial house of representatives, the legislature being then in session. A bill was introduced appropriating $3,000 for a bronze plaque or tablet, to be placed in a suitable location at the Baldwin Home at Kalawao, Molokai. Other suggestions were likewise made to the effect that a suitable memorial for Brother Dutton should be something which would serve the lepers on Molokai in a practical way, and it was expected that decisions as to just what form the memorial would take would be made within a few days.

From all over the world there are coming telegrams testifying to the affection and esteem in which Brother Dutton was held by thousands, and probably millions, who have never seen him.

Honolulu, Territory of Hawaii,
March 28, 1931.

*The latest photograph of Joseph Dutton, taken in January, 1931,
at the St. Francis Hospital, Honolulu, to which he was removed
for an eye operation. When he went to Honolulu he left Molokai,
and his work among the lepers, for the first time in 44 years.*

STATE OF NEW YORK
EXECUTIVE CHAMBER
ALBANY

FRANKLIN E. ROOSEVELT
GOVERNOR

March 7, 1932.

Dear Father Hanz:

It is very difficult to word a suitable tribute
to Brother Dutton. The man of faith perceives in Brother
Dutton a providential supplement to Father Damien with
whom he labored. These two lives linked together in the
heroic and gentle ministrations to the unfortunate lepers
on Molokai stand out as beacons, guides to better things,
encouragement in distress and inspirations to sacrifice for
our fellowmen.

While the name and fame of Brother Dutton like
his courageous predecessor, Father Damien, are deathless,
the maintenance of the Brother Dutton Junior High School
and the erection of a national memorial to him will serve
to remind us constantly of his deeds and nobility of
character.

I wish you every success in your undertaking.

Very sincerely yours,

*Franklin D. Roosevelt*

*Tribute from N.Y. Governor Franklin Roosevelt*

THE WHITE HOUSE
WASHINGTON

May 14, 1932.

My dear Father Hanz:

I am deeply interested in the romantic
story of Brother Joseph Dutton, whose life as
pioneer, soldier and great humanitarian is so
characteristic of our people in its variety,
picturesqueness and idealism. His service to
the lepers of Molokai crowned his life with a
saintly glory. It is a privilege to pay tribute
to his memory.

Yours faithfully,

Herbert Hoover

Father Joseph E. Hanz, Rector,
Brother Dutton School,
Beloit, Wisconsin.

*Tribute from President Hebert Hoover

## *Joseph Dutton on a Christian Death*

In fact a christian must hope for death – so called, to be taken into the true life – the eternal life in Gods own good time – with great joy. This is the harvest from all our labors, the ultimate object of all there is in this so called life. Whatever we do

that does not aim at a happy death is all vain, and worse than wasted. This is expressed strongly – but it is Gods own truth.

# JOSEPH DUTTON

## HIS MEMOIRS

Appendices and Additional Materials
from the original book

AND

New Content
the reader may find interesting and enlightening

*Joyfully yours*
*Joseph Dutton*

*"To Brother Joseph Dutton*
*with all good wishes from Theodore Roosevelt, July 10th, 1905"*
*President to Penitent.*
*The autographed photograph which President Theodore*
*Roosevelt sent to Joseph Dutton in 1905.*

# Correspondence

As the story of Father Damien's martyrdom has gone around the world, so has the story of the life work of Brother Dutton, the man who took up the burden at Molokai upon the death of the famous Catholic. And as the story of Brother Dutton's life has become better known, and has penetrated into the far places, the world has awakened to a more clearly defined realization of what his isolation and his labors mean. Consequently, the world has not been slow in showing its appreciation through the expression of kindly thoughts toward the man who has carried on this work, and who has never accepted one penny by way of remuneration.

## Correspondence with President Warren G. Harding

The late President Warren G. Harding, beloved by all Americans and an especial and sincere friend of the Territory of Hawaii, was among the thousands to pay tribute to Brother Dutton's long period of unselfish service. On May 10, 1923, not so very long before his untimely death, he sent Brother Dutton the following letter from the White House at Washington:

My dear Brother Joseph:

At various times, over many years, my attention has been called to the splendid Christian service you have been rendering to the unfortunate members of the leper colony at Molokai. Only quite recently my attention was drawn to the fact that now, at the age of eighty, you are still carrying out this wonderful service, and are still enjoying good health. It is difficult to feel that this is less than one of those miraculous compensations which come at times to men and women who make the supreme sacrifice. I think it cannot fail to be a lesson, a great inspiration, to all who feel the urge to great human service.

The other day a friend of mine spoke of the work of Father Damien and yourself. I had known, through the writings of Robert Louis Stevenson, something about his story of Father Damien, and more recently of how you had carried that work forward after Father Damien's death. I do not know why I have been moved to write a letter to you. I know very well that those who do the great self-sacrificing tasks of the world, have to find their satisfaction in the work which comes to their hand. I am very sure that nothing I can say can possibly add to the satisfaction which you must feel in having thus carried on a service to the bodies, the minds, and souls of men and women, for which we find few parallels. But it has seemed not improper, I hope not an intrusion, for me to say to you that your work is not unknown, is not unappreciated; that all over the world there are people who regard you and Father Damien as men whose lives have been well-nigh perfect examples of self-abnegation, sacrifice and service. You have set for us a model which I wish might be raised up for the view and emulation of many others, for it is in the selfless service of all our brothers that all of us must at last find the great satisfactions and consolations of this life.

So I shall end, as I began, by saying that I realize how impossible it is for me to say anything which will add to the satisfactions which you must deserve from the

consciousness of a noble and chivalrous work, thus splendidly performed. I hope you may be spared many, many
more years to carry it forward; and it would be one of the
great pleasures of my official service, if I might be able
to at any time, or in any way, extend a helping hand or
influence in behalf of yourself and of those to whom you
have given your life. "Most sincerely yours,

(Signed) Warren G. Harding.

To this letter Brother Dutton replied, on July 27, 1923, as follows:

My dear Mr. President:

It was a beautiful letter, yours to me, of May 10th, last.
Am wishing to be really so good and useful as you think.
Have done, and am doing my bit to help the lepers, and
to keep things in order. But the service has done me
good; it is fully an offset. In fact my main feeling is one
of intense gratitude toward Almighty God for giving this
opportunity—in health and strength—to enjoy the life
and to feel so greatly benefited. Also am thanking Him
that there are many old-fashioned, sober people yet living. You and Mrs. Harding are two. Am inclosing a little photo of my dear old mother for Mrs. Harding. And
hearty thanks to you, dear friend, for your good letter.

Yours, cordially and joyfully,
(Signed) Joseph Dutton.

Like the well-beloved Mark Twain, Brother Dutton found it necessary in 1913 to inform his friends that "the report of my death has been greatly exaggerated." On numerous occasions it was reported throughout the United States that Brother Dutton had passed away, and many columns of newspaper space were devoted to his obituary. On other occasions it was reported that Brother Dutton, like Damien, had contracted leprosy, all of which were, of course, wholly without foundation. After the reports of his death had been denied, Brother Dutton received many letters congratulating him upon being still alive and active and in good health.

## Correspondence with
## Mrs. Augustus E. Willson

Under date of May 11, 1913, Mrs. Augustus E. Willson, wife of the governor of Kentucky, and daughter of General Ekin of Civil War fame, wrote to Brother Dutton as follows:

My dear Mr. Dutton:

We were especially glad to receive your Easter greeting today, as we had read in the papers that God had taken you home. Several papers had long obituary accounts, and we were greatly distressed that you had been taken from your noble work, so that we were doubly glad to see your familiar writing.

The first intimation we had that the bad news might not be true was when the papers you sent Mr. Willson came. But as they were of a date in March, we were still afraid. But your greeting of today, for which we thank you, removes all doubt, and I congratulate you with all my heart and hope the report of your illness is also incorrect.

My dear brother's widow, Mrs. Ekin, wrote me expressing sorrow, and sending me a Chicago paper with an account of your death. I have written her this morning of your letter received today. When you write again, tell us of your health. I hope God in His mercy will spare your life and give you perfect health for many years to come.

## Correspondence with
## Brevet Brig.–Gen. James A. Ekin

The General Ekin referred to in the foregoing letter was Brevet Brig.-Gen. James A. Ekin who, after the Civil War, appointed Brother Dutton as a special agent of the quartermaster department for the investigation of claims. Among his possessions Brother Dutton has the following letter which was handed to him by General Ekin on June 16, 1884, at Louisville, Ky.:

I have the honor and the pleasure to state that in the month of November, 1875, Capt. Ira B. Dutton was appointed by me, under proper authority, an agent of the Quartermaster's Department in the army, charged with the investigation of claims, and that he served in that capacity with zeal and fidelity until honorably discharged on the 31st of December, 1883, a period upwards of eight years.

Captain Dutton's duties were discharged in a faithful, efficient and intelligent manner, and to my entire satisfaction. His record is clear and without a blemish, and I have always regarded him as an honorable, conscientious gentleman. He enjoyed my confidence to the fullest extent and was held in high estimation.

Captain Dutton was paid a salary and a per diem allowance for his services. He had no property accountability or responsibility to the government, and did not become liable or indebted to the United States in any way as such agent. Payments for his services were made by me, and his accounts were always right, and always just and proper.

It affords me more than ordinary gratification to furnish this certificate of non-indebtedness to Captain Dutton.

## Certificates of Non-indebtedness
## for the Trappist Order

Brother Dutton possesses eight certificates of non-indebtedness, which, with the exception of one from the Treasury Department, were applied for by him at the time when it was possible that he might remain permanently at Gethsemani as a member of the Trappist Order, which would have required that he show himself to be clear of all monetary obligations. As he did not enter the order, remaining at the monastery only 20 months, he retained the papers.

The following letter was handed to Brother Dutton on December 19, 1865, near Memphis, Tenn., aboard the steamer Ruth of the Atlantic & Mississippi Steamship Co., by Brig.-Gen. Charles C. Doolittle of United States Volunteers :

> "The bearer of this, Mr. Ira B. Dutton, late regimental quartermaster, 13th Wisconsin Infty., is commended to the favorable consideration of my friends. He is a young man of high character and of thorough business qualifications, and can be trusted in any position. He served with me as brigade and post quartermaster, at Decatur, Ala., and closes his business of twenty millions without loss to government, and as an honest man."

On November 29, 1876, Brother Dutton was appointed a United States commissioner by H. B. Andrews, clerk of the sixth circuit court, Western division of Tennessee. At that time he was special claim investigating agent. He resigned as commissioner on April 22, 1884, and on November 18, 1903, at the leper settlement, he wrote:

> "I will just add a notation here that this appointment was intended and made use of for a special purpose. Though I could have charged fees, I never did so. It was simply to facilitate my work as investigating agent of the War

Department, having hundreds—I may say thousands—
of witnesses to examine, often having some when there
was no one authorized to administer the oath, until I got
this appointment."

The following letter was handed to Brother Dutton by A. W. Wills,
an attorney of Nashville, Tenn., and Washington, D. C., who served as a
lieutenant colonel during the Civil War, on April 30, 1884:

"To whom It May Concern:
Ira B. Dutton, now of Gethsemani, Ky., in the year 1867
was in my employ as an agent of the Q. Mrs. department,
and I take pleasure in stating that all of his accounts were
faithfully and accurately rendered, and that at the expi-
ration of his term of employment he was in no wise indebted to the United States government."

The same writer, on February 14, 1868, sent the following letter to
Brother Dutton :

"Having completed your duties in connection with the
Qr. Mr. Dept. under my direction, I desire to bear testimony to the thorough and business-like manner in which
you have always conducted the business pertaining to
the department, and cordially wish you that success and
promotion warranted by the actions of an honest, industrious, sober and reliable young man. You have served
the Qr. Mr. Dept. honorably and faithfully, and may you
merit your just reward is the fervent wish of your friend."

A commission, issued to Brother Dutton on August 5, 1882, by
the War Department, as agent of the office of the quartermaster general,
bears the signature of Robert Lincoln, son of Abraham Lincoln and
then secretary of war. To this commission Brother Dutton has attached
the following memorandum:

"This commission, issued by Mr. Robert Lincoln (son of Abraham Lincoln) on August 5, 1882, was merely a matter of form. I had been filling the place (not in the office of the quartermaster general, U. S. A., but in Tennessee, Kentucky and Ohio), since November, 1875, under authority of the quartermaster general. But Mr. Lincoln, while in office as secretary of war, ruled that it was a position requiring appointment by the secretary. Hence the new appointment."

On October 22, 1868, while Brother Dutton was a clerk in the quartermaster department, he received the following letter from Capt. C. H. Hoyt, A. Q. M., in charge of cemeterial operations for the department of Louisiana:

"Having been relieved from duty in this military department, I wish to express to you my entire satisfaction at the manner in which you have performed your duties while a clerk in my office. I take pleasure in recommending you to any one who may require the services of a thoroughly competent and trustworthy clerk."

To this letter Brother Dutton has since attached the following notation :

"This follows, in order of service, the letters of Col. A. W. Wills, and is the close of my work in cemeterial operations. Here I wish particularly to refer to this Captain Hoyt, A. Q. M., who was a stranger to me when I went to him, and not an old friend like Captain Wills. I shall always remember the kind manner in which he handed me this—as he did to all his office force, if I remember correctly, when he was changed to other duty. But very specially the observation he made to me, showing that he had noted I was for the moment down in the ranks.'

How, I do not know. Possibly he knew I had been an officer. Anyway, he said:

"I ask you to take this letter, but you will hardly use it. You will do better. I hope you will not get into the departmental rut. It's hard to break away, once in it."

I knew that, but it was in the period when I had lost ambition for the moment. For quite a while, I may say; even did worse later on; but regained somewhat still later.

While still an agent of the quartermaster department, Brother Dutton, on June 19, 1877, received the following letter from Gen. James A. Ekin, already referred to, at the Jefferson, Indiana, depot of the claims branch of the quartermaster department:

"You were on the 24th day of May notified that in consequence of the failure of Congress to make an appropriation for the support of the army, out of which appropriation your services, as an agent of the quartermaster department, is paid, you would be relieved from duty at the close of the present fiscal year, the 30th of June, instant.

In separating officially—I trust only for a limited period—I desire to take the opportunity of expressing my appreciation of the intelligent and faithful manner in which you have discharged the delicate duties committed to your charge. Not a single complaint has been made from any source, and whilst the interests of the government have been protected, claimants have been treated with courtesy, and opportunities afforded them and their attorneys of presenting their cases in a manner that no injustice was done the parties.

For the fidelity with which you have investigated the large number of claims placed in your hands, you are entitled to my thanks. I wish you health and prosperity."

From the office of the inspector of the quartermaster department at Nashville, the following letter was sent to Brother Dutton on April 14, 1866, by Col. James F. Rushing, inspector:

"The bearer, Mr. Ira B. Dutton, late 1st Lieut. Vols. and A.Q.M., in the department of the Cumberland, I have known very well for the past three years, and I take pleasure in thus certifying to his ability and integrity. He is well conversant with the QM department and is of very correct habits in general, and I commend him to the courtesy and consideration of the army and the patriotic generally."

The following letter, written June 30, 1877, was handed to Brother Dutton by John T. Flynn, superintendent of the Louisville & Nashville Railroad, Memphis division:

"To R. R. Officers:
The bearer, Mr. Ira B. Dutton, was in the employ of this company in the freight department at Memphis, Tenn., for several years. On separating from the road, I take pleasure in testifying to the ability and integrity of Mr. Dutton. Any R. R. Co. needing the services of one in the freight department cannot find a man better qualified to fill the position."

The foregoing are but a few examples of the testimonials which were in Brother Dutton's possession at the time he resolved to give himself up to a life of penance. That he was well thought of not only in the army, both before and after the war, and during his several employments after he had left army service, is testified to by all of them.

## Correspondence with
## Herbert Hoover

On February 17, 1921, Brother Dutton received from Herbert Hoover, then with the general committee of the European Relief Council, a letter thanking him for a contribution to aid the destitute children of Europe.

Following is the text of the letter:

Dear Brother Dutton:

Both I and all of my colleagues in the General Committee of the European Relief Council have been greatly touched by the contribution that you have made towards supporting the destitute children of Europe. I know of no contribution from all this broad land of so touching a character, and it is the wish of the committee that I should acknowledge to you their feeling in the matter. The real appreciation of such gifts comes from the hearts of those who are served.

This is something about which Brother Dutton knows nothing. He made no personal contribution toward the fund for the relief of the destitute children of Europe for the simple reason that he had no means with which to make it. However, a contribution was made—and a generous one—by the patients at the leper settlement proper, and Brother Dutton says it is quite likely that, when the money was received, the officials were of the impression that he had contributed it and sent it along.

## Dutton's 1920
## Christmas Correspondence

To all of his close friends, and they number hundreds, Brother Dutton never fails to send cards of greeting on their birthdays, and upon appropriate occasions such as Easter, Christmas and the New Year. He keeps a card index of the names of these friends, and upon each card is the birth date, and usually the birth date of a close relative or two. Hardly a year goes by that each of these persons is not remembered on his natal day. In 1919-20, however, Brother Dutton was so overwhelmed with work that he could not find time in which to remember all of his friends on Christmas, New Years' and Epiphany, and so, during the latter year, after his labors had eased up somewhat, he mailed to each a single greeting to cover all three of the occasions. He said:

Dear Friends All:

So loyal and steadfast, even to the children, to the grand-children, and in several instances to the great-grandchil-dren, of the ones I personally know. To you all this comes as a hearty acknowledgement of your faithful remem-brance, and of my seeming neglect. That you feel sure these appearances are backed by good reasons I have no doubt. You will, however, be interested in knowing the reasons, and I hope to make them apparent.

The greetings that go with these slips were ready in time for everyone, but were delayed in the hopes of hav-ing letters to go along, for I'm in debt to nearly all of my correspondents.

May God bless you.
Very affectionately,
Joseph Dutton.

## *Dutton's Censorship Memorandum*

It was on July 14, 1921, that Brother Dutton issued his famous "Memorandum" to his friends explaining in detail just why it was that every paper, magazine, book and other bit of reading material that went into the boys' home at Kalawao was carefully "censored" by him and every picture tending to be salacious in the smallest degree cut out, before the literature was placed in the boys' reading room.

Although it probably has never until now found its way into public print, copies of this "Memorandum" were sent to practically all of Brother Dutton's friends, and was prepared in response to numerous questions concerning his censorship. The text of the "Memorandum" is as follows:

> "The dear friends, here and there, will recall a quaint way I have of cutting out, from periodicals, etc., pictures of bad characters. As of immodest suggestion, by reason of indecent dress, or of wanton expression, inviting and lewd.
>
> Having myself suffered from these, and similar evils, long ago, this action may be considered just and wholesome. For some irregular portions, and certain incidents, of my life—am now in the 39th year of voluntary penance, having made, on 40th birthday, April 27, 1883, a vow to Almighty God for devoting the rest of this life in reparation, by work at some retired place without pay. This to cover, if may be, all of the "sowing of wild oats," as the common expression goes. For the soul is greatly injured when pleasure or satisfaction is derived from evil pictures, or by immodesty in any form. Am not mentioning the "Movies" as I've never seen one.
>
> The special purpose in this, rather disgraceful, confession is the fact of having a lot of magazines with good pictures interspersed with some very bad ones. For some years I have been sending out various periodicals, many

requiring very little censoring; but in the past three years a considerable number required so much that they were put aside for a general overhauling. When these begin to arrive "over there" you will know the wherefore of such a coming of old magazines, and will enjoy them. For the "remains" will be good, with many fine pictures. Have not read the articles, but a glance over indicates fairly good matter.

Another point: These will partly take the place of letters I owe. As a correspondent am "getting no better very fast"; rather becoming worse and worse.

Now am prompted to make this a sort of all-around letter, for the thought comes that many of you, in two or three states I can think of, will recall the capers I cut, somewhat like "a boy out of school."

Having carried unusual responsibilities in the latter part of our Civil War—"unusual" for one so young, 21 and 22 years—everything was closed and settled in good order. Also, it was tolerably well known there were expectations concerning the regular army, with kind words volunteered by four major generals.

Just at the close of the war an incident occurred (one of a private nature) that caused me to forsake the plans of that time. You know about this in part. Some of you know all, and of some wild years that followed. You know if I ever injured anyone but myself; I am not conscious of doing so, at least seriously. You have all been wonderfully good to me. This is very comforting, in a social way, among dear friends, but it does not excuse the sin associated with some of those "capers."

The old time friends are not the only ones, for there are very many dear ones on these islands. Was not expecting this, nor thinking of it, in coming here. Was seeking only good work—suitable for penance. This was made easy by sincere friend. ship on all sides and by the companions here at our leper settlement. We are like a family.

The above is also to explain a little the high value these good friends put upon my little work-chores and trying to help; surely, to find good, useful work was a part of the vow, but not really the incentive. This was more personal—for the good of my soul; and this we all know is the chief responsibility of every Christian.

Am now glad the little memo—as begun—has merged into quite a letter, for all these things will be appreciated by the dear friends everywhere. Of 173 I have birthday dates, and would suggest that others send me their dates of birth, as there is less chance of overlooking them. You see, I have these names and dates in a little book always near by. They are entered by months. Before each month I put the greetings in envelopes, sending by dates, or aim so to do. Certainly I do not fail all the time, and there is a chance, when anyone goes, that unanswered letters from the same person may get some sort of reply. At best, my part will be very defective."

Begging prayers and forgiveness,
Yours cordially,
Joseph Dutton.

## *Correspondence with*
## *Charlotte Cameron*

One of Brother Dutton's staunchest friends is Charlotte Cameron, the English authoress, their first meeting having been in 1921 when she visited Molokai and the leper settlement as a guest of members of the Territorial Legislature. At that time Mrs. Cameron was touring the South Seas, and her book, "Two Years In the South Seas," was published some months later. In this volume she tells of conditions at the leper settlement, and mentions Brother Dutton and his work prominently.

On Easter Sunday, 1923, she wrote to Brother Dutton as follows:

"Peace, and good will be to you, dear Brother Joseph Dutton, on this Easter Day. Christ is risen! I thank you very much indeed for your Christmas and New Year card, which I received at Singapore. I appreciate it more than those of princes or queens, because I realize what a good and wonderful work you are accomplishing for God— and the lepers. May your life be spared for many years yet. The enclosed clipping will tell you of my latest work.

I passed through Honolulu two days ago. Met Senator and Mrs. (Charles F.) Chillingworth. He will be at Molokai on the 7th. My thoughts will be with you and the lepers on that day. It's just two years ago since my visit. I presume that you have received my new book, and trust you like what I said. Senator Chillingworth was delighted with the work. I also gave one to Dr. (W. J.) Goodhue. Am on my way home to London now and should arrive on May 6. My addresses are the same. Mail follows me all over the globe. I should have liked to visit Molokai, and seen you once more on earth, but it was not possible.

A tiny prayer for me, I should appreciate sometimes. May God bless you until you stand in the Great Presence."

Charlotte Cameron.

## Correspondence with
## Lucius E. Pinkham

For many years, and in fact up until the day of the death of the latter, a warm friendship was maintained between Brother Dutton and the late Lucius Eugene Pinkham, a Democrat, at one time president of the territorial Board of Health, and later governor of Hawaii. After Pinkham's term as governor expired, he removed to the Mainland, where he entered sanitariums, as his health was not of the best.

Under date of June 24, 1920, while in a sanitarium at Worcester, Massachusetts, he wrote to Brother Dutton as follows:

Dear Brother Joseph Dutton:

For ten months, the past year, I have been in sanitariums and there is no immediate prospect of my being able to leave. While at Dr. Sawyer's sanitarium at Marion, Ohio, I gradually dispensed with crutches and cane, and for several weeks walked about the large grounds without.

With the doctor's approval, I accepted the invitation of Senator and Mrs. Harding to become their guest in Washington. The third day my hip gave way and I was put to bed. The senator and his wife were extremely kind. The two days I was at the capital I met many of the senators and representatives I had known formerly, both in Washington and in Hawaii, and I met at Senator Harding's residence more than one-quarter of the members of the senate. It was a great pleasure to me. People would be generally quite surprised to see the leaders of both parties enjoying each other's society in golf, breakfasts and other popular sports.

Should Senator Harding be elected President, you would find the people had selected the most courteous and conscientious of men, at the same time just and firm.

He is free from all vulgar methods in speech, and is fair and square. Of course we do not know who is to be the candidate on the other side.

Harding and Coolidge have the virtues and abilities we hear talked about and desired, but so seldom see. Neither are wealthy. Governor Coolidge lives in a double house in Northampton and pays $32 per month, and hopes his landlord will not raise it to $35.

It was very kind of you to send me the Easter cards. The photographs of yourself and the foliage are most pleasant to look at and bring to me agreeable reminiscences. You appear to be holding your own quite well. I infer the pension the legislature provided for you does not tempt you to leave your home or the sight of your charges. I wonder if your associated brothers are still content. You must give them my regards and best wishes.

Old Chaulmoogra oil seems to be coming into its own. If you see Mr. Van Lil, tell him I think of him. Mr. Hutchinson, too, if still alive. I note Mr. McVeigh (superintendent of the leper settlement) has been traveling more or less on public sanitary work. Won't you call him up and tell him I am sending my "aloha nui' to him through you, and give the same to all those who know me?

Tell Dr. Goodhue I received a letter from his brother, E. S., since I began to fill this last sheet, and give my sincere regards to him and his wife and those of her family still living.

I hope that ample funds are provided not only for a satisfactory subsistence but to keep the buildings and grounds in good order. May your heart keep and grow young as your years advance. I am about in the same fix as you respecting correspondence.

Sincerely yours,
Lucius E. Pinkham.

On October 12, 1920, Pinkham wrote to Brother Dutton from Worcester, Mass., as follows:

Dear Brother Dutton:

Permit me to thank you for the kind birthday remembrance and the letter that accompanied it. The day before it arrived my cousin, Capt. C. H. Pinkham, a Civil War veteran now 70 years old and wearing the Congressional medal for bravery, handed me a clipping from an article relative to yourself. I said to him: 'I have just passed my birthday, and I know Brother Dutton has, as is his custom, sent me a birthday card, due here now.' Sure enough, it reached me the next day.

The Legislature was just in voting you the pension and you were very wise in declining it. You could hardly have remained at the Baldwin Home and settlement had you taken it. So long as you remain at your work you will be a man of interest to the world. You would find, when circulating in it, that it would chill your heart. Eminent men step aside from pressing interests, or die, and promptly pass from men's minds. For instance, not long since, Andrew Carnegie, Henry C. Frick, George W. Perkins, Georges Clemenceau, to say nothing of rulers and would be rulers. They rise and fall so rapidly one can hardly retain in mind their names.

Men are praised inordinately and men are maligned to the limit. The world is frightfully unsettled. Altruism takes the place of common-sensed, righteous living. Entities created by law and governed by it, if the authorities see fit, have so superseded individuals and individual practise and conscience that the human problem seems to almost call for a new creation.

You can rest under your vines and foilage and look back over 34 years of devotion to those whom the world and literature consider to suffer and to have suffered the most tragic disease.

I believe your life has been a happy one and that resting as you are will be a happy one to the end.

I thank you for your kind words. If ever a man tried to be just and wise in his public and private duties, I think I can claim that distinction. I believe I am, though very slowly, regaining in some degree my health. I hope to leave here on the 23rd for Kansas City, Missouri, to remain with my only niece this winter.

With my kindest regards,<br>Lucius E. Pinkham.

The last letter which Pinkham wrote to Brother Dutton, and probably the last letter to be received in Hawaii from its former governor, was mailed from Kansas City, Mo., on August 7, 1921. It read as follows:

My dear Brother Dutton:

I have owed you a letter or two, and thanks for your remembrances, for a long time. If ill health is any excuse for such neglect I have ample excuse, particularly as my nerves have been punishing me for overwork and refuse to be comforted.

November 5th, last, I dined with President-elect Warren G. Harding and his wonderful wife, and delivered to them the congratulations of Capt. Charles H. Pinkham who, it chanced, as a telegram informed me during that night, died, so I could not deliver your card and message to him. I have been in Kansas City since November 12, last year. I shall change residence before October 1, destination unknown, but it will not be either

Washington or Honolulu, as my lameness will not permit me to travel any distance.

A letter from our mutual and loved friend, Charles A. Brown, tells me you are content at your home, though retired from active responsibility. It is most fortunate you can spend your last days where your work has been done and where your heart is and where you can see the prospect of overcoming the disease that has had such a tragic setting in the history of the world.

My most attentive friend is an old Civil War veteran who did live in Worcester, but was so soft-hearted he recently married a well-provided widow of Pittston, Pa., though he was 79 years of age. I think his wife has eye trouble somewhat corresponding to yours. Mr. Brown writes you have lost the sight of one eye and are apprehensive as to the other. If you would take a trip away from Molokai, your sight might be restored by an operation; but that is against your practice to date.

I have taken some interest in politics and possibly successfully in the two or three efforts I have made. I have had no personal objects in view. The island of Molokai should change some under the 'Hawaiian Homes Commission Act. It is a problem, however. In fact the whole world is a problem.

Mr. McVeigh seems to hold onto his work wonderfully. Please remember me to him and Dr. Goodhue, Mr. Hutchinson and Mr. Van Lil and others I know.

Please telephone Sister Benedicta my deep Aloha nui, and tell her I have just received letters from 11 of the Kapiolani Home girls and Sister Helena and the card for Sister Helena's 50th anniversary. It is a great comfort to one as ill as I am.

I hope the U. S. government is treating you as liberally as other veterans of the Civil War. Let us hope greed may be restrained and ambitions curbed until peace and justice may prevail. Now I must bid you goodnight and wish you patience to bear your ills and freedom from pain or grief.

Most sincerely and faithfully,
Lucius E. Pinkham.

## *Letter to the National Tribune from D.H. Wood*

The following letter was published in the National Tribune, Washington, D. C., on November 26, 1914:

Editor National Tribune:

A picture of Ira B. Dutton in a late issue awakens memories of the days of half a century or more ago. I knew Dutton in his boyhood in Janesville, Wis. He was, as a boy, clean, correct in speech and deportment, and evidently a lover of home and of his mother, who was his teacher and companion. He had few companions, but was reserved and dignified even in his boyhood. About the year 1857 he and Ed. H. Woodman, some three years his senior, formed a friendship that became like the friendship of David and Jonathan, and was a strong influence with Woodman at his death in 1912. In the summer of 1861, Woodman organized a company, which later become Co. B., 13th Wis., and of which he served as captain. Of this company Dutton was a member, but upon the organization of the regiment in October, 1861, he became quartermaster sergeant. He had a rare gift for business; was quick, accurate and courteous, and handled the quartermaster's supplies with satisfaction to his superiors and to the boys. About the fall of 1863, or possibly in 1864, he was commissioned lieutenant of Company I. After the war he served in the quartermaster's department for some time in the South.

D. H. Wood,
1st Sgt., Co. A, 13th Wis. Vol.

## *Letter confirming*
## *Brother Dutton's war record*

Brother Dutton's war record may be stated briefly as follows:

> Quartermaster Sergeant, 13th Wis. Volunteers,
>    to February 10, 1863.
> Commissioned 2nd lieutenant
>    February 10, 1863.
> Commissioned 1st lieutenant
>    February 15, 1865.
> Appointed regimental quartermaster
>    March 24, 1865.

Was recommended for appointment as captain, U. S. Volunteers, by Majors General George H. Thomas, J. L. Donaldson, L. H. Rosseau and Robert S. Granger. (Dutton was unaware of this recommendation)

Served on the staff of the latter from June, 1864, until about October, 1865.

3–014.

ACT OF FEBRUARY 6, 1907.

# DECLARATION FOR PENSION.

THE PENSION CERTIFICATE SHOULD NOT BE FORWARDED WITH THE APPLICATION.

Territory of *Hawaii*
County of *Kalawao* } ss.

On this *20th* day of *January*, A. D. one thousand nine hundred and *Eleven* personally appeared before me, a *Notary Public* within and for the county and State aforesaid, *Joseph Dutton*, who, being duly sworn according to law, declares that he is *67* years of age, and a resident of *Kalawao* county of *Kalawao*, Territory of *Hawaii*; and that he is the identical person who was ENROLLED at *Janisville, Wisconsin* under the name of *Ira B. Dutton* on the *in the summer of 1861 - Mustered in fall of 1861* as *Q.M. Serg't, 13th Wis. Inf. Vols (2nd Lt. Co. 76 10 1863, 1st Lt. 5 C? Feby 15. 1865, 1st Lt RQM, mch 24. 1865 on staff Gen. com'ly. Dist 1864-5)* in the service of the United States, in the *Civil* war, and was HONORABLY DISCHARGED at *Madison, Wisconsin*, on the *20th* day of *January*, 1866. That he also served as *Q.M. Agent Constur'd of* *dating Nov 24, 1865. Same as reg'r* *1867 - 68. as Investigating Agent Q.M.D. Nov. 1875, to Dec 31st 1883, in Tennessee, Kentucky and Ohio.*

That he was not employed in the military or naval service of the United States otherwise than as stated above. That his personal description at enlistment was as follows: Height, _____ feet _____ inches; complexion, _____; color of eyes, _____; color of hair, _____; that his occupation was _____; that he was born *April 27th*, 18*43*, at *Stowe Vermont*.

That his several places of residence since leaving the service have been as follows: *Early part of 1866, Mount Vernon, Ohio. rest of 66 Valhermoso, Ala. 1867 - 70 Pittsburg Landing Tenn, Chattanooga, New orleans La. Corinth Miss., 1870 - 75 Memphis Tenn. 1875 - 83. Tenn. Ky, Ohio, Ind. & Augustin* That he is *not* a pensioner. That he has *never* heretofore applied for pension *Memphis, Chattanooga, Nashville Tenn, Louisville Ky, Cincinnati O. Ind. &c* _____ (If a pensioner, the certificate number only need be given. If not, give the number of the former application, if one was made.)

That he makes this declaration for the purpose of being placed on the pension roll of the United States under the provisions of the act of February 6, 1907. *To aid a charity in Tennessee* That his post-office address is *Kalawao*, county of *Kalawao* Territory of *Hawaii*.

                               *Joseph Dutton*
                               (Claimant's signature in full.)

Attest: (1) *Louis M. Leisen*
       (2) *Liborius Hengst*

Also personally appeared *Louis M. Leisen*, residing in *Kalawao* and *Liborius Hengst*, residing in *Kalawao*, persons whom I certify to be respectable and entitled to credit, and who, being by me duly sworn, say that they were present and saw *Joseph Dutton*, the claimant, sign his name (or make his mark) to the foregoing declaration; that they have every reason to believe, from the appearance of the claimant and their acquaintance with him of *15* years and *7* years, respectively, that he is the identical person he represents himself to be, and that they have no interest in the prosecution of this claim.

                               *Louis M. Leisen*
                               *Liborius Hengst*
                               (Signatures of witnesses.)

SUBSCRIBED and sworn to before me this *20th* day of *January*, A. D. 191*1*, and I hereby certify that the contents of the above declaration, etc., were fully made known and explained to the applicant and witnesses before swearing, including the words *Ira B. & Liborius Hengst* erased, and the words *Territory* added; and that I have no interest, direct or indirect, in the prosecution of this claim.

[L. S.]

                               *Emil Van Li?*
                               (Signature.)
                           *Notary Public 2nd Judicial*
                           (Official character.)

*Brother Dutton's pension documents from Stowe Historical Society*

# Brother Dutton's Civil War Pension

Although having received a pension of $50 a month from the United States government as a veteran of the Civil War, Brother Dutton has never at any time used any of this money for personal use. It has been devoted to the benefit of those to whom he ministers at the leper settlement, or to some other good cause. For it should be remembered that when Brother Dutton decided upon a life of penance, he vowed that whatever work he should do on behalf of his fellow men would be carried out without thought of monetary remuneration. As he expresses it:

> "Although always praising the government for its generosity in the pension system, I would not accept a pension for myself, unless in actual need. I feel that the government has always paid me well for actual service performed."

The first actual request for Brother Dutton's pension money was received by him in 1910 from an association engaged in charitable work in Memphis, Tenn. A check was forwarded to this institution by Brother Dutton on November 21 of the same year. From February 4, 1911, to March, 1912, the checks were sent to a Miss Linder for use at the St. Catharine's Industrial School at Memphis. On March 17, 1912, the checks were transferred to the Good Shepherd Sisters, Memphis, who are still getting them. Many a glowing letter has been received by him from them, expressing their appreciation of his generous assistance. A record of Brother Dutton's pension disposal is on file in the office of the commissioner of pensions at Washington, D. C.

3—447.

## DEPARTMENT OF THE INTERIOR
### BUREAU OF PENSIONS
#### WASHINGTON, D. C.

_February 15, 1911_

Mr. Joseph Dutton,
Kalawas,
Hawaii

SIR: To aid this Bureau in preventing any one falsely personating you, or otherwise committing fraud in your name, or on account of your service, you are required to answer fully the questions enumerated below.

You will please return this circular under cover of the inclosed envelope, which requires no postage.

Very respectfully,

_Commissioner._

1. When were you born? Answer. _April 27th 1843._
2. Where were you born? Answer. _at Stowe, Vermont._
3. When did you enlist? Answer. _In Summer of 1861._
_you enlist?_ Answer. _at Janesville, Wisconsin._
5. Where had you lived before you enlisted? Answer. _at Janesville Wisconsin_
6. What was your post-office address at enlistment? Answer. _Janesville, Wisconsin_
7. What was your occupation at enlistment? Answer. _Was Clerk in a Book store_
8. When were you discharged? Answer. _Jany 20/1866. dating Nov 24/1865_
9. Where were you discharged? Answer. _at Madison, Wisconsin_
10. Where have you lived since discharge? Gives dates, as nearly as possible, of any changes of residence. _Early part of 1866 at Mt Vernon Ohio, Rest of 1866 at Baltimore, Md. Ala. 1872-'75. Memphis Tenn. 1875-'83. Tenn. Ky. Ohio — Henderson Ky, Corinth Miss, Chattanooga, Nashville, Tenn, Louisville Ky, Cincinnati + Mt Vernon O._
11. What is your present occupation? Answer. _Servant of the lepers on Molokai island._
12. What is your height? Answer. _5_ feet _7_ inches. Your weight? _140 lb, abt_; The color of your eyes? _Gray_ The color of your hair? _Brown + Gray_ Your complexion? _Light_ — Are there any permanent marks or scars on your person? If so, describe them. _One on right knee, accidental cut about 58 yrs ago._
13. What is your full name? Please write it on the line below, in ink, in the manner in which you are accustomed to sign it, in the presence of two witnesses who can write.

_Joseph Dutton_

WITNESSES: { 1. _Louis M. Leisen_     2. _Maternus Gaschet_ }
[Witnesses who can write sign here.]

Date: _March 10th 1911._

6—1760

---

_* Brother Dutton's pension documents from Stowe Historical Society_
_1911 questionnaire from the Bureau of Pensions_

WAR DEPARTMENT,
THE ADJUTANT GENERAL'S OFFICE.

*Respectfully returned to the*

**Commissioner of Pensions,**

*with the information that in the case of*

Ira B. Dutton

Co. B, 13 Reg't Wis Inf

*the records show the following:*

Age 18, height 5 feet 7 inches,
complexion Fair
eyes Blue, hair Light
place of birth Stowe, Vt
occupation Clerk
enrolled September 9, 1861
and is reported on M/o roll of 7th S
dated San Antonio Tex Nov 24, 65
as Q. M. with remark, on detached
service as A.A.Q.M. Decatur Ala
no discharge furnished, and on *
*and the rolls on file for that period do not
show him absent without leave or in deser-
tion,* ~~except as follows~~:

---

* Individual M/o roll dated Madison
Wis Jany 20, 1866 as 1st Lt & R.Q.M.
M/o to date Dec 23, 65. with remark
at the time of M/o of org'n was on
det. serv. as act Q.M at Decatur
Ala. Discharged by reason of M/o of
org'n.

He was transfd from Co B to 7th S
Oct 61, transfd to Co D. on M/i as
2d Lt March 63, transfd to 7th S
May 65.

F. C. Ainsworth
The Adjutant General,

Per 7

Washington, D. C. FEB 17 1911

(Commissioner of Pensions.)

---

*\* Brother Dutton's pension documents from Stowe Historical Society*
*1911 verification of Dutton's military history from the War Deparment*

Kalawao. Molokai.
Hawaii. May 28/1915.

Hon G. M. Saltzgaber,
Commissioner of Pensions,
Washington D.C.

My dear Sir:

First. I beg your pardon
for allowing this reply to yours of Jan'y
2. 1915. to be delayed. For some months
we have been more or less on a strain
with a large number of unusual cases,
our working force being much broken
down.

Anyway I wished merely to have
a typed copy of one of Commissioner
Davenports letters to send you which
has now come – from Honolulu, and
in thinking it will cover the case
in question. I have a number of
beautiful letters from Mr Davenport,
and in one of them he gives me liberty
to make what use I like of any of them.
This one refers to the circular that
is apparently the basis for your
letter of Jan'y 2. 1915. The circular was
sent in error. There is not any

*Brother Dutton's pension documents from Stowe Historical Society
1915 Letter from Dutton to Commissioner of Pensions requesting his
pension be sent to the Sisters of the Good Shepherd at Memphis*

living person who could possibly give
you any inconvenience in this matter.
I never consented to take the
pension until about four years ago.
My reason had nothing whatever to do
with the subject of this letter, nor
with any part of the subject.
Blanks for pension were sometimes
times sent me by friends - comrades
I always stated the fact - that Uncle
Sam had treated me so well I
should be ashamed to take it
without necessity, acknowledging
the beauty of the pension idea.
and having all my life to work
for a living I never saw the
actual need of it for me.
Then finally, in 1911, I took it,
but for the Memphis, Tenn, Good
Shepherd Sisters. More funds were
needed. Memphis ladies were helping.
Some suggested my pension - as
they knew I did not take it.
When I am dead there will be no
one having the slightest claim upon
it.
Six piece memoranda -
enclosed may be useful
or interesting. I have many such

Very sincerely
Your obedient
servant,
Joseph Dutton

---

*Brother Dutton's pension documents from Stowe Historical Society.*
*1915 Letter page 2*

(from the Memphis Gazette, July 14, 1928.)

## *A Beautiful Tribute to Brother Joseph*

### Sisters of Good Shepherd at Memphis
### Send Tribute to Far Off Hawaiian Islands.

One of the handsomest tributes of Brother Dutton's work among the far off Leper colony in the Pacific Ocean, in memory of his silver jubilee was sent him by the Sisters of the Good Shepherd at Memphis. It is a dainty hand painted, hand illuminated poem, which is printed below. Brother Joseph sent the gift to the Sisters of Mercy of the city . . . the Gazette is privileged to reprint the beautiful tribute to Brother Joseph and his work.

> How little do we reck' the ills
> Of those that near us dwell;
> And what of those beyond our ken,
> What griefs their bosom's swell.
>
> We murmur when some petty wrong
> Our daily life o'er casts;
> And think not of the noble souls,
> That face life's bitter blasts.
>
> We step aside and blanch with fear,
> When pestilence is nigh;
> And there are souls like Damien,
> With Lepers, live and die.

He's passed away, a Dutton stands,
Upon a shore of death;
Amidst the Lepers daily lives,
Inhales their fetid breath.

"Unclean, Unclean", that ancient cry,
Heard through Gehenna's Vale,
How sad, how more than sad the tones
Of that despondent wail.

Christ Jesus heard that heartfelt cry,
"Unclean", but Thou canst heal
Decaying flesh the ulcerous sores:
O, Christ thy power reveal.

An outcast from the haunts of men,
Can Nature's beauties cheer?
Who but a Damien, Dutton brave,
Can solace, bring them here.

The tranquil Ocean laves the shore,
. . . seems their Isle;
. . .
. . . Dutton's smile.

. . . feared the foe
        2 lines missing
On Kalawao tread?

We say he's reached the Silver term,
Men sound his praise loud,
A column in the daily news,
A whisper in the crowd.
"A living death" they trembling say,

An Exile from his King,
Ah surely not for gold, his aim,
Scant recompense he'll find.

Ah no, the world has no reward,
For such a life as this;
A recompense the Saviour'll give,
In realms of joy and bliss.

The Silver years, He'll crown brave soul,
Reward He'll surely meet;
When pillowed on his Sacred Heart,
You'll hear his welcome sweet.

Was to Him, a Leper he,
No semblance of a man,
When at pillar prone He lay,
Scourge by the Roman's hand.

He thinks he saw you in that hour,
Upon that lonely shore,
Comforting a stricken race,
Of lepers sad and poor.

Dear Brother Joseph, list we pray,
Your Memphis friends unite
In wishing you, all grace and joy,
And a crown of bliss, all bright.

From the Sisters of the Good Shepherd, Memphis, Tenn.

# The Leprosy Situation in Hawaii
## 1931

Leprosy was undoubtedly present in the Hawaiian Islands as early as 1830, and in 1848 it was noted in many of the Chinese coolies who had been brought in as laborers. However, it was not until 1864 that its rapid spread caused the alarm among the people which resulted in the founding of the leper settlement, first at Kalihi, in Honolulu, and then on the island of Molokai.

The disease in all probability was known to the ancients. The mere fact that, in the earliest sacred writings, there are allusions to an affliction which had evidently more than all others impressed the primitive peoples by its gravity and terrible nature, at once points to leprosy as the malady which was likely to stamp itself on the popular imagination.

But the records of ancient literature in all countries are so vague that it is impossible to strictly identify diseases as they are classified today, and the description of leprosy in the Bible forms no exception. It is clear, however, that leprosy existed among the Jews, their history indicating this. The first accurate description of the disease was written by Aretaeus in the first century of the present era. Leprosy appears to have been very prevalent all over Europe from the second to the seventh century, and it is supposed that later the returning Crusaders brought it with them. At one time in England alone there were one hundred and nine hospitals for lepers.

At the present time, leprosy occurs in almost every country in the world, but it is more prevalent in those countries which have a seaboard. In the United States leprosy occurred first in Minnesota among people recently arrived from Norway and Sweden; in Louisiana among emigrants from Arcadia, and in California among the Chinese. From 1912 to 1917, both inclusive, 276 cases of leprosy were reported in America from 25 states, the majority of which bordered on the ocean. After a study of these data, it was concluded that a large proportion of these cases contracted the disease outside of the United States.

There are two distinct types of the disease; first, the one in which the skin is principally affected, and, second, the one in which the nerves are the seat of the trouble. One general theory of scientists is that in a virgin race the disease affects the skin for the most part, while in the older races the nerves are the portion to be involved.

In 1914 Dr. Arthur L. Dean, A.B., Ph.D., arrived at Honolulu from Yale University to become president of the College (now University) of Hawaii, and also professor of chemistry. At that time Chaulmoogra oil, obtained largely from India, was in use for the treatment of leprosy at the Kalihi receiving station and at the leper settlement.

Some weeks after his arrival, Dr. Dean was called upon at his office at the college by Miss Alice Ball, a young part-American Negro, who was a graduate of the University of Washington at Seattle, and who had contracted with the Department of Public Instruction at Honolulu to teach in a government school on the island of Kauai. Dr. Dean noted that Miss Ball wore the emblem of Sigma Xi, a scientific research society, and was convinced immediately that here was a young woman of unusual ability.

Miss Ball, it appears, had become intensely interested in the awa root, which possesses medicinal properties and which at that time was grown rather extensively in the Hawaiian Islands. Her theory, as she explained to the college president, was that the awa root contained an alkaloid, and she desired to obtain from the college laboratory apparatus which would enable her to carry on her experiments while on the island of Kauai.

At that time the college was not completely organized, and had no spare laboratory apparatus which might be loaned to Miss Ball. Dr. Dean, however, suggested that if she was not concerned too greatly regarding salary, he would give her a position at the college as an assistant in chemistry. His plan was that she help him in laboratory work in freshman chemistry, and that this would give her an opportunity to proceed with her studies for a master's degree, which was really what she sought.

Miss Ball accepted this proposal and severed her connection with the Department of Public Instruction. She worked steadily during the entire college year, 1914-15, obtaining much interesting data through her experiments with awa root. The following year, in 1915, she obtained her master's degree at the college, and her thesis dealt with awa root.

As a result of her experiments, Miss Ball had isolated a number of the properties of awa root, and desired to make a test of their psychological effect. At that time the college possessed no animals for experimental purposes, and it was through a search for animals upon which Miss Ball might test the properties of awa root that Dr. Dean first met and became acquainted with Dr. George W. McCoy, then in charge of the United States leprosy investigation station in Kalihi, and a surgeon with the United States Public Health Service. Dr. McCoy is today head of the hygienic laboratories at Washington, D. C. Dr. Dean met Dr. McCoy through Prof. Arthur R. Keller of the college faculty.

The leprosy investigation station kept a number of animals for experimental work, and Dr. Dean asked Dr. McCoy if a few of these could be used for the purpose of testing Miss Ball's properties of awa root, and the latter gave his consent. Dr. Dean and Miss Ball made the necessary injections, and in this way became acquainted with the other members of the station staff, including Dr. Harry T. Hollmann, at present a practising physician at Honolulu, and the late Dr. Donald Currie.

One day, during the fall of 1915, Dr. Hollmann called on Dr. Dean at the college, taking with him a bottle containing Chaulmoogra oil in the crude form in which it was then being used in the treatment of leprosy. This was Dr. Dean's first acquaintance with the oil. He had never seen a sample of it before, although he knew what it was and was acquainted with its general uses.

It was about this time that Dr. McCoy was relieved from his duties at the investigation station and transferred to Washington, his place being taken by Dr. Currie. Just previous to this, Drs. McCoy, Currie and Hollmann had been experimenting with a Chaulmoogra oil formula worked out by Dr. Victor Heiser, then at the head of the United States Public Health Service in the Philippines. In its crude state, Chaulmoogra oil is very thick, making its injection into the human patient very difficult and often impossible. Dr. Heiser had mixed it with equal amounts of olive oil so as to make it thin enough for a more satisfactory injection, and had obtained rather good results in preliminary experiments in the Philippines. The Heiser experiment, as repeated in Hawaii, resulted in an improvement in forty-two cases of leprosy.

Dr. Hollmann, however, believed that a still more effective formula could be worked out. He took a bottle of Chaulmoogra oil to Dr. Dean and explained to him that literature on the subject of leprosy had stated that Chaulmoogric acid had been isolated from the oil, and he wanted to know whether Dr. Dean, being an expert chemist, would undertake to isolate this acid from the sample of oil which he had with him. He had also taken a sample of the acid to the United States Experiment Station, he explained, with the request that it undertake a similar experiment. Dr. Dean offered to undertake the experiment. Miss Ball was available to assist him, and he felt that, between them, they would be able to isolate the acid desired.

Dr. Dean immediately took up the matter with Miss Ball, who was willing, and they decided they would "beat the U. S. Experiment Station to it," if possible; failing in this, they would at least make a good showing.

The first thing they did was to look up the references to which Dr. Hollmann had alluded, these having been published in the journal of the Chemical Society of London. They showed that Chaulmoogric and Hydnocarpic acids had been isolated from the oil proper, and gave the extensive formulas. Miss Ball went to work on the oil sample in the college laboratories and succeeded in extracting a small quantity of Chaulmoogric acid by methods which today are considered as being very crude. The federal experiment station, by the way, was unable to isolate the acid, the reason being, probably, that other work prevented the experiment ever being made.

Hawaii does not take any credit for the method by which the Chaulmoogric acid was isolated. The formula had been published in full in London, and no formula was worked out by anyone in the territory.

The small quantity of Chaulmoogric acid obtained at the college was turned over to Dr. Hollmann, and, although it was of unusual interest, he, nor anyone else, knew of any method by which it would be administered to a person suffering from leprosy. A little later Dr. Hollmann explained what really had been in his mind for some time. He said he was strongly of the belief that the experiments had not been carried far enough, and that there was still something well worth following up. In his opinion, the oil was not in a suitable physical condition to be injected properly, as it was too thick and heavy and caused irritation at the point of injection. His theory was that the oil, or something from it, should be injected intravenously, or directly into the blood stream, which was something that could not be done with the oil in its original state, owing to its thickness.

Again, it was felt that an injection of the bulk oil would not accomplish the required results, and Dr. Hollmann desired to have taken from the oil, if possible, the active agent; in other words, that fraction of the oil which actually was beneficial in the treatment of leprosy. Briefly, it was desired that the curative principle believed to be present in the oil should be isolated, or at least concentrated into smaller bulk, and that some form of the oil better adapted to subcutaneous injections be found. Dr. Hollmann believed firmly that the Chaulmoogric acid was the fraction he was looking for; but when he obtained it finally, there was no method known to him by which he could make use of it.

Dr. Dean and Miss Ball were then faced with the following problems: First, to obtain something which could be injected properly, and, second, to isolate the active agent in the oil. Dr. Hollmann had worked out no formulas for either problem, and left the matter in the hands of the college.

The first suggestion by Dr. Dean was that the acids be converted into soaps, which are soluble in water, and that these be injected. But Dr. Hollmann said that he did not desire to do this as it would cause

haemolysis, or rupture of the red blood corpuscles. This suggestion, therefore, was never carried out, but it is interesting to note that at that time,
although it was not known in Hawaii, Sir Leonard Rogers was working
upon precisely the same experiment in India at the School of Tropical
Medicine, Calcutta. Although this method has since been abandoned
to a considerable extent, some promising results were obtained. It is still
used in India today to a certain extent.

Dr. Dean and Miss Ball then set about to obtain a thinner liquid.
The former hit upon the idea of converting the fatty acids of Chaulmoogra oil into their ethyl esters. It was found that this could be done,
the resultant product being a fluid a little thicker than kerosene, and
easy to inject into the human patient. It was found out later that other
scientists had produced the ethyl esters, although this was not known
in Hawaii at the time they were obtained at the college. However, Dr.
Dean and Miss Ball had succeeded in obtaining a thinner oil, and they
felt that that particular problem had been solved, in part at least.

The next step was to isolate the active principle in Chaulmoogra
oil from the whole. It was decided to proceed in this way: Take the
mixed fatty acids and fraction them into four fractions. Then convert
each fraction into the corresponding ethyl esters, which would give liquids. Then experiment with each of the four fractions and determine
which produced the best results in the treatment of leprosy. This was
done, and in strict accordance with Dr. Dean's idea of attacking the second half of Dr. Hollmann's problem.

The four fractions were:

A. Ethyl ester of Chaulmoogric acid.

B. Ethyl esters of acids crystalizing from alcohol with
    Chaulmoogric acid in the initial separation.

C. Ethyl esters of acids soluble in 92 per cent alcohol in first
    separation and which form ether soluble lead salts.

D. Ethyl esters of acids forming lead salts insoluble in ether.


In the fall of 1915 small quantities of each of the four fractions
were obtained at the college and turned over to Drs. Currie and Holl-

man at the leprosy investigation station, where they were tried out. Interesting results, and little else, were reported, and the station asked for more of the liquids.

Miss Ball, in the spring of 1916, was compelled to return to Seattle because of her health, her physician believing that she had tuberculosis. That same fall she returned to Honolulu, but remained only a few weeks and then went back to Seattle, where she died shortly after. On December 21, 1916, Dr. Dean wrote a letter to Dr. Hollmann in which he enclosed a brief statement of Miss Ball's work in connection with Chaulmoogra oil. This work was held to be of such great importance that it was decided to continue with it, and Dr. Dean carried on where he and Miss Ball had left off at the time of her departure.

It is interesting to note that good results were obtained from the use of each of the four fractions of the fatty acids of Chaulmoogra oil, although it was indicated that the first and the second might be better than the others, but with differences not very striking. At about this time Dr. Hollman left the investigation station, and Dr. J. T. McDonald took charge, becoming very enthusiastic over the experiments with the new Chaulmoogra oil derivatives.

Dr. Dean next arrived at the conclusion that the methods of separation then in use were not absolutely accurate; in other words, that pure compounds should be obtained to take the place of what were then known to be mixtures. In other words, his theory was that pure Chaulmoogric acid and pure Hydnocarpic acid should be obtained, and then converted into absolutely pure ethyl esters. Steps were taken to carry out this theory. It proved to be a difficult task, especially to produce the liquid in quantities, but in the end Dr. Dean was successful.

At about this time Dr. Richard Wrenshall, now professor of chemistry at the University of Hawaii, arrived at the college to join the faculty, and he worked with Dr. Dean on methods for producing the liquids in large quantities, for obtaining pure acids, for converting them into ethyl esters, and in testing out the latter on groups of patients at the leprosy investigation station. After Dr. McDonald took charge of the station, Dr. Dean had considerable to do with planning the treatment of the patients, and helping to plan experiments with patients, and his relations with Dr. McDonald became very cordial.

The treatment of patients with the four fractions has proved that the acids are effective in cases of leprosy, and that the acids, when suitable for injection, produce the same beneficial effects that are obtained from the mixed esters, and that the curative property resides in the acids of this type. It is not held that there are no other acids which will accomplish the same results, but it is held that these are the only acids which it has been proved will do it.

For practical purposes, the mixed esters, either with or without combined iodine, are used, as these are cheaper to prepare and do the same work as the pure esters of the pure acids will do. Today university executives and those in charge of the investigation station are striving to obtain something which is even more effective, and which will work more rapidly; something which will increase the action of Chaulmoogric acids and make them more poisonous to the bacteria of leprosy.

In a report to the Territorial Legislature of 1919, Dr. Dean said, in part:

> "It is believed that further investigations will result in making products which will prove still more effective, and it may not be too much to hope that treatments may be developed through the cooperation of the Kalihi station and the college which will arrest the disease in a large proportion of the cases taken in their early stages."

And now Dr. Dean's forecast has, in many instances, come true, for many patients at Kalihi hospital have not only been paroled after an examination showing that the disease has been arrested, but have later been discharged as being entirely free of the disease.

The leper settlement on Molokai, and the Kalihi investigation and receiving station at Honolulu, are under the jurisdiction of the Territorial Board of Health.

Kalihi Hospital at Honolulu is maintained solely as a receiving station for lepers, and all patients there are given the regular treatment. Nowadays when a person is found to have leprosy he places himself voluntarily in the custody of the Board of Health and is admitted to the Kalihi Hospital, where treatment begins immediately. This voluntary submission is of extreme importance, for scientists and others who have made an exhaustive study of leprosy in recent years declare that the disease can be arrested, and probably permanently, if treatment is begun while it is in its earliest stages.

When treatment is begun in the early stages of the disease, the patient, provided he responds normally, is subject to parole within about eighteen months, the disease having been arrested sufficiently to permit him to have his freedom without being a menace to those with whom he comes in contact. After parole, however, the Board of Health does not relax its surveillance over him. One of the conditions of his parole is that he report regularly for treatment to the designated government physician or other agency, and this treatment after parole continues for a period of about three years. When the three years have expired, the paroler is eligible to go before an examining board which determines whether the disease has been arrested sufficiently to permit him to be declared not a leper.

If he is held to be not a leper, he is given a full release. In a number of instances there have been recurrences of the disease in parolers, and they have been returned to the receiving station for continued treatment. Patients at Kalihi Hospital who are held finally to be incurable are sent to the leper settlement at Molokai. When this action is necessary, the patient submits willingly, sensing, apparently, the fact that the government will do everything within its power to make him happy and comfortable during the remainder of his lifetime.

The following statistics, taken from the official records of the Board of Health, are interesting in that they indicate the rise and fall of the disease, and the disposition of lepers, in the Territory of Hawaii from 1912 and 1913 until the present:

## Kalaupapa Settlement

Period, October 3, 1913, to October 25, 1922. Patients treated by Dr. James T. Wayson, now chief sanitarian of the Board of Health; Dr. McCoy, Dr. Currie, Dr. Hollmann, and Dr. W. J. Goodhue, medical superintendent at the settlement:

Released on parole—Male, 49; female, 29; total, 78.

Reexamined after parole, declared to still be lepers, and returned to the settlement—Male, 10; female, 4; total, 14.

Reexamined after parole, declared to be non-lepers, and granted full discharges—Male, 13; female, 8; total, 21.

Of the whole number paroled, four men and five women, a total of nine, died.

## Kalihi Hospital

Period, February 13, 1912, to September 14, 1918, or prior to the introduction of the new Chaulmoogra oil specific:

Released on parole—Male, 25; female, 15; total, 40.

Reexamined after parole, declared to still be lepers, and returned to the hospital—Male, 4; female, 3; total, 7.

Reexamined after parole, declared to be non-lepers, and granted full discharges—Male, 13; female, 8; total, 21.

Period, December 24, 1918, to May 7, 1924, or after the perfecting of the new Chaulmoogra oil specific:

Released on parole—Male, 141; female, 118; total, 259.

Reexamined after parole, declared to still be lepers, and returned to the hospital-Male, 26; female, 21; total, 47.

Reexamined after parole, declared to be non-lepers, and granted full discharges—Male, 14; female, 14; total, 28.

Of the whole number paroled in this period, 13 patients, 8 men and 5 women, died.

PATIENTS SENT TO MOLOKAI

1920 . . . . . . . . . . . . . . . . . . . None
1921 . . . . . . . . . . . . . . . . . . None
1922 . . . . . . . . . . . . . . . . . . None
1923 . . . . . . . . . . . . . . . . . . 92
1924 (to May 7) . . . . . . . . . . . . . 49

The sending of large numbers of lepers to Molokai from Kalihi Hospital during 1923 and the early part of 1924 was due to the fact that the latter institution was "clearing house," as it were. These were old cases which had been under treatment for some years at the receiving station, which failed to respond to the treatment, and which were declared finally to be incurable. However, these were the first patients to be sent to the settlement in many years, and form one indication that the method of treatment which prevails in the territory today is accomplishing worthwhile results.

Within the last several years there has developed almost a worldwide demand for the new Chaulmoogra oil specific as produced in Hawaii, and the Board of Health has received letters from many countries requesting supplies or information regarding the formula. Insofar as it has been able, the Board has complied with this request, furnishing the specific free of charge. But it is at present being produced only in limited quantities in the islands and for that reason there is little more than enough for local use.

Sensing the apparent great value of this specific, the Territorial Board of Agriculture and Forestry has planted a large area of land to the trees which bear the seeds from which Chaulmoogra oil is expressed, and within a few years the territory will have a vast Chaulmoogra-oil-producing plantation.

Medical and other scientists in Hawaii, in handling the treatment of leprosy, have performed one other noteworthy public service: They have been instrumental in ridding the community—and Hawaii's population is highly cosmopolitan—of that inherent fear of leprosy which existed up until only a few years ago.

# Kalaupapa Today (1931)

Kalaupapa, the main leper settlement on the Molokai peninsula, is today a thriving village of more than 500 inhabitants, and all traces of the early days, when the Hawaiian government was striving to curb the disease to the best of its limited resources, have disappeared.

Good government, aided by science, has wrought wonderful changes there, and a more happy and contented people will probably not be found any. where else in the United States. They used to call Molokai the "Lonely Island" simply because it was associated always with leprosy. But it is called that no longer, for no resident of Kalaupapa is unhappy, and certainly none is lonely.

The leper settlement, as a political subdivision, is known as the county of Kalawao, and is a part of the county of Maui, one of the larger islands of the group. There is equal suffrage there, all men and women who are citizens and qualified as to age voting in all territorial and county elections; and some warm political battles are waged on that tiny peninsula. Candidates for office may, provided they obtain authorization from the Board of Health, visit the settlement and deliver campaign speeches. The late Prince Jonah Kuhio Kalanianaole, for 20 years Hawaii's delegate to Congress, visited the settlement regularly every two years. And there is nothing a Hawaiian enjoys better than hearing a political speech, unless, perhaps, it is making one himself.

For many years Kalaupapa has been laid out into streets, and these are today bordered by scores of pretty, comfortable cottages in which the lepers live. Many of these cottages are surrounded by walls fashioned from lava stone, and within them are a myriad fruit trees and shrubs bearing gorgeous blossoms the year around, for the Hawaiian has always been an ardent lover of flowers. There are well-kept gardens, and many of the patients own their own horses, cattle and hogs, to say nothing of poultry in great numbers.

A glimpse into any one of these cottages indicates the comfort in which the occupants live. They have all sorts of musical instruments, books without number, excellent furniture, modern stoves, player pianos and phonographs, and there are a few radio outfits. New records for pianos and phonographs are obtained regularly from Honolulu. Many of the patients discarded the old-fashioned cookstoves years ago, and are now using modern ranges which burn oil.

The territorial government, through the Board of Health, has done everything within its power to provide for the comfort and accommodation of these people, and the Legislature appropriates thousands of dollars every two years for the maintenance of the settlement. The patients expressed their appreciation of this attention when, during the World War, they invested in countless Liberty Bonds and war savings stamps. Naturally none of the patients saw any active service.

Kalaupapa from one end to the other is lighted by electricity. There is also an ice plant, several stores maintained by the government, a butcher shop, a storehouse for the distribution of poi, the staple food of the Hawaiians made from the root of the taro plant; machine shops, carpenter shops, and a battery-charging station.

It is interesting to note that more than a score of automobiles of a popular, inexpensive make are owned by the patients. Several of these are in use as taxicabs, and are patronized to a great extent by the patients at the boys' home at Kalawao. During the past year or so, several new automobiles have been shipped to the settlement every month.

Members of the legislature, who gather at Honolulu every two years for a 60-day session, always visit the Kalaupapa settlement, as well as the boys' home at Kalawao, during this period. This visit is always looked forward to by the patients, for it means new faces, in some instances the renewal of acquaintances, and, always, plenty of speeches. And the patients retaliate with some of the finest instrumental and vocal music to be heard anywhere, for they are marvelous musicians.

The center of attraction at the settlement is the Amusement Hall, a very large building near the seashore. Here entertainments of all sorts are held, dances are given, and motion pictures exhibited regularly. The hall is quipped with billiard tables and also with a complete radio outfit which is operated skillfully by one of the patients. This outfit is able on certain occasions to pick up pro grams broadcast from stations on the Mainland. Programs are broadcast nightly from Honolulu. The first motion pictures were exhibited at the settlement many years ago by the late R. K. Bonine, at one time Honolulu's leading photographer and, previously, connected with the Pathe company.

Mail is received at the settlement several times a week. Some of it comes direct by steamer to Kalaupapa, and the rest is brought by a mailman who rides down the narrow trail along the face of the 2,000-foot cliff at the back of the settlement. Time was when this trail was guarded constantly to prevent the escape of patients. This custom was discontinued years ago, and since then there has never been an attempt by a patient to leave the settlement. The trail has been widened and paved with stone, and fences have been erected at some of the more dangerous curves.

Apart from the comfortable cottages of the patients, there are three separate homes at the settlement: The McVeigh Home, the Bay View Home, and the Bishop Home for Girls. The latter institution is managed by four Catholic sisters, who are devoting their lives to the care of their young charges. The Bishop Home, as well as the other homes, are splendidly equipped institutions where nothing is lacking for the comfort of the patients.

The Catholic Mission at Honolulu, established not long after the arrival of the first New England missionaries in Hawaii in 1820, cannot be praised too highly for the work that it has done, and is now doing, on behalf of the lepers. It was the Catholic Church which took the initiative when the call went forth, after the establishment of the settlement, for "clean" people to work among those afflicted with the dread disease. It was the Catholic Church which sent the famous Father Damien to

Molokai, and the same faith impelled Brother Dutton to go there to spend the remainder of his life. There is no question that Catholic workers will outnumber all others until such time as leprosy is eliminated completely in Hawaii, and the settlement closed. Catholicism is at its high tide in the territory today, and its influence has always been for the good. The Catholic schools are among the finest in the Islands.

At Kalaupapa the casual visitor sees but little of actual leprosy. The reason for this is that the patients never come into close contact with visitors; not that they are forbidden to do this, but because they do not care to have the visitor "take any chances," to use a common expression. For leprosy is a strange disease. Scientists know little or nothing about it; they do not know what causes it, how it spreads, or how it is transmitted from a patient to a "clean" person.

For example, a patient at Kalaupapa would not think of shaking hands with a visitor. He would not knowingly touch or handle anything which he knew might later be handled by a "clean" person. After a visitor has gone through the settlement, and especially if he has made the rounds of the hospitals, he is taken to the home of the superintendent, where he is asked to wash his hands with a liquid soap containing a high percentage of carbolic acid. This is the only precaution taken. There is no case of record where a visitor to the settlement has afterward contracted leprosy.

The hospitals at Kalaupapa are interesting. They are big, clean, airy buildings in which patients needing hospital attention have rooms to themselves, equipped with large, comfortable beds and all other modern conveniences. They are especially excellent from a sanitary standpoint, and at regular intervals are scoured and scrubbed from top to bottom. Each hospital has its staff of nurses, kitchens, storerooms and laundries. Many Hawaiians who are not lepers are employed here. Only the worst cases of leprosy—especially those in which the disease has affected the eyes—are cared for in these institutions. Of course, all patients needing attention other than for leprosy are given hospital accommodations if they need it.

Another interesting feature at Kalaupapa is the "kokua" or "helper" system. For instance, if a married man goes to Molokai as a leper, his wife, although she be a non-leper, may go there also to live with and help him. The same applies to a married woman who is a leper. This system no doubt has done a great deal to preserve morale and general order at the settlement. If a "kokua," or helper works for the government besides attending to home duties, he or she receives pay from the government. No one is asked to do anything for nothing. All lepers who work in and around the settlement receive so much pay per day. The government stores sell all varieties of provisions and equipment at cost price.

The government of the leper settlement is simple, and there is seldom any interference by the territorial government at Honolulu. There is a regularly appointed district magistrate and sheriff. The former hears and determines all cases brought before him by the sheriff, the superintendent or other persons in the settlement. But there are few cases for trial; now and then a matter of gambling, or a domestic difficulty. Kalaupapa has a jail, and the record sentence thus far is said to have been six months. All cases of divorce on the ground of one of the two parties having leprosy are handled through the office of the Attorney General at Honolulu.

Many babies are born at the leper settlement every year, and the territorial government provides funds for their care and maintenance until they become of age. Another peculiar thing about leprosy is that a child born of leprous parents is in 99 cases out of a hundred, free from the disease. Since the establishment of the settlement there have been but few cases in which children of leprous parents have later on contracted the disease.

As soon as a baby is born at Kalaupapa, it is taken from the mother and placed in a special hospital devoted solely to the care of infants, and staffed by a corps of trained nurses. Here the little ones remain, under close observation, for a year. If, at the end of twelve months, the baby is normal physically, and shows no symptoms of leprosy, it is sent to the proper institution at Honolulu. At Honolulu the government maintains two separate institutions, one for boys and the other for girls, in the Kalihi district. When they reach the proper age, the children are sent to school and otherwise cared for until they complete their minority, when they are free to go where they will.

In the latter-day history of Kalaupapa settlement, two men stand out prominently as having established praiseworthy records in the service of the lepers. One is the late John D. ("Jack") McVeigh, who was superintendent of the settlement for nearly a quarter of a century. The other is Dr. William J. Goodhue, who was medical director for more than a score of years.

McVeigh, who was known from one end of the territory to the other, was an interesting personage with an interesting history. He had been dubbed the "Uncrowned King of Molokai," and this, in a way, was true, because his authority in the settlement was supreme, and he was seldom if ever disobeyed. Yet he was one of the kindliest of men, young no longer but surprisingly active and alert. The patients at Kalaupapa loved him and, to them, his word was the law.

At one time a "bucko" mate on sailing vessels plying between Australia and Hawaii, McVeigh, in his youth, learned to use his fists, and use them well. Quitting the sea, he entered the employ of the Board of Health at Honolulu and then later went to Kalaupapa as superintendent, where he has been ever since.

Days were rather wild in the settlement a quarter of a century ago, and McVeigh, during the first year or so, had his hands full. In the first place, he was a white man, which did not gain him a great deal with the patients. Several attempts were made to take his life, but on each occasion he outguessed the conspirators and then punished them—with his bare fists. When it was seen that he meant business, and that he had nothing but kind feelings toward the patients, and desired to give them all a square deal, this sentiment against him was gradually abated. The result has been that there hasn't been a bit of trouble worth mentioning at the settlement for years.

McVeigh was responsible for practically all of the modern improvements at Kalaupapa. Working hand in hand with McVeigh was Dr. Goodhue, with a splendid record of service behind him. With more than 500 patients to attend to, he set an example of loyalty and fidelity that is probably without equal in Hawaii, and was beloved by all of his patients.

Another man who has worked steadily for the betterment of conditions not only at Kalaupapa and Kalawao, but at the Kalihi receiving hospital, is Dr. Frederick E. Trotter, president of the Board of Health for several years. Dr. Trotter was surgeon and chief quarantine officer of the United States Public Health Service at Honolulu when he was offered the presidency of the board during the administration of the late former Governor Charles J. McCarthy. The chief of the U. S. P. H. S. protested vigorously against Dr. Trotter resigning from the service; and finally offered him an indefinite leave of absence in order that he might connect up with the territorial government. It was not until recently that Dr. Trotter insisted that his resignation from the U. S. P. H. S. be accepted.

Dr. H. E. Hasseltine, former superintendent of the Kalihi receiving hospital, is another whose work in connection with lepers and leprosy is praiseworthy. He experimented exhaustively with the new Chaulmoogra oil specific for the treatment of leprosy, and the records of paroles and discharges show that very good results have been obtained.

SERVANT OF GOD
# JOSEPH DUTTON
HIS LIFE * HIS SERVICE * HIS LEGACY

# Kalaupapa Today (2023)

*St. Philomena Church 2018 as seen from the site of the Baldwin Home*

*Brother Dutton Grave at St. Philomena*

*View from Kalawo at the former site of the Baldwin Home*

*St. Damien Grave at St. Philomena,*
*with the site of the Baldwin Home in the background*

*St. Marianne's grave at Kalaupapa*

*St. Marianne Cope statue at Honolulu Park*

*Detail of plaque at St. Marianne statue*

SAINT MARIANNE COPE, OSF

January 23, 1838 – August 9, 1918

| | |
|---|---|
| 1883 – 1888 | KAKA'AKO BRANCH HOSPITAL, O'AHU |
| 1888 – 1918 | KALAUPAPA, MOLOKA'I |
| MAY 14, 2005 | BEATIFIED IN ROME, ITALY |
| JANUARY 23, 2010 | STATUE DEDICATED |
| OCTOBER 21, 2012 | CANONIZED IN ROME, ITALY |

MOTHER MARIANNE COPE AND SIX SISTERS OF ST. FRANCIS OF SYRACUSE, NEW YORK, RESPONDED TO KING DAVID KALĀKAUA'S PLEA TO CARE FOR HAWAI'I'S PEOPLE AFFLICTED WITH LEPROSY (HANSEN'S DISEASE).

UPON ARRIVAL IN HAWAI'I IN 1883, HER FIRST TASK WAS OVERSEEING THE KAKA'AKO BRANCH HOSPITAL, A RECEIVING STATION FOR PEOPLE SUSPECTED OF HAVING HANSEN'S DISEASE. MOTHER MARIANNE IMMEDIATELY SET TO WORK ON MAKING THE DIRTY, OVERCROWDED HOSPITAL MORE LIVABLE. IN 1888, SHE WENT TO KALAUPAPA, WHERE MEN, WOMEN AND CHILDREN WERE EXILED. SHE BROUGHT HOPE, JOY AND DIGNITY TO THESE OUTCASTS.

IN ALL THE YEARS OF CLOSE CONTACT WITH PATIENTS, MOTHER MARIANNE AND THE SISTERS MIRACULOUSLY NEVER CONTRACTED THE DISEASE. THIS STATUE, ERECTED IN HER HONOR, SERVES AS AN INSPIRATION TO NEVER GIVE UP CARING FOR THOSE WHOM SOCIETY HAS ABANDONED.

WWW.SOSF.ORG

*Memorial Plaque*
*at the entrance to Blessed Sacrament Catholic Church*

# *Blessed Sacrament Church*
## STOWE, VERMONT

Young Ira B. Dutton lived his childhood in two places where he continues to be remembered and honored: Vermont and Wisconsin. These chapters of the book describe how Blessed Sacrament Church (BSC) in Stowe, VT and St. Jude Church in Beloit, WI came to honor the Servant of God Joseph Dutton.

At his birthplace in Stowe, VT, the Knights of Columbus were instrumental in having the church dedicated to Brother Joseph Dutton when it was built in 1949. The church stands on farmland where he was born to Ezra Dutton and Abigail Barnes Dutton.

The history of the church and the artwork by French artist, Andre Girard preserves the legacy of Brother Dutton, linking Stowe and Molokai. This chapter includes

- Pastoral Letter from Rev. Jon Schnobrich, Pastor
- Blessed Sacrament Church history and content from the book, *Painting on Light,* used with permission of Reverend Jon Schnobrich, Pastor of Blessed Sacrament Church.
- Murals showing Dutton, Damien, Marianne on Molokai
- Celebrations of Brother Dutton's 179th and 180th birthdays

## *The life of Servant of God Joseph Dutton has Enriched Blessed Sacrament Church*

### REVEREND JON SCHNOBRICH, PASTOR, 2020 TO PRESENT

It is considered a gift and privilege to encounter someone whose life so powerfully embodies the Gospel principles taught by our Lord. Jesus is the way, the truth and the life, which means that to follow in his footsteps one must strive to live as He lived. When Jesus began his 3-year public ministry, he was poor but was provided for; he was homeless, yet always was given shelter. He lived close with the people of his day, and His great love for them in their need moved him to the generous outpouring of love that we celebrate at every Mass—his self-sacrifice on the cross of Calvary.

When Joseph Dutton responded to the movement of grace in his soul to leave everything and dedicate his life to serving the lepers on Molokai, he was responding to the desire of God who sanctifies, that is, makes holy. This holiness, that manifested in his tireless care and selfless hospitality for the community of lepers in Kalawao, was a holiness that literally made visible the teaching of Jesus from Matthew's Gospel through Dutton's way of life ("Whatever you did for one these, the least of my people, you did it for me.").

The parishioners of Blessed Sacrament in Stowe have received this great inheritance of coming to worship God in a Church built on the very grounds where back in the early 1840s, Ira Dutton was born, and played as a toddler before his family moved to Wisconsin. Blessed Sacrament Church in Stowe marks the beginning of Dutton's earthly story. With such unique art and now, with his cause for canonization open, the parish has the gift and privilege of spreading the story of God's grace that moved Servant of God Jospeh Dutton to give everything for the Kingdom of Heaven.

With gratitude for our vacationing visitors, we extend Dutton-esque hospitality in welcoming them to pray and worship with us. Always with an eye towards serving those in need, the parishioners live out the spirituality of Dutton by serving each other and those in our community and beyond.

Wherever there are people in need, we remember the inspiring and challenging words of Servant of God Joseph Dutton:

> *"I wish to guard you against having too high*
> *an estimate of the work here.*
>
> *Work performed with good intention*
> *to accomplish the Will of Almighty God,*
> *is the same in one place as another.*
>
> *One's Molokai can be anywhere."*

~ Servant of God Joseph Dutton

## A History of
## Blessed Sacrament Catholic Church
(EXCERPT FROM *PAINTING ON LIGHT*)

STOWE, VERMONT 1949

B lessed Sacrament Church has a unique and extraordinary history. Its humble beginnings started with a small congregation which gathered on Sundays in the basement of the Town Hall of Stowe to attend Mass, because they did not have a church building of their own. In 1947 when Bishop Ryan assigned Rev. Francis E. McDonough to be Pastor of The Holy Cross Church in Morrisville, he also asked him to be Pastor of the Stowe Parish and to eventually build a church for their small congregation.

Much earlier the Knights of Columbus had planned to build a church in Stowe that was to honor the memory of Brother Joseph

Dutton. The 19th Century Stowe native was remembered and admired for his work with Father Damien (who is now St. Damien), in caring for the lepers on the island of Molokai. Although the new church was to be dedicated to The Blessed Sacrament, it was decided to fulfill the earlier plans of the Knights by having the church also serve as a memorial to Br. Joseph Dutton.

After several unsuccessful attempts to find a suitable property on which to build the church, Fr. McDonough thought he had found the perfect site. Although the property was not for sale, Fr. McDonough approached the owner about the possibility of selling a portion of his land as a location for a church. The owner, Mr. McCutcheon, said he might consider it, but would have to think about it. After several days, Fr. McDonough again spoke with the owner, and happened to mention that the church was to be built in the memory of Br. Joseph Dutton. Mr. McCutcheon's reply surprised Fr. McDonough. "Well," he said to the Pastor, "that's interesting. You know he was born in the house I live in and my grandmother was a younger sister of his grandmother."[1]

In Fr. McDonough's remembrances of the building of Blessed Sacrament Church, he expressed his own reaction to this astounding coincidence as follows: "Well, if the Angel Gabriel had appeared to me on the spot, and said this was the place to build a church, I couldn't have been more sure of it."[2]

It was with great enthusiasm that Fr. McDonough visited Maria von Trapp and her family to ask for their prayers for the success of his efforts to acquire the property. However, when the Pastor presented the offer to Bishop Ryan, the Bishop did not consider the property to be a suitable site. Feeling completely frustrated, Fr. McDonough reported the Bishop's response to Maria von Trapp, who offered to speak with the Bishop the very next morning. Mrs. von Trapp's powers of persuasion must have been considerable, because by the afternoon of that same day the Bishop had approved the purchase of the property, and directed Fr. McDonough to start building the church. On November 2, 1948 Fr. McDonough had the satisfaction of turning the first sod for the construction of Blessed Sacrament Church.

Since winter was approaching, construction on the church was immediately begun. The architectural firm of Wittier and Goodrich from Burlington, Vermont designed a rustic church suited to the needs of its small congregation and characterized by its simplicity and harmonious proportions. Local natural materials were used such as basic pine panels for the walls of the church, and green Vermont marble for the floors with the sanctuary space being done in red marble.

After receiving permission from Bishop Ryan, Fr. McDonough was finally able to say the first Mass for the congregation in their own church. The Trapp Family Singers returned from a tour in England to sing at this special Mass. Fr. McDonough described this day as "a glorious occasion".[3]

The church was officially dedicated with the title Blessed Sacrament Catholic Church on March 6, 1949 by His Excellency Most Rev. Edward F. Ryan, D.D., Bishop of Burlington. The feast of Corpus Christi, the official feast of the Blessed Sacrament, was celebrated by Bishop Ryan on June 16th. This was the official public dedication of the Church. In his remembrances Father McDonough describes it as, ". . . a beautiful day, the Trapps sang the *Missa Brevis* by Mozart. It was absolutely magnificent."[4]

Before making any specific plans for the decoration of the church, Fr. McDonough decided to consult with Maurice Lavanoux, who was a personal friend and the Editor of *Liturgical Arts Quarterly Magazine*. Father received more than the expert advice he had sought. Mr. Lavanoux spoke to him about the possibility of receiving a set of 14 paintings of the *Way of the Cross* which Mr. Otto Spaethe had commissioned to be donated to a new church. The 14 *Stations of the Cross* had been painted by the French liturgical artist, André Girard.

Several months later, Fr. McDonough was pleasantly surprised to receive a visit from not only Maurice Lavanoux, but Mr. and Mrs. Otto Spaethe and the artist, André Girard. They had all come to see if it was a suitable site for the commissioned paintings. Within a few days, Maurice Lavanoux was able to give Fr. McDonough the good news that the *Stations of the Cross* were to be donated to Blessed Sacrament Church.

He also reported that the artist, André Girard, had expressed the desire to decorate the entire church. Since the parish had very limited funds, Mr. Girard had said he would be willing to do the work if he would be provided the necessary art materials and lodging for himself and his family.

The fourteen paintings making up the *Way of the Cross* that André Girard had painted for Mr. and Mrs. Spaethe measured two feet square and were well suited in scale to the proportions of the church. However, Girard's interpretation of the suffering of Christ as He struggled on the way to Calvary was very moving. His dramatic use of color and light as well as the beauty of each painting created an impact that was far beyond their size. Girard, like Rembrandt, also effectively employed the chiaroscuro technique, which utilizes a darkened setting for a scene and bathes the main action with a glowing light. This creates an atmosphere of drama and mystery through which we are drawn into each scene to more completely understand what is taking place. As we follow each painting we begin to have a sense of experiencing the events of Christ's journey to His crucifixion and death. Nine of the original fourteen paintings are reproduced on the facing page.

The triptych André Girard created for Blessed Sacrament Church was highly personalized. It is presently located on the wall to the right of the altar. Traditionally, triptychs have three panels with the central panel having a formal image of Christ or he Madonna in a historic or ethereal setting. What makes Girard's triptych unique is that the central panel portrays Joseph, Mary, and the Infant Jesus in a Vermont setting with a recognizable image of Blessed Sacrament Church in the distance. It is referred to as *Our Lady of Stowe*. The panel to the left portrays a series of homey and informal scenes of the early life of Christ. Mary is first shown caring for the baby Christ, then walking with the growing child, teaching Him and also playing with Him. They are scenes that any contemporary mother and child can identify with. The right panel is more traditional, in that it depicts Christ's Public Life, Passion, and Death. Although the triptych is a small-scaled work, it encompasses the total life of Christ in a fresh, new, and engaging manner.

The Altarpiece depicting the Communion of Saints

Father Benedict Kiely Raising the
Chalice during the Consecration

One of André Girard's most important works in Blessed Sacrament Church is the large-scaled oil painting on stretched canvas that covers the wall behind the altar. This piece presents a significant and appropriate setting for the services that take place there, which include the consecration of the Blessed Sacrament at Mass. The focal point of the painting centers on the images of the Father, Son and the Holy Spirit, which provide a visual manifestation of the Triune God, and is a specific reminder of the Divine Presence in the church.

André Girard designed the altarpiece to express the concept of the

*The Annunciation*

*The Nativity*

*Jesus among the Doctors*

Communion of Saints, which in the Catholic Church signifies the union with God, the blessed in heaven and His people on earth. Therefore the painting encompasses the settings of the heavens and the earth. In the upper section the images of the angels, painted in tones of gold and bronze, become somewhat ethereal as they are bathed in a radiance of light emanating from the sacred figures. The painting has such an overall effect of light, that for those who choose to use it as an inspiration during Mass, the images can reinforce what is taking place. However, the painting is so slight in its definition that it would not be a distraction for those who choose not to focus on it. The lower portion of the painting represents the people on earth looking upward to the heavens.

The faces of angelic hosts are continued following a panel to the side of the altar and extending from there to the entire church, serving as a unifying element behind the *Stations of the Cross*, and giving them a sense of movement and connection. Looking upward at the ceiling, angelic faces again provide a subtle continuity to Girard's overall church decoration.

Although it was his paintings of *The Way of the Cross* that brought André Girard to Blessed Sacrament Church, it was upon seeing these small works in this empty rustic space that set Girard's creative mind soaring. He began to envision how he might decorate the entire church with his paintings, an opportunity given to very few artists.

Fr. McDonough remembers that when Girard first visited Blessed Sacrament Church, he kept looking at the windows and saying "C'est magnifique!"[5] The Pastor wondered why Girard considered these ordinary windows to be so special, but Girard's artistic mind was actually envisioning what a magnificent opportunity they would provide for his illustrations of the life of Christ in the innovative painting technique he had developed which he called "Painting on Light." Using this technique Girard would paint on the clear glass against the light of the sun passing through the windows. Juxtaposing translucent and opaque paint in multiple layers, Girard could create subtle as well as dramatic effects.

André Girard was artistically and emotionally inspired when he learned about the life of Br. Joseph Dutton. Instead of doing a singular static portrait of him as might have been expected, Girard decided to illustrate his story by painting twelve large-scale murals in black on the exterior walls of the church. The murals begin with his arrival in Molokai, and end with the salute to Br. Dutton by the American battleships sent to Molokai on the specific orders of President Theodore Roosevelt. A viewing of these murals is to witness Br. Dutton's life and dedication.

In 1974 Blessed Sacrament Church realized André Girard's paintings on the windows as well as the exterior murals were deteriorating due to the constant exposure to Vermont's extreme weather conditions. If left untended, they might be lost forever. Josephine Belloso, who had studied with Girard, was selected to do the restorations. During two summers, she restored the windows, the exterior murals, the doors, and the pediment.

Twenty years later, the exterior panels again needed restoration which was done by Wolfgang P. Kier.

*Brother Dutton Takes Over*
*Additional Responsibiities*

*The Distribution of Holy Communion*

*Father Damien in the Confessional*

In 2005 a major expansion of Blessed Sacrament Church was undertaken. A Parish Center was constructed, and a narthex or vestibule, was added to the entrance to the church. In addition to this, the expansion of the nave with a transept provided fifty percent more space for those attending services. In 2010 André Girard's artwork again required restoration. Matthew H. Strong, a local artist, restored Girard's paintings of the exterior murals, the doors, and the pediment.

Unfortunately, the paintings on the windows were so dried out, that they could no longer continue to be restored by repainting. However, Josephine Belloso recreated the paintings in collaboration with Sr. Jean Dominici, by digitally restoring photographs of the windows. These digital images were then printed on special vinyl and attached to a new set of windows. The replacement of Girard's original artwork was a tremendous loss, but the eventual deterioration of his extraordinary imagery would have been a tragedy. This digital process, introduced by Miss Belloso, en-

sured that André Girard's window illuminations would remain permanent images, and never have to be restored again.

It is extremely rare that a single artist has been given the opportunity to decorate an entire church. During Medieval times, churches were
decorated by hundreds of artisans over generations. Even Michelangelo
in the Renaissance did not decorate the entire Sistine Chapel. So André
Girard truly experienced a unique opportunity to develop and express
the spirited character of Blessed Sacrament Church through his art.

The artistry of André Girard is an integral part of the history of
Stowe, as well as of Blessed Sacrament Church. An internationally ac-
claimed artist, he gifted this small town and this small church with a
treasure of his creation. His artistic vision encompassed not only the
religious aspect of his subject matter, but was also sensitive to Stowe's
heritage in commemorating the life of a most important native son in
an exceptional manner.

He also respected the natural rustic aspect of the environment and
made use of the natural wood walls of the church as the background
for the Dutton murals. He incorporated the setting of Vermont for a
painting of the Holy Family, and embraced the natural daylight into
his window illuminations. Thus, Blessed Sacrament Church reflects an
important part of Stowe's history. It is a unique church that provides a
place of respite to reflect not only on the beauty of Girard's paintings,
but also on the lives that inspired them.

The congregation of Blessed Sacrament Church is comprised of

about 200 families,
but the church's dai-
ly attendance is in-
creased by the many
visitors who travel to
Stowe throughout the
year to enjoy its many
offerings.

*Matt seeks to reproduce
the original images*

# *Mural Restoration*
## Summers 2010–2014

*Matthew H. Strong restoring one of the murals*

In 2010, Blessed Sacrament Church needed to restore the twelve exterior murals which André Girard had painted, telling the story of Brother Dutton in Molokai. Due to the passage of time, exposure to the elements, and extremes in weather conditions, not only the paint needed to be restored, but the wood base for the murals required restoration as well.

Fortunately, Matthew H. Strong, a local artist, was selected for the commission. Matthew was well-qualified to meet the challenges of the work. He was a recognized artist and master carver, and therefore would be able to develop the best approach to restoring the paintings as well as the deteriorating wood on which they were done. Matthew Strong's first approach to the restoration was to sand around the painted areas, in order to try to preserve the original artwork by André Girard. However, after being informed that the murals had been completely stripped down to the wood by the second restorer in 1994, he decided to sand the panels down completely as well. In this way, he was able to remove the top layers of the deteriorated wood to the more solid pine underneath.

The surprising result was that when the paint was removed, the wood behind the paint was lighter than the darker weathered wood around it. Over the years, the paint had protected the wood underneath it. The value of this lighter image left on the wood was that it created a negative of the original mural that could provide a basic pattern for the restoration. I had also given Matthew photographs of the murals so these could also provide the necessary details that might have faded over the years of the murals' existence.

The final system that Matthew devised for the restoration he described as follows; "My first step was to sand each panel down to clean wood. I then applied clear exterior polyurethane and lightly sanded again. Patterns were then drawn following the negative images and the photographs, after which Black Sign Painter's Paint was used to re-create the original artwork. After several layers of polyurethane and urethane were applied and sanded, the restoration was completed."

This may seem easy to accomplish. However, one has only to compare the murals before and after the restoration to understand the skill, experience and attention to detail that was required to achieve such a successful result. Before the restoration, the murals were rather dark due to the deteriorated state of the wooden panels. By stripping down the wood to the more solid and lighter layers underneath, Matthew achieved a greater contrast to the black painted images, thus making the murals more impactful. The crisp lines of the recent restoration and re-discovered details also added much to the successful re-creation of the originals.

During the restoration of the murals, Matthew had a young helper. His daughter, Isabelle, donated her time and efforts the first year, and was so diligent and accurate in her work, that Blessed Sacrament hired her the second year. She was allowed to work on one of the murals following her father's drawings. Isabelle became so inspired by the selfless lives of Brother Dutton and Father Damien, that she used the money she earned to go to Central America with her high school the next summer to help the poor and disadvantaged.

André Girard's idea of painting the exterior of Blessed Sacrament Church with murals illustrating the life of Brother Dutton was a bold and inspiring concept. However, since the church was to be dedicated to the Stowe native, the murals seemed the perfect way to make visitors aware of Brother Dutton and the valuable contribution he had made in going to Molokai to help Father Damien in his mission of mercy. Without these extraordinary murals Brother Dutton's accomplishments would probably have been limited to a few words on a plaque which most visitors might overlook. Girard's murals are large and dramatic and draw one's immediate attention and interest.

The scenes Girard painted of Brother Dutton's life in Molokai are devoid of distracting color. Boldly painted in black against the raw wood, they are suited for the rustic tropical setting. The rich, lush vegetation of large leaves and overgrown vines also add a sense of beauty to each scene, despite the serious nature of the subject matter being represented.

André Girard cleverly draws us into each scene by providing a particular vantage point from which we view each event. In most instances, we view the scenes at a distance from behind tropical foliage. In other instances, we view the event inside an architectural setting; or we are brought closer to the scene as if we were standing directly behind the lepers. By changing our vantage point we literally become engaged in the viewing process as we follow in the lives of Brother Dutton, Father Damien and their congregation.

André Girard's narrative of Brother Dutton's life in Molokai is: dramatic in its presentation, expressive in its bold, primitive style; impactful and moving in its effect on the viewer; authentic and true to reality in the portrayal of the challenges Brother Dutton, Father Damien and their flock were facing. The result: once the murals have been experienced, and one has followed in the footsteps of Brother Dutton, the events become enduring images in our memory.

André Girard selected most of the scenes he would illustrate in the murals based on accounts described in *Damien the Leper* by John Farrow, published by Sheed and Ward in 1937. The quotes are under each panel.

*A—The Arrival of Brother Dutton in Molokai*

In this first mural, André Girard artistically engages us in following Brother Dutton as he begins his new life of service in Molokai. By enclosing the scene of his arrival with tropical vegetation, Girard creates the illusion we are witnessing the event by peering through an opening in the the foliage.

In this momentous encounter, Brother Dutton is portrayed as vigorously striding forward with eagerness to meet Father Damien, who is shown in a more reserved pose. By positioning both men as they clasp hands, Girard symbolizes their newly-formed alliance.

Upon closer inspection, we can observe greater details that enrich the experience of the event. Huge mountains are visible in the background as well as the sea surrounding the island. Girard also suggests what this moment might have signified for Brother Dutton by portraying the ship that brought him to Molokai as it sails away in the distance, leaving him to face new and unknown challenges.

*B—Father Damien Introduces Brother Dutton to the Lepers*

André Girard portrays this dramatic scene with little emotional reaction on the part of Brother Dutton as he views the lepers for the first time. The most expressive figures of the scene are the lepers whom Girard portrays eagerly leaning forward as they try to decide if Brother Dutton truly has come to help them. Father Damien initially must have been uneasy about the response of Brother Dutton and whether his resolve would weaken when he realistically confronted the challenges he was facing. The relieved expression on Father Damien's face demonstrates his realization that here at last was a kindred spirit willing to assist him in caring for his flock.

By placing the figures within a structural setting, André Girard gives the viewer the impression that they are within the enclosure as the scene is taking place. The tropical setting is established by having large openings on the walls revealing the sunlight as well as tropical foliage outdoors.

*C—Father Damien and Brother Dutton at Work among the Lepers*

André Girard in this mural illustrates one of the many tasks Br. Dutton had to fulfill since Father Damien's health was beginning to fail. The cleansing and changing of the wrappings for the lepers' wounds had to be accomplished on a regular basis as well as the completion of the many unfinished projects begun by Father Damien.

When Matthew was restoring this mural, he found it puzzling that Father Damien was missing from the scene even though the above quote from the book specifically mentioned him (see picture opposite). By referring to an earlier photograph of the mural, Matthew was able to re-create the original mural as Girard had painted it. We can now clearly decipher Father Damien standing behind Br. Dutton ready to provide assistance. A missing woman and a man were also re-created. Restoring these missing figures was an important accomplishment in preserving the integrity of Girard's work. Matthew was amused by this situation and liked to refer to this mural as illustrating, "The years that Father Damien and some of the lepers were lost in the jungle."

*D—Brother Dutton Assisting Father Damien at Mass*

Dutton was to take care of the two churches and to assist, although he doubted his worthiness, the priest at Mass. As the latter's hands were rapidly becoming too swollen to be of such use, it was also agreed that the newcomer would gradually assume the unpleasant duty of dressing and washing the sores of the lepers at the hospital . . . p. 181[30]

*Section of mural where Father Damien was missing*

*E—The Distribution of Holy Communion*

A major focus of Father Damien and Brother Dutton was to provide for the spiritual needs of their leper congregation. André Girard on this page creates a scene of Mass being conducted in the great outdoors by Father Damien assisted by Brother Dutton. The lepers are depicted kneeling on the ground in poses that suggest fervent attitudes as they pray and receive the Blessed Sacrament.

*F—Father Damien in the Confessional*

Another way in which Father Damien provided religious services was by hearing confessions. The section of the wall on which this mural was painted had an opening for the door of the church sacristy. This presented an arstic challenge, but André Girard cleverly solved the problem by making the door into a confessional, with Father Damien inside and Brother Dutton kneeling to make his confession as several lepers await their turns. The amusing aspect when I was doing the original mural restoration, was to see the figure of Father Damien suddenly swing out from the wall as the priest appeared to hop out behind him when he exited the church after Mass.

The scene also seemed to captivate visitors' attention, and sometimes children posed for photos going to confession with Father Damien. The door was sealed shut when the church building was renovated but it is still possible to discover the outline of the door as well as its hinges.

*G—The Burial of the Dead*

*I (Damien) have also buried a large number. The average of deaths is at least one a day. Many are so destitute that there is nothing to defray their burial expenses. They are simply wrapped in a blanket. As far as my duties allow me time, I make coffins myself for these poor people . . . p. 119.*[31]

In addition to attending to the spiritual needs of their community, Brother Dutton and Father Damien also had to attend to their physical needs. Food, lodging, and medical attention had to be provided on a daily basis. At the end of their life's journey, provision for their burial had to be made as well. André Girard in his portrayal of the burial scene shows Father Damien lowering a deceased leper into a coffin, as Brother Dutton and others kneel to pray.

*H—Anguished Lepers Witness the Loss of Supplies*

*Bad weather would occasionally cause a capsize and, of course, the loss of provisions. Many a time there was enacted the tragedy of starving lepers standing on the sea-beaten beach and watching with anguished eyes while their only hopes for food were engulfed by the angry waves. These were the conditions when the priest came to Molokai. He rapidly caused a change . . . p. 120.*[32]

This mural is particularly expressive because it depicts the disappointment of the lepers, when greatly needed provisions could not be delivered, and they realized the possibility of starvation. Girard portrays their skeletal figures in silhouette as they stand on the shore in attitudes of sheer frustration and anguish. In the distance they can see the boat that was to deliver the needed supplies getting farther away. Brother Dutton is seen rushing to the shore, while Father Damien follows quietly with his hands clasped in prayer.

*I—Brother Dutton Takes Over Additional Responsibilities*

*"There is so much left to do." A horizon of achievement continued to beckon him. A new chapel was planned and at the hospital a new building was commenced. In vain Dutton begged him to desist, to rest. His only answer was, "Off I am, Brother Joseph!" and although his pace was sometimes but a stagger off he would go . . . p. 186* [33]

In this third panel, Girard portrays Brother Dutton trying to complete the many plans and projects begun by Father Damien as well as trying to take care of the daily needs that required his attention. Some of the figures are shown surrounding Brother Dutton and waiting in line so he can assist them. Others are shown on their knees and reaching out to touch him to try to get his attention.

*J—The Burial of Father Damien*

*His grave was dug in the cool shadow of the pandanus tree and around it the long line of mourners shuffled in sad and grotesque parade, clad in the pitiful paraphernalia of the burying associations he had founded. Their friend "Kamiano" was dead but they did not want to accept the mournful fact that he had gone and even when the grave was filled they refused to go. They sat on the ground, beating their breasts, swaying their bodies with misery, after the custom of their ancestors . . . p. 199*[34]

In portraying the death of Father Damien, Girard describes one of the saddest days for the leper colony. Father Damien had been the first person ever to give the lepers hope. He had taken care of them and given them dignity. He had shown them how to cope with their illnesses, and how to prepare for death. He was always there for them, as their most caring friend.

Girard creates a solemn setting by using a dominance of the color black in this composition. The vantage point of the viewer is different in this mural when compared to the others. André Girard does not portray the event as seen from a distance, but rather brings the viewer up close, directly behind the rows of lepers quietly mourning the loss of their beloved priest. Brother Dutton is shown silently praying beside the casket, accompanying Father Damien to the very end.

In the distance, we encounter figures in attitudes of unbridled frustration, showing their anger that Father Damien had been taken from them. Thus Girard expresses the full range of emotions that were brought about by Father Damien's passing. This makes the panel more compelling and touching to the viewer as they reflect on what the loss of Father Damien must have meant to his beloved congregation.

The news of Father Damien's illness and death drew much attention to the selfless work he and Brother Dutton had been doing. In addition, it made known the tremendous need for assistance to be given in order to improve the difficult conditions that existed in the Colony. Fortunately, it also brought relief to Brother Dutton whose burdens had been ever increasing.

*K—Brother Dutton Receives Recognition and Assistance*
*Another priest came to minister to the spiritual wants of the Colony; Sisters came*
*to aid in the works but Dutton's work went on increasing. About this time Robert*
*Louis Stevenson, the well-known author, came to visit Molokai and was shown*
*about by Brother Dutton. Well-to-do business men in Honolulu, neither of whom*
*was a Catholic, donated money for a boys' home and a girls' home, respectively. And*
*when the United States Government took over the Islands, conditions improved*
*still more. (From booklet on Brother Dutton written by Father McDonough.)*[35]

In this mural, Girard commemorates the arrival of the first nuns who came to Molokai. Brother Dutton is shown greeting the Franciscan Sisters, who came to assist him and Father Damien in their work. One has only to look at Brother Dutton's eager stride, his tightly clasped hands and the blissful expression on his face to understand what the arrival of the Sisters must have meant to him. Behind Brother Dutton, a few lepers are depicted bent over with cane in hand, coming to welcome their new caregivers. The nuns, under the guidance of Mother Marianne, (now St. Marianne) cluster together for moral support as they embark on this overwhelming new venture.

*L—American Battleships Salute Brother Dutton*

As we complete our visual journey following Brother Dutton's life in Molokai, Girard presents us with a rendering of this historic moment which must have filled Brother Dutton's heart with pride and joy. Having served in the army and worked for the United States Government for many years, Dutton was very patriotic and proud of his American heritage.

André Girard depicts Brother Dutton and a few figures on the shore raising and saluting the American flag as was their daily custom. Suddenly they are transfixed by what they see in the distance—the silhouettes of the United States battleships precisely rendered, passing by in battle formation saluting Brother Dutton. The composition has a formal and ordered quality, suggesting a significant event is taking place. It illustrates an exceptional tribute by President Theodore Roosevelt and the United States Government for a man who had sacrificed his life in the service of others.

# The Twelve Murals
## Blessed Sacrament Church

## Murals on West Elevation

A — Brother Dutton Meets Father Damien in Molokai

B — Father Damien Introduces Brother Dutton to the Lepers

C — Father Damien & Brother Dutton Working among the Lepers

D — Brother Dutton Assisting Father Damien at Mass

E — The Distribution of Holy Communion

F — Father Damien in the Confessional

G — The Burial of the Dead

H — Anguished Lepers Witness the Loss of Supplies

 I — Brother Dutton Takes Over Additional Responsibilities

J — The Burial of Father Damien

K — Brother Dutton Receives Recognition and Assistance

L — American Battleships Salute Brother Dutton

## *Reflections*
### Matthew H. Strong

It was a crisp, clear morning in late summer when I put tools to the wood panels to start on my odyssey of restoring 12 murals on the Blessed Sacrament Church. I have spent months in research trying to get photos of the original paintings to no avail. The research on paints and varnishes had yielded what I thought would get the most durable final products. I had no idea how much the technique I had in mind would change by the end of the restoration, or how much more my own understanding and appreciation for the artwork and for the men in the story that the artwork was about, would change as well. As I worked on the peeling varnish, two women stopped to talk and asked about what I was doing. This turned out to be the providence of God as one of the women, Sr. Joy, said she had done some of the sanding of the murals herself, when her teacher had done a major restoration of the artwork at Blessed Sacrament in the early 1970s. Fortunately, Sr. Joy was able to get me in contact with her teacher, Josephine Belloso, who had studied under André Girard, himself.

Her knowledge and resources of photos were invaluable to me in bringing the paintings back as close as possible to their original form. The process of restoring the paintings ended up taking over 4 summers. The paint and varnish I used changed as I learned what did and did not work. To my surprise, I was told by a member of the Restoration Committee at Blessed Sacrament that a secondary restoration of the murals had taken place in 1994 and that the second restorer had chemically removed the original paint from the murals.

Therefore, my process went from trying to save what I thought was original paint to scraping down the whole panel and starting over with the image left on the wall from weathering and using photos from the past. Through my working on the restoration I gained an insight into what Girard intended to convey through the paintings. To most of us, the paintings are rather unusual and to some extent disturbing. This is as it was meant to be, for it portrays the sacrifice that Father Damien and Joseph Dutton made for the sake of those who suffered from leprosy. If one takes the time to look at the paintings and lets the story and the message come through, it is clear that the sacrifice is not glamorous, but the eternal glory brought about by that sacrifice outshines anything here on earth. I am truly richer in spirit from having had the honor and privilege of being part of the restoration of the artwork on the outside of the Blessed Sacrament Church here in Stowe, Vermont.

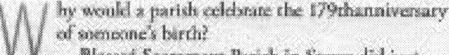

# Stowe parish celebrates birth of Stowe-born
# Servant of God Joseph Dutton

Why would a parish celebrate the 179th anniversary of someone's birth?

Blessed Sacrament Parish in Stowe did just that on April 24 to mark the Stowe birth of Ira Dutton — a Civil War veteran who joined St. Damian of Molokai in his ministry to lepers — who since the 178th anniversary of his birth was declared a Servant of God, the first step toward canonization.

Blessed Sacrament Church, built on land that was once the Dutton farm where Ira was born on April 27, 1843, is dedicated to him.

He entered the Catholic Church on his 40th birthday, taking the name Joseph after his patron, St. Joseph.

"We are proud to have the birthplace of this remarkable man from Lamoille County marked by one of our churches, and every year moving forward we will honor the work of grace that God accomplished in him, leading him to a life of penance and a life love and charity poured out in serving Christ in the poorest and most abandoned," commented Father Jon Schnobrich, pastor of Blessed Sacrament Parish and Most Holy Name of Jesus Parish in Morrisville.

Brother Dutton's birthday celebration — on Divine Mercy Sunday — included Mass, a tour of the exterior of the church that depicts his life on Molokai, Hawaiian music and dance, videos relating to his life and a Hawaiian-style luncheon. Many of the participants wore leis or floral hair clips.

"Our Servant of God Joseph Dutton's life bears a beautiful witness to the mercy of God," Father Schnobrich said in his homily. "That mercy accompanied him through war ... [and] alcoholism and opened the door to a life of mercy, seeing God in the ... most poor."

God's mercy transforms, heals and makes new, he added. Brother Dutton's life "inspires us with hope for those great and holy things God desires to accomplish though us," Father Schnobrich said.

He spoke of Brother Dutton as being ordinary, simple and uncomplicated: "How much our God loves the ordinary, the simple and the uncomplicated."

A portrait of Brother Dutton stood on one side of the altar and one of the Jesus's Divine Mercy on the other; colorful flowers between them were brought to the sanctuary by children at the beginning of the Mass.

Claudia Kanile'a Goddard of New York City sang a song, the lyrics of which were composed by the boys of the Kalawao Band, leprosy patients, in 1879 to express their love for St. Damien.

SUMMER 2021

*Brother Dutton's 179th Birthday Celebartion in Vermont Catholic magazine*

## Blessed Sacrament Parishioners
## Celebrates Joseph Dutton

The pastors at BSC have actively supported bringing Joseph Dutton's story to the world. The invitation by the 2018 DMCC to Monsignor Ruthier renewed the enthusiasm for Dutton and the understanding that BSC has an key role in the story of Servant of God Joseph Dutton's canonization.

Pastor Father Jon Schnobrich led the BSC Parish to celebrate Dutton's 179th birthday in April 2022. In spite of Covid-19, the Mass was well attended. Featured guests included musician Claudia Goddard and Patti Danko came with the Dancing Ladies of New York.

In 2023, the Parish ramped up for Dutton's 180th Birthday celebration. The Mass was celebrated by Bishop of Honolulu, Reverend Larry Silva and five priests. The Mass was joined by Zoom to people living in Rome, across the continental US and Hawaii.

The weekend activities included a Saturday brunch hosted by pastor, Fr. Jon. Parishioners led the visitors on a tour of the artworks that make BSC a special church. In 1949, French artist, Andre Girard, painted 36 windows with scenes from the Life of Christ. On the outside walls, Girard painted twelve large murals with scenes from the life of Joseph Dutton on Molokai.

Saturday evening, the Stowe cinema showed The Wind and the Reckoning, a movie about the impact on a Hawaiian Family diagnosed with leprosy, based on an 1893 true story. The screen play was written by John Fusco and directed by David Cunningham. They held a Q&A session after the viewing.

The Mass was the highlight of the weekend of celebration activities. Claudia Goddard performed the song, Hallalujia, in Hawaiian with the entire congregation singing the chorus. Children led a procession with flowers followed by five priests and the bishop. Bishop Silva's homily seamlessly connected gospel reading about the Road to Emmas with the Joseph Dutton's service on Molokai.

A Vermont Picnic was served to everyone by Charlie Shaffer and his staff at the Matterhorn that featured lobster rolls with all the trimmings.

Members of the Joseph Dutton Guild took advantage of being in Vermont to conduct business for the "cause", led by Monsignor Sarno and Roxanne Torres.

The Blessed Sacrament Parish is humbled to be a part of the Joseph Dutton Story. This book was created and funded by members with essential contributions of the Guild.

Joseph Dutton, pray for us.

180th Birthday Celebration for

Servant of God,
Joseph Dutton,
Layman

April 23, 2023

Blessed Sacrament Church

Stowe, Vermont

Later, at the luncheon, she accompanied members of "Gracious Ladies" of New York who performed authentic hula dances.

Blessed Sacrament parishioner Jim Brochhausen called the birthday celebration "quite amazing" and said it is "phenomenal" to have such a connect with Servant of God Dutton.

Another parishioner, Susi Clark, said, "We are so happy to celebrate Brother Joseph Dutton because now he has achieved the first level toward sainthood. And to have a lay person from Stowe [so recognized] is extraordinary."

Brother Dutton would be the third saint who cared for the lepers on Molokai: St. Damien de Veuster and St. Marianne Cope are the others.

According to one of the attendees at the Stowe celebration, Sister Cheryl Wint of the New York-based Sisters of St. Francis of the Neumann Communities, St. Marianne's order, "their sense of a penitential life and of community is part of our charism."

Brother Dutton was born in Stowe, but his family moved to Wisconsin in 1847. He served in the Civil War and married in 1866. But his wife left him a year later, and he began a period he later called the "degenerate decade," drinking heavily, something he later discontinued.

Brother Dutton was determined to do penance and atone for his "wild years," and after studying the Catholic faith, he decided that being Catholic would best enable him to lead a penitential life.

He learned about Father Damien and the Kalaupapa leprosy settlement in Hawaii and decided to go to there to help carry on the work of Father Damien, who had been diagnosed with leprosy, and soon became an expert in caring for the patients' medical needs.

Brother Dutton died in Hawaii in 1931.

Father Schnobrich said the celebration in honor of Brother Dutton was a "great way" to honor and celebrate Divine Mercy Sunday by honoring Brother Dutton who lived Divine Mercy and whose life testified to God's grace.

Celebrating a 179th birthday is "an odd birthday to go big on," he said, but the parish did so as a "way of honoring the new movement of raising up Brother Dutton" for canonization.

*VTC - Cori Fogere Urban*

THE DUTTON SCHOOL, BELOIT, WISCONSIN

*Brother Dutton School.*
*Beloit, Wisconsin*

# The Legacy of Brother Dutton School
## at St. Jude Parish
### BELOIT, WISCONSIN

## Editor comment

*Servant of God Joseph Dutton Layman has thousands of people who contin-
ue to remember his example of service they learned while attending Brother
Dutton School in Beloit, Wisconsin. The story written here was collected from
several newpaper stories and booklets sent to Blessed Sacrament Church by
Cathy Simplot, a graduate of the school. The school is a credit to an extraordinary priest, Reverend Joseph Hanz.*

*The following text is edited from the madisoncatholicherald.org, writ-
ten by Edward O'Brien. August 23, 2018. Mr. O'Brien was the principal at
the Brother Dutton School from 2007 to 2011.*

In 1903, Father Hanz came to Beloit to serve as the curate to Father
Mathias Brown at St. Thomas Parish. Fr. Hanz was a graduate of
Marquette University in Milwaukee. The Catholic population of Beloit
continued to grow and the need for a new Parish was determined.

In 1908, Father Hanz was appointed pastor of the newly organized St. Jude Parish. The St. Jude Church was dedicated on June 26,
1910, home to 125 families. Fr. Hanz continued to lead his parishioners
as the parish grew along with the west side of a growing Beloit. The
rectory building was added in 1911.

Father Hanz served the Knights of Columbus and was the state
chaplain 1915 to 1917. He was a gifted and effective speaker who was
often asked to present his views on faith, public service and patriotism
both locally and at statewide events. He became very concerned that
the United States would soon become involved in the Great War of the
European Nations.

In April 1917, the United States declared war on Germany due to her unrestricted submarine warfare and broken promises of peace. President Woodrow Wilson called for soldiers and sailors to enlist. Over three-million men answered the call. Father Hanz was very well known by state officials in Madison. Governor Phillip appointed Fr. Hanz the chaplain of the Wisconsin National Guard as a Captain. Captain Hanz also served on the Board for War Relief and the American Red Cross Chapter in Beloit. Father Hanz organized a Boy's Service Corps made up by young boys of St. Jude Parish to assist the families of men serving in France.

During the war, Father Hanz frequently gave his patriotic speech on "The Cross and the Flag." He was proud of the 90 young men from St. Jude Parish who were serving and the three young women who served as Army nurses. The Parish mourned the deaths of four men who died – two killed in combat and two who died of influenza during the epidemic of 1918. Father Hanz spoke of the example these four men gave to the Beloit community through their faith in God and devotion to their country. A granite plaque is attached to the church with the four names.

St. Jude Parish added many families during the 1920s. Under the leadership of Father Hanz, St. Jude Parish went on to build the first Catholic school in Beloit. The new school would be named for Brother Joseph Dutton, who left nearby Janesville to serve in the Civil War as captain in the Union Quartermaster Corps.

Joseph Dutton would later in life devote himself to the service of lepers in the Colony on Molokai in the Hawaiian Islands. Joseph Dutton was called "Brother Dutton" by Fr. Damien De Veuster, who later died of leprosy. Brother Dutton served from 1886 until he died in 1931.

Father Hanz held the conviction that "Education which embraces religion is the most vital thing anywhere." With his convictions on the social impact of religion, it follows that to impress the great lesson of religion, the love of neighbor, on the children in the new school, he chose to name the school after the greatest and most vital exponent of that law living at that time, the Hero of Rock County, Brother Dutton. As he often quoted the patriarch of Molokai: "Your Molokai is wherever you are. To perform your duties faithfully and bear yours patiently, constitutes your Molokai."

*Bishop Murphy, layng the cornerstone of Brother Dutton School*

Bishop Joseph Murphy of Belize laid the corner stone for Brother Dutton School on June 27, 1926. The school opened later that year with 135 pupils, instructed by seven Sisters of St. Agnes from Fond du Lac. The school soon built a fine reputation for quality educational programs, recognized by the state governor and clergy. For many years, the children of St. Jude Parish attended the Joseph Dutton School at no tuition cost. St. Jude Parish sponsored all expenses for the school's operation.

The Brother Dutton School graduated its first class of seven students from 9th grade in 1930. The entire school that year had 285 students. Their activities were beautifully chronicled in the first of a remarkable series of yearbooks entitled "Fraira."

In a word made famous by Father Hanz, "Fraira – it is a charmed term. To the school students, it stands for an ideal. And this ideal, it is the aim for the pupils to emulate. Fra means brother. Ira is the name of Captain Dutton, U.S.A. in the days of Lincoln and the Civil War. Fraira then is Brother Dutton, in whom one finds no finer type of hero. He belongs to the lepers of Molokai. He belongs to us – to the Rock – to Wisconsin – to America – to the world. He was a service man true to Cross and Flag – his, the only love worthwhile. Fraira then teaches well by holding up before us this ideal. May it spur us on to tread in his hallowed footsteps, the footprints, after all, of the Master."

By the late 1930s, the school enrollment reached 400 students. Classes were expanded to include a program for freshmen and sophomore high school subjects.

In response to the challenges of the depression, Fr. Hanz organized a variety of cultural activities for the students and the community: school-wide dramas, a Drum and Bugle Corps that marched in all the Beloit parades. Fr. Hanz also had a plan for a national memorial high school to be named for Brother Dutton, but it was never built.

Father Hanz was elevated to Monsignor in 1946. He was well known for his spiritual leadership, speaking abilities, patriotism and expectations of educational excellence for the students of Brother Dutton School. He composed a school song in 1935 called "Aloha Then" that the students sang at school events.

A total of 205 young men of St. Jude Parish served in WWII; thirteen of those brave men gave all in service to their country. Monsignor Hanz served St. Jude Parish for 47 years. He died October 8, 1950. He never forgot his priorities: his faith, his people and his love of his country. He was, himself, a model in the image of Joseph Dutton!

*The Brother Dutton School Drum and Bugle Corps marching in a
Memorial Day Parade in downtown Beloit during the 1940s.*

*April 23, 1943 – Field Mass in observance of the 100th anniversary of the
birth of Brother Dutton. On Memorial Day, Father Hanz, in the presence
of distinguished representatives of church and state, preached a great sermon
entitled: "Brother Dutton, Soldier of Cross and Colors." From booklet,
Called to Glory, St. Jude's Church Beloit, Wisconsin, 1908 – 1983.*

(FROM THE MADISON CATHOLIC HERALD)

# *A Final Tribute to Brother Dutton School*
## 06/23/2011

Saturday, June 4, 2011 was declared "Brother Dutton School Day
throughout the State of Wisconsin." The proclamation was signed by
Governor Scott Walker and also by Secretary of State Douglas LaFol-
lette.

Memories, traditions, and stories of the revered Catholic grade
school prevailed at the Brother Dutton School Homecoming and Re-
union event celebrating 85 years of quality education and service to St.
Jude Parish and the Beloit community. The school ceased operations at
the close of the academic year in June.

The school and all associated with it for the past 85 years were
honored during a special Mass, tours of classrooms, historical displays
and photographs, and social time with a casual dinner attended by more
than 500 people. Not only parish families and school students from the
past years, but also Beloit area community leaders and the general public
attended.

To launch the celebration, an overflow crowd of 450 attended the
Mass celebrated by St. Jude Pastor Fr. John Hedrick. Concelebrants were
Bishop John McNabb, Brother Dutton alumnus, and former pastor Fr.
Steve Kortendick, now pastor of St. Jerome Parish, Columbus, and St.
Patrick Parish, Doylestown. St. Jude Deacon James Davis preached the
homily. Bishop McNabb, O.S.A., was ordained as a member of the Au-
gustinian Order and long served the Church in Peru, South America,
until his retirement.

Deacon Davis shared a message of faith, encouragement, and support based on the day's Gospel, asking that each person share the light of

the Paschal candle, keeping faith alive and radiating all the love around us. "As Oprah said, use your life to serve the world," he said.

After Mass concluded, Brother Dutton Principal Ed O'Brien proudly presented the proclamation sent from the State of Wisconsin acknowledging Brother Dutton Grade School's faith and service to Beloit the past 85 years. Mentioned were the quality of the school's academics and the hundreds of students, the Sisters who once staffed the school, staff, teachers through the years, parents, and volunteers who unselfishly gave service.

Superintendent of Diocesan Schools Michael Lancaster brought greetings on behalf of Bishop Robert C. Morlino. He presented an official commendation to the school and students, noting that many vocations to the priesthood and religious life and one bishop were fostered at Brother Dutton, as well as an exemplary education given to all students. He also expressed appreciation for the priests, Sisters, staff, faculty, parents, and volunteers who have contributed to the school during its long history.

A well-organized tour through 12 classrooms allowed visitors to view school historical displays, artifacts, and memorabilia beginning with the years after World War I when the first St. Jude pastor Msgr. Joseph Hanz led planning for a parish school. Each Sister and priest who had attended Brother Dutton School was featured on a poster with pictures and information about their respective vocations.

Parishioner Clare J. Landry said the historical displays were made possible by the Exhibits Sub-Committee of the 2008 St. Jude Parish Centennial Celebration three years ago. At that time, Landry, chair of the sub-committee, documented the parish and school history from each year.

Landry said as he arranged and organized all the historical material, it became clearly evident that the school was a focal point for the parish. "Enrollment was in the hundreds, from early days to the present. Our students were a cross section of Beloit and the Stateline area. History shows that parents wanted a parochial Catholic education for their children," stated Landry. He said that Brother Dutton School was a very prominent educational facility from its early years on, especially in the 1940s, 1950s, to the 1970s when enrollment peaked. The school was well known and respected not only for its academic environment but also for its music, traditions, and involvement in the community. "There was a phenomenal staff of Sisters," he added.

"From what I kept reading as I arranged the exhibits, pastors called the school a focal point of the parish, the center of the parish. There were, all through the years, many outstanding athletic teams," stated Landry.

In the display about first pastor and school founder Msgr. Joseph Hanz, a 1946 quote pointed out that he felt the school was "the center of parish activity with an unusual force of unity."

Highlighting the yearly exhibits were pictures of teachers from the Sisters of St. Agnes who came to the school in 1929. Many visitors commented on the strict discipline demanded by the Sisters, "and we really learned," repeated many former students.

Prominent also was notable information about the school's name-sake, Brother Joseph Dutton, a "hero" to Father Hanz. It was pointed out that the school is a monument to Brother Dutton who gave courageous devotion and unselfish sacrifice to lepers on the island of Molokai. Joseph Dutton, pray for us.

A measure of success for the Brother Dutton School is the number of vocations
that the school produced. In the booklet, by Reverand Richard J. Lenarz,
"Call to Glory" the number of 'sisters' from St. Jude / Dutton school by
1983 was 23 plus 5 mentioned on p 40; total 28 Religious women.

In the 1983 "Call to Glory", the number of priests include three men who came to
celebrate their first Mass at St. Jude plus Bishop McNabb. Rev James Johnson was
the 1st in 1946. Later, three priest-sons of the parish celebrated the St. Jude 50th
Anniversary Mass – Fr. Johnson, Fr. McNabb and Fr. DeBock.
Fr. McNabb became Bishop McNabb and served in Peru.

Soon, three more priest-sons, Fr. Michael Trainor and Fr. Thomas Gillespie
and Fr. Monte Robinson celebrated their first Mass at St. Jude.
Conclusion – six priests from 1908 to 1983.
Thank you Servant of God Joseph Dutton.

*Dutton School — 8th Grade Graduation — 1962*

*From left to right*
*Back row, fourth: Linda Newton, Barb Scott, David Quick,*
*Tom Sauser, Willard Staron, David Kuehe, Cathy Eichman*
*(provided this photo), Donna Martin, Marianne Pody.*

*Third Row: Jean Hamill, Mary Mitchell, Sally Kohloff, Virginia*
*Belvedere, Geraldine Pea, Getrude Pocius, Vera and Joy Sperl,*
*Sharon Wragella, Kathy Dennison, Virginia Daily.*

*Second Row: Sister Gilbertine (principal of BDS in 1962), Jane*
*Hamill, Angela Brown, Barb Demos, Jean Behrman, Carol Gannon,*
*Karla Carroll, Mary Koehler, Veronica Meyers, Donna Torres.*

*Front Row: Patrick Monahan, Jim Hills, Jim Hudson, Gerald Kobus, Louis Kluck,*
*Wayne Katuin, Bernard Kielich, Tom Garstecki, Harold Raymont, Karl Perkins.*

*Not Pictured: Robin Brooks, Linnea Shufelt, David Kuntz.*

# *Wisconsin Epilogue*

Stephen Skelly of Janesville, Wisconsin is blessed with the discovery of a treasure trove of Brother Dutton documents that have been hidden away since 1982. Here is his story :

I have known about Joseph Dutton for most of my adult life. My daughters played basketball against Brother Dutton School in Beloit when they were in school at St. Mary's in Janesville.

In 2008 my daughter, Erin Skelly Olver, got the job as the Director of Religious Education (DRE) at St. Jude Church in Beloit, the home of Brother Dutton School. I started asking her if there were any Brother Dutton files at the now closed school. She told me she never saw any, but I kept bugging her about it for the next 14 years.

My cousin Pete told me he does a 45-minute presentation on Joseph Dutton's time in the Civil war as he had read everything he wrote while in the army. April 25, 2023 the Gazette in Janesville printed a story called "Hometown Brother" about Joseph Dutton with the help of my cousin Pete Skelly and me. On May 3rd, Pete called me telling me the Catholic Herald had posted their article on line. I thought my job helping Servant of God Joseph Dutton's path towards canonization was complete, but Brother Dutton had other plans for me.

This year the Madison Diocese assigned a new team of priests to live together in the rectory at St. Jude where the Brother Dutton School served the parish for 85 years. In June work began on repairs to the rectory and my daughter Erin asked me to help with cleaning up. That morning I went to work with Fr. John Hedrick who was working to straighten up the basement, pitching outdated books, papers and accumulated junk. Fr. John was retiring in July and had been pastor there for more than 10 years and knew what was junk. The incoming priests, Fr. Bart Timmerman and Fr. Lawrence Oparaji were also working in the rectory.

After lunch, back in the basement I came across two poster boards about Brother Dutton with pictures and photocopied letters. I was excited to see them but deep down I was let down thinking, is that all there is after all these years. I wanted more. In the basement was an old coal room with a steel door that was the next place to clean. The room was full of church records and looked to be made water proof. As we went through boxes, I was the one to carry them out of the basement. At some point while in the room, I broke the light bulb with my head and a new bulb was put in. As I was helping clean up glass on the floor and picking up some loose papers, I looked to my right and saw two banker boxes sitting in the corner. One box was inscribed "Brother Dutton scrapbooks KEEP" and the other "PRICELESS Brother Dutton's Papers DO NOT DESTROY 1/3/82". My heart started pounding and tears were in my eyes, I had found what was thought to be lost.

Since that day we have been working with Pat Boland, historian with The Joseph Dutton Guild. Some of the materials we have found

have never been seen before - letters to Brother Dutton from St Marianne Cope and a letter from president Theodore Roosevelt. I will continue to scan information to be shared with Hawaii and Vermont as requested.

Steve is searching for a suitable place where the documents and scrapbooks will be safely archived. Until then, Steve will guard these boxes. For more information, contact Steve at s.mikeskelly@gmail.com. Perhaps these papers will be in a sequel to this book.

# Hansen's Disease in the 21st Century

## Editor comments

*The Cleveland Clinic website is the source for this update on Hansen's disease (Leprosy). The fear associated with the disease has been erased because the cause and treatment are well understood. To better grasp the past fear in the 19th century, recall the initial protocols we followed as Covid-19 entered our world in 2019.*

Hansen's disease is an infectious disease caused by the bacteria *Mycobacterium leprae* (my-co-bak-TEER-ee-um LEP-pray). It can affect your eyes, skin and mucous membranes and nerves, causing disfiguring sores and nerve damage. Leprosy has been around since ancient times. For centuries, people isolated and shunned those with leprosy because the disease wasn't understood. Today, effective treatment is available, and there's no need to quarantine people with leprosy.

Although it's rare, Hansen's disease still exists today. According to the World Health Organization, approximately 208,000 people around the globe have the disease, with most cases found in Asia and Africa. In the United States, about 150 people receive a Hansen's disease diagnosis every year. Research suggests that over 95% of people infected with Mycobacterium leprae don't actually develop the disease because their bodies fight off the infection.

Although it is not highly contagious, Hansen's disease can spread from person to person. Experts don't fully understand how the disease spreads from one person to another, but the bacterium is likely transmitted through airborne droplets when an infected person coughs or sneezes. When bacterium is released into the environment, other people can inhale it. Hansen's disease can't be spread through hugging, shaking hands, sitting next to an infected person or intimate contact.

Thanks to modern medicine and the discovery of antibiotics, Hansen's disease is curable. Over the past 20 years, over 16 million people have beat the disease. It is treated with multidrug therapy (MDT), an approach that combines different types of antibiotics. In most cases, healthcare providers will prescribe two to three different kinds of antibiotics at the same time. This helps prevent antibiotic resistance, which occurs when bacteria mutate (change) and fight off the antibiotic drugs that usually kill them. Common antibiotics used in the treatment of Hansen's disease include dapsone, rifampin and clofazimine.

Antibiotics can't treat the nerve damage that may occur as a result of Hansen's disease. Healthcare providers may also prescribe anti-inflammatory drugs, such as steroids, to manage any nerve pain. On average, Hansen's disease treatment takes one to two years to complete.

Hansen's disease was shrouded in mystery for centuries. Today, we understand it as a curable disease. Prompt treatment is the first step toward healing and a better quality of life.

# *Kalaupapa — A Brief History*

FROM THE NATIONAL PARK SERVICE (NPS) WEBSITE.
LAST UPDATED DECEMBER 19, 2022.

**Kalaupapa** is now a property co-managed by the Hawaii State Department of Health and the US National Park Service. Both entities have managerial responsibilities, albeit for different functions. The current status is an important part of Joseph Dutton's Story. The article will help the reader understand the impact of Dutton's service to the people under his care.

Few places in the world better illustrate the human capacity for endurance or for charity than the remote Kalaupapa Peninsula on the island of Molokai. The area achieved notoriety when the Kingdom of Hawai'i instituted a century-long policy of forced segregation of persons afflicted with **Hansen's disease**, more commonly known as leprosy.

This mysterious and dreaded disease reached epidemic proportions in the islands in the late 1800s. At the time, there was no effective treatment and no cure. With new cases threatening to eradicate the native population and no knowledge of what caused the disease, officials became desperate. To government officials, isolation seemed the only answer. In 1865, the Legislative Assembly passed, and King Kamehameha V approved, "AN ACT TO PREVENT THE SPREAD OF LEPROSY", which set apart land to isolate people believed capable of spreading the disease.

This place was chosen to isolate people with, what was at that time, an incurable illness. The peninsula was remote and fairly inaccessible. To the south, the area was cut off from the rest of Molokai by a sheer *pali*, or cliff, reaching nearly 2000 feet. The ocean surrounded the rest of the area to the east, north and west. Boat landings were practical in good weather only. Hawaiians had inhabited this peninsula for over 900 years, so the land could support people. Vegetables such as sweet potatoes, taro, and fruits could be grown in the valleys and on the flatlands. The ocean and tidal pools provided seafood. Fresh water was available from Waikolu and Waihanau valleys.

Once the decision was made, and the law passed, the government proceeded to purchase lands and move the Hawaiian residents to other homes, severing their long connection to the land. The village Kalawao on the isolated Kalaupapa Peninsula thus became the home for thousands of leprosy victims subsequently moved here from throughout the Hawaiian Islands. On January 6, 1866, the first group of nine men and three women were dropped off at the mouth of Waikolu Valley, the closest accessible point to Kalawao on the southeast side of the peninsula. By October of the same year, 101 men and 41 women had been left to die at Kalawao.

## The Early Years: 1866 - 1900

The government's expectation was that these patients would move into the houses left behind by the Hawaiians who had lived in the area previously and the ill would tend crops and sustain themselves. But this belief soon proved to be wrong. It soon became apparent that most patients were too ill or demoralized to be self-sufficient. With no hope or will to live, some patients fell into vice and immorality.

Reports of the insufficient housing and lack of supplies were soon filed by the patients and their families, by the resident superintendent, and by the Board of Health agent Rudolph W. Meyer, who lived on top of pali overlooking the settlement. As stories of the deplorable conditions spread, many Hawaiian people hid their afflicted relatives and friends, hoping to prevent their discovery and banishment to a certain death. Others chose to go into isolation with their loved ones as a kokua, a helper.

In spite of the Board of Health's efforts to improve conditions, including building a hospital and homes, supplies of food and clothing, housing, and medical care could not keep up with the numbers of people being sent to Kalawao. Starting in 1873 major improvements were made due to the arrival of **Father Damien** and the interest and support of the next two Hawaiian Kings, William Charles Lunalilo and David Kalakaua.

During the years 1888 to 1902 the isolation laws in Hawai'i were strictly enforced and the population at Kalawao swelled to over 1,100 people. During this period the Bishop Home for Girls opened in Kalaupapa and was managed by **Mother Marianne Cope** and the **Sisters of St. Francis**. In Kalawao, the Baldwin Home for Boys was being run by **Brother Joseph Dutton** and **Brothers of the Sacred Heart**. During this time people began gradually moving to the peninsula's west side Hawaiian fishing village of Kalaupapa. In 1893-1894 the Board of Health took steps to deal with the last remaining non-patient Hawaiians living in Kalaupapa and on the peninsula. The isolation settlement was expanded to include not just Kalawao, but the entire peninsula and all trails and lands to the top of the pali. The last remaining private property was purchased and all non-patients removed. The centuries-long habitation of the Kalaupapa Peninsula by non-patient Hawaiian people came to an end.

The Board of Health began relocating patients to the Kalaupapa side of the peninsula, because the climate was warmer and dryer, and freight and passengers could be landed more easily. Water lines were extended from Waikolu Valley to bring Kalaupapa a fresh supply of water.

As the ramifications of the disease unfolded, husbands were separated from their wives and children, diseased children were removed from their mothers and fathers, and babies born to patients were immediately taken by health officials to be placed in the care of relatives or taken to orphanages. Although Hawai'i did more for its people with Hansen's disease than any country in history up to that time, it was still a frightening experience for the patients and difficult for the health care workers and clergy who ministered to the sick.

*Kalaupapa Historical Society Collection*

## *The 20th Century: 1900—1945*

Starting in 1900 the Board of Health implemented a plan to provide high quality services, facilities, utilities, and medical care for patients at Kalaupapa. A major construction program began, with individual cottages, dormitories, hospital facilities and other buildings being built. In 1902 Dr. William J. Goodhue became resident physician and John D. McVeigh became the settlement's superintendent. These two men worked to improve the quality of life within isolation by promoting sports and other activities, improving medical procedures, and by treating patients with respect and human decency.

The Board of Health records over the years reveal how the disease knew no racial or ethnic boundaries. In the Board of Health's annual report for 1903, the records show the total patient population at Kalaupapa to be 888 people – 541 males and 347 females. Of that number, 459 males and 338 females were Hawaiian. Among the other major racial groups represented were 40 Chinese men and 3 Chinese women; 12 Portuguese men and 2 Portuguese women; and seven "American" men and one "American" woman.

In the 1900s the Federal Government of the United States of America built two facilities on the peninsula. The Molokai Light was built on the northern tip of the peninsula to help guide westbound vessels into Honolulu Harbor on O'ahu. Opened in 1910, a succession of lighthouse keepers and their families lived at the station, segregated from the patient population. Over in Kalawao, a hospital complex was built to conduct Hansen's disease research. The Public Health and Marine Hospital Service operated the US Leprosy Investigation Station from 1909–1913. In spite of superior facilities and generous funding, isolation and an inability to attract patients willing to undergo medical experiments led to its early closing.

By 1919 treatments of chaulmoogra oil, derived from seeds of trees found in India and Southeast Asia, offered hope as a cure for Hansen's disease. People dared to think Kalaupapa settlement could be closed. After 10 years however, belief in the curative powers of the oil waned.

Despite the years of medical research a cure still seemed as remote as ever.

By 1924, the patient population had been reduced by almost half. Among the 485 patients remaining, the largest racial groups represented were 169 Hawaiian men and 101 Hawaiian women; 53 part-Hawaiian men and 43 part-Hawaiian women; 28 Japanese men and 4 Japanese women; and 24 Filipino men and one Filipino woman.

By the 1930s Kalaupapa's physical infrastructure was in need of an overhaul. Territory of Hawai'i Governor Lawrence M. Judd reorganized the leprosy control program in the early 1930s and undertook ambitious construction and rehabilitation projects. State-of-the-art water and power systems were installed; roads were paved; and facilities such as a hospital, store, service station, and houses were built.

## *The 20th Century: 1945 - Today*

After World War II, dramatic changes in both the treatment of Hansen's disease and in social attitudes towards patients occurred with the discovery of sulfone drugs. Essentially a cure for the disease, the drugs were introduced into Hawaii in 1946. The new medications brought almost immediate reductions of symptoms and vast improvements in the quality of health and life.

In 1947, Former Governor Lawrence M. Judd became Kalaupapa's resident superintendent and he and his wife Eva Marie promoted social activities and adult education classes. Boy Scouts, Girl Scouts, Lion's Club, American Legion, and other organizations opened Kalaupapa to the wider world. Many of the physical barriers separating patients from workers were removed.

With the new drug therapies, Hansen's disease patients were no longer contagious. There was no further need for isolation. In 1969 the century-old laws of forced quarantine were abolished. Former patients living in Kalaupapa today have chosen to remain here, most for the rest of their lives.

Kalaupapa has been home for 100 years for people once banished from society, but it is in transition due to its ever decreasing patient population. The settlement is much quieter than it once was. There are fewer buildings. Life today is lived at a somewhat slower pace. But Kalaupapa remains a remarkable place with an extraordinary history – a place exhibiting the worst and the best of human responses to the challenge of sickness.

# *The American-born Saints*

The United States Conference of Catholic Bishops website introduces us to several saints with a connection to the New World. Just
three American-born people have been canonized as of 2023.

- St. Elizabeth Ann Seton, S.C
- St. Katharine Drexel, S.B.S.
- St. Kateri Tekakwitha

## *St. Elizabeth Ann Seton, S.C.*

Founder of the Sisters of Charity of St. Joseph. Considered founder of
the Catholic School system in the US.

St. Elizabeth Ann Seton was the charming "belle of the ball" as a
young woman in New York City, linked to all the first families. At the
age of 19, she fell in love and married the wealthy, handsome William
Magee Seton. The two had a very happy marriage, raising five children.
Ten years after they were married, William's business and health both
failed, and Elizabeth was left a poor widow with five children to raise
alone. Her love for the Eucharist led her to convert to Catholicism and
founded the first order of religious women in America, the Sisters of
Charity of St. Joseph, a religious community based on the Rule of St.
Vincent De Paul. She was able to still raise her children, as well as live
the life of a sister and found several schools. She became the co-founder
of the first free Catholic School in America. She was canonized by Pope
Paul VI in 1975.

*St. Elizabeth Ann Seton, S.C.*

*St. Katharine Drexel, S.B.S.*

*St. Kateri Tekakwitha*

## St. Katharine Drexel, S.B.S.

School builder and founder of the Sisters of the Blessed Sacrament for Indians and Colored People

When she asked Pope Leo XIII to send more missionaries to Wyoming, he asked her, "Why don't you become a missionary?" As a young, wealthy, educated girl from Philadelphia, this was hardly the expected lifestyle for young Katharine Drexel. But raised in a devout family with a deep sympathy for the poor, Katharine gave up everything to become a missionary to the Indians and African Americans. She founded schools in thirteen states for African Americans, forty mission centers and twenty-three rural schools. She also established fifty missions for Indians in sixteen different states. She died at the age of ninety-six and was canonized in the year 2000.

## St. Kateri Tekakwitha

Native American and consecrated virgin

Nicknames are generally silly, entertaining names given to people by affectionate relatives or friends. It's rare to hear an enviable one. But "Lily of the Mohawks?" Now, that's an elegant nickname. This is the nickname of St. Kateri Tekakwitha. Orphaned at the age of four, she was raised by her uncle, the chief of the Mohawk village. When priests came to the village, Kateri was drawn by their teachings, and converted at the age of 19, heedless of the anger of her relatives. Because she refused to work on Sundays, she was denied meals that day. Finally, a missionary encouraged her to run away to Montreal, Canada, to practice her faith freely. She followed his advice, and lived a life of extreme prayer and penance, taking a vow of virginity. She was beatified in 1980 and canonized on October 21, 2012.

*Joseph Dutton, born in Stowe, Vermont,*
*could be the fourth American-born person canonized.*

# *Acknowledgements*

This book is the inspiration and cooperation of five people. In April 2023, Dr. Maria Devera, President of the Joseph Dutton Guild, attended the Joseph Dutton 180th Birthday Celebration at Blessed Sacrament Church in Stowe, Vermont. She proposed a book project to Lynn Altadonna of Stowe that would incorporate the 1931 book, *"Joseph Dutton – His Memoirs"*.

Barry Kerrigan of Desktop Miracles, a Stowe publisher, was consulted to suggest how to proceed within copyright rules, what to include, and to design and produce the book. The objective was to create a book that would advance the mission of the Guild—the canonization of Joseph Dutton.

We are eternally grateful to Phil and Chris Sabado for donating the cover illustration and his testimony about Brother Dutton

The concept was to expose the reader to the Dutton autobiography and present the continuing Molokai story to the present day. The artworks at Blessed Sacrament Church have spoken to Vermonters since 1950. Stowe is Dutton's birthplace. The Dutton family soon moved to Wisconsin and raised the young boy to manhood and a Civil War soldier. Brother Dutton School there taught several thousand students for 85 years. Recently, we re-discovered wonderful stories in Wisconsin from Cathy Simplot and Stephen Skelly. These communities have been added to the book.

We trust the reader will be enriched by the history incorporated in this book and blessed by a deeper understanding of Joseph Dutton and his self-less example serving others for 44 years on Molokai.

# *Prayer to Servant of God Joseph Dutton*

*Beloved and eternal Father,*

*You chose the Servant of God*

*Joseph Dutton as an ardent*

*Apostle of Your Divine Mercy.*

*I humbly pray that, through the*

*Intercession of the Servant of God,*

*You grant me this favor that I now request*

*(here mention your request)*

*Through Christ our Lord. Amen*

If you have received a favor or miracle through the intercession of the Servant of God, please write to :

The Joseph Dutton Guild,
PO Box 3344,
Honolulu, HI 96801 (USA)

Made in the USA
Columbia, SC
07 March 2025

54778277R00189